HOW TO WIN MEDICARE APPEALS

HOW TO WIN MEDICARE APPEALS

DAVID MULLENS, DPM, JD

AMERICAN BAR ASSOCIATION
Senior Lawyers Division

Cover design by Kelly Book/ABA Design

Printed in the United States of America.

24 23 22 21 20   5 4 3 2 1

A catalog record for this book is available from the Library of Congress.

Library of Congress Cataloging-in-Publication Data

Names: Mullens, David D., author. | American Bar Association. Senior Lawyers Division, sponsoring body
Title: How to win Medicare appeals / David Mullens, DPM, JD.
Description: Chicago : American Bar Association, 2020. | Includes index. |
Summary: "This book is about how to successfully fight for the payment of medically reasonable and necessary services when Medicare erroneously denies payment, or when Medicare erroneously demands a repayment of overpayment"—Provided by publisher.
Identifiers: LCCN 2019059051 | ISBN 9781641055987 (hardcover)
Subjects: LCSH: Medicare—Law and legislation. | Administrative procedure—United States. | Medicare beneficiaries—Legal status, laws, etc.—United States. | Medicare—Claims administration—United States.
Classification: LCC KF3608.A4 .M85 2020 | DDC 344.7302/26—dc23
LC record available at https://lccn.loc.gov/2019059051

Contents

Introduction

What is this book about?

There are a lot of books on Medicare appeals. I think I have most of them. The one thing they have in common is that they are not very useful when you are faced with an appeal and you want direct, practical answers for the questions in front of you: **What do I do next? Why is that the best choice? Exactly how do I do that?**

This book is about how to successfully fight for the payment of medically reasonable and necessary services when Medicare erroneously denies payment, or when Medicare erroneously demands a repayment of overpayment.

Who is this book for?

If you are a **contracted Medicare provider (provider or supplier)**, and you must submit claims to Medicare in order to get paid for the services or supplies you provide to Medicare beneficiaries, **this book is for you.**

If you are a **biller/coder/billing service** for contracted Medicare providers and/or suppliers, and you want to continue fighting for payment after your redetermination appeals are denied, **this book is for you.**

If you are a **health care attorney** representing Medicare providers and suppliers, **this book is for you.**

What is this book *not* about?

This book is **not** about selecting the correct codes and modifiers for a service. Every provider group has coding experts who publish widely and are far more knowledgeable than I will ever be regarding the selection of the correct codes and modifiers for the services billed by that group.

Why does this book target the ALJ hearing?

The ALJ (Administrative Law Judge) hearing is the provider's first and last chance at a fair review of a denied claim by a truly neutral third party. As a result, most appeals are not won before you get to the ALJ hearing and will not be won in an appeal after the ALJ hearing. The information in this book will help Medicare providers, Medicare billing companies, and health care attorneys who represent Medicare providers to prepare for ALJ hearings—and will help you win those ALJ decisions.

Is there a lot of repetition in this book?

Yes. I know no one is going to pick this book up and read it cover to cover. People use this kind of book when they are in the middle of an appeal and want to know what to do next and how to do it. I purposefully included enough information to allow each section to stand on its own, and that requires repetition.

If you have practical suggestions for future versions, please do not hesitate to email me at dmullens@mullenslawoffice.com.

1

The Underlying Problem

OUTLINE

1. What is the underlying problem?
2. If Congress won't pay for Medicare, what can Medicare do?
3. Who is getting squeezed as a result of this payment dispute?
4. Why are you helping Medicare to avoid paying for your services?
5. How did we get here?
6. What does the future hold?
7. What does all this mean for providers?
8. Are providers being treated as adversaries by Medicare?
9. What is the only cure for this problem?

1. What is the underlying problem?

Medicare has an impossible task. Congress expects Medicare to provide quality medical care for the Medicare beneficiaries. However, Congress does not give Medicare enough money to meet this goal.

2. If Congress won't pay for Medicare, what can Medicare do?

Medicare is doing the only thing it can do: Medicare is rigidly enforcing all the rules that apply before payment is made, and Medicare is aggressively going after any "improper" payment after payment is made.

3. Who is getting squeezed as a result of this payment dispute?

The providers are the ones caught in the middle of this quality care versus inadequate funding dispute.

4. Why are you helping Medicare to avoid paying for your services?

A lot of providers tell me they don't want to appeal denied claims because it will be at least three years before an Administrative Law Judge (ALJ) will hear the dispute. But if you have a pipeline of denials, you will eventually reach the end of those three years with a litany of claims that will be adjudicated, one after the next, by the ALJs.

You should be looking at your denied claims as an annuity that won't start paying out until three years from now. You **must** look at it like this. Otherwise, you will be giving up income you cannot afford to surrender. Take the long view.

5. How did we get here?

The answer is simple: When Medicare went into effect in 1966, there were 19 million people receiving Medicare benefits and life expectancy for the average American was 70 years. By 2015, there were 55.5 million people receiving Medicare benefits and life expectancy was 78.8 years.

In addition to three times as many beneficiaries and a longer average life span, the annual cost of care for the average beneficiary has skyrocketed due to new technology (e.g., MRI studies, CT scans, and artificial joints). And the enhanced safety of general anesthesia enables Medicare patients to undergo surgical procedures not considered reasonably safe in 1966.

6. What does the future hold?

If things weren't bad enough, the Congressional Budget Office (CBO) projected a $25 billion cut to Medicare in 2018 alone as a result of the GOP tax bill. And that tax bill calls for automatic annual cuts to Medicare going forward.

7. What does all this mean for providers?

The Medicare provider must know the Medicare billing rules that apply to all of the provider's services. And the provider must know how to appeal when a claim has been erroneously denied or when the provider receives an erroneous demand for repayment of overpayment.

Providers who cannot successfully appeal erroneously denied claims or appeal erroneous demands for repayment of overpayment are looking at financial disaster.

8. Are providers being treated as adversaries by Medicare?

Unfortunately, yes.

Are most of your denied services or supplies medically reasonable and necessary based on the clinical facts? If Medicare appeals were limited to this question, this book would not be necessary because providers would be winning their appeals without any extra help.

9. What is the only cure for this problem?

Unless and until providers unite and fight back, it is only going to get worse.

2

Why This Is a "Must Read" Book

OUTLINE

1. When it comes to Medicare billing, how much do you know?
2. How will this book change your view of Medicare and your grasp of the Medicare appeals process?
3. Why are there no other books like this on the market?
4. Why is this book a bargain?

1. When it comes to Medicare billing, how much do you know?

Here is the plain truth: In spite of your years in practice/business, when it comes to Medicare claims and appeals, you still don't know what you are doing!

And for many of you, Medicare patients represent a large share of your practice/business. But it doesn't stop there. Medicare sets the gold standard for the billing and payment guidelines all the insurance companies follow. As a result, what you don't understand about Medicare claims and appeals reappears in your failed billing and appeals experiences with other insurance companies.

2. How will this book change your view of Medicare and your grasp of the Medicare appeals process?

This book will clear up your misconceptions regarding Medicare. More importantly, it will guide you through the Medicare appeals process in a common-sense fashion, enabling you to defend yourself against incorrect denials.

3. Why are there no other books like this on the market?

I don't know. This book seems like a natural response to a huge problem. And I know personally about incorrect demands for repayment of overpayments.

While I was fortunate to practice podiatric surgery and to be a member of the Stanford University community orthopedic surgery service for more than 30 years, I decided to go to night law school after I was on the receiving end of a Medicare audit. I won the audit but was not treated well by the Medicare special investigator. In fact, that bad treatment was the reason I went to law school.

My personal Medicare audit experience allows me to understand your frustration. And my experience representing Medicare-contracted providers enables me to guide you successfully through the Medicare appeals process.

4. Why is this book a bargain?

I spent thousands of hours writing this practical approach to Medicare appeals. I wish I'd had the current "me" to turn to when I was going through my Medicare audit. I didn't, but you do.

3

How to Find the CFR Codes Cited in This Book

OUTLINE

1. How can you find the CFR codes cited in this book?
2. How should you use the Medicare website?

1. How can you find the CFR codes cited in this book?

Short answer: Put 42 CFR plus the section number I am referring to into your Internet search bar and click!

Longer answer: The rules of the Medicare appeals process are published in the Code of Federal Regulations (CFR), Title 42, Public Health, Chapter IV, Centers for Medicare and Medicaid Services, Department of Health and Human Services, Section 405.900 et seq. To make this easy, any time you want to read the actual rule about the subject being addressed, just put 42 CFR and the section number into your Internet search bar and that CFR section will come up.

For example, when I tell you doctors are "suppliers" and are not "providers" under section 400.202, you can check on this by putting "42 CFR 400.202" in your Internet search bar and reading the definitions for *provider* and *supplier.*

2. How should you use the Medicare website?

Do **not** try to use www.Medicare.gov—you won't find anything because that website is for the Medicare beneficiaries. Instead, go to www.CMS.gov. When you get to the CMS.gov web page, click on the **Medicare** tab at the top of the page. Then, scroll down to find the topics you want.

If you know you are in the right topic area but what you are looking for is not listed, go to the top of the page and put your keyword(s) into the search bar. For example, you won't find headings for RACs (Recovery Audit Contractors), UPICs (Uniform Program Integrity Contractors), CERT (comprehensive error rate testing) contractor, or SMRC (supplemental medical review contractor) on the Medicare page of the www.CMS.gov website. However, if you enter RACS, UPICs, CERT, or SMRC in the **search bar** at the top of the Medicare page, a list of publications will appear.

In addition, I will tell you how to find Medicare website information on each section's topics.

4

Your Target Audience in the Appeals Process

OUTLINE

1. Who is your target audience in the appeals process?
2. What simple thing can you do that will convert your notes into powerful weapons when you are appearing before the ALJ?
3. What do you have to do before you can appeal to the ALJ?
4. How far will you have to go to win your appeal?
5. What is the biggest procedural stumbling block in the appeals process?
6. Why should you write a letter explaining your appeal and what should the letter say?
7. How long should the letter be and what should the explanation in the letter be based on?
8. How long do you have after you receive the redetermination denial to get the letter to the QIC?

1. Who is your target audience in the appeals process?

The Administrative Law Judge (ALJ) is always your target audience. Every progress note you write and every report you dictate should be done with the thought that an ALJ will decide whether you should be paid based on the content of that note or report.

2. What simple thing can you do that will convert your notes into powerful weapons when you are appearing before the ALJ?

In layman's terms, include a couple of sentences in plain English that explain the patient's problem and what you did about it. For example, instead of telling the judge, "The margins of the neurotrophic ulcer were sharply debrided," think about telling the judge something like this: "Due to diabetic neuropathy, the patient has a lack of sensation on the bottom of the foot. And due to a combined bunion and adjacent hammertoe deformity, his second toe joint is pushing down against the skin on the bottom of the foot. What started as a callus under the second toe joint has developed into a pressure sore (i.e., ulcer). The hard, calloused margins of the ulcer that prevent healing were sharply removed (debrided). Without this debridement procedure, the hard, calloused edges make the pressure sore larger and deeper. In order to allow the ulcer to heal, custom shoe inserts (orthotics) were fabricated to remove weight-bearing pressure from the bottom of the second toe joint."

3. What do you have to do before you can appeal to the ALJ?

Getting your appeal of the denied payment in front of the ALJ is another matter. When Medicare denies payment, you must submit a first-level "redetermination" appeal to the same Medicare contractor that denied the original payment. When that contractor denies your first-level redetermination appeal, you must submit a second-level "reconsideration" appeal to a Qualified Independent Contractor (QIC). After the QIC denies your reconsideration appeal, you are then allowed to submit a request for the third level ALJ appeal.

4. How far will you have to go to win your appeal?

The first and second levels of appeal work when a claim is denied because of an entry error on a claim form. However, if a claim is denied for any reason other than an entry error on the claim form, chances are you won't win payment until you get to the ALJ hearing.

5. What is the biggest procedural stumbling block in the appeals process?

It's very important to note: Medicare requires **all** evidence for an appeal to be submitted when the second-level reconsideration appeal is requested. If you do not submit the patient's medical records when you ask the QIC to perform the reconsideration appeal, you will probably not be allowed to submit the medical records when you request the ALJ appeal.

6. Why should you write a letter explaining your appeal and what should the letter say?

Without a letter explaining what you did, why you did it, and how recognized authorities support the denied service, the patient care documents you send to the QIC as "evidence" for the reconsideration appeal will be an unorganized pile of documents the ALJ's staff attorneys may not spend time organizing. And even if they are willing to organize your documents, without a letter explaining the evidence, the ALJ and her staff attorneys may not understand why your claim should be paid.

7. How long should the letter be and what should the explanation in the letter be based on?

Your letter should be **no longer than three pages**. The letter should explain why you should be paid for the service in question and should be based on the patient care documents you will organize and staple to the letter as numbered attachments. The letter plus the stapled attachments is your "letter brief."

8. How long do you have after you receive the redetermination denial to get the letter to the QIC?

You have 180 days (six months!) to get the letter brief to the QIC after you receive the redetermination denial. You can do this. You have to do this.

See the chapter on reconsideration appeals for a detailed explanation of the letter brief you must submit to the QIC for the ALJ.

5

But I Need Help Right Now!

OUTLINE

1. Can you submit a claim for services provided more than a year ago?
2. Does Medicare provide appeal request forms for each level of appeal?
3. Your initial claim was denied. What should you do?
4. Why was your claim denied?
5. Was it a clerical error, a violation of a Medicare policy billing rule, or both?
6. What should you do if the claim was denied because of a clerical error?
7. Is it okay to ask for a reopening of the claim if you still have time to submit a redetermination appeal?
8. What if your claim was denied because of a Medicare policy billing rule?
9. What if the denial was due to both a clerical error and a Medicare policy billing rule?
10. Your redetermination appeal was denied. What should you do?
11. Where will the judge look for support of the clinical facts in your letter?
12. What will the conclusions regarding effectiveness, safety, and cost be based on?
13. If you late-send a letter brief to the ALJ, will the ALJ consider your letter brief?
14. Will the ALJ make sense out of patient care documents sent without a letter?
15. If you send the patient care documents to the QIC without a letter, can you later send a letter brief to the ALJ?
16. If you are facing the deadline for a reconsideration appeal, what should you do?
17. You missed the deadline to submit a redetermination appeal. What can you do?
18. If your redetermination appeal was "dismissed," what do you absolutely have to do?
19. Why was your appeal dismissed?
20. You have time to resubmit a dismissed redetermination appeal. What should you do?
21. Your redetermination was dismissed and you are past the time limit. What should you do?
22. If you are past the time limit to appeal and the contractor says you didn't send the required information but you can prove you did, what should you do?
23. If you are past the time limit to appeal, but you can meet the good cause requirement of "circumstances beyond your control," what should you do?

24. Your reconsideration appeal was denied by the QIC. What should you do?
25. You submitted a photograph to the QIC. Why should you request a video teleconference (VTC) ALJ hearing?
26. The patient is willing to appear at the hearing. Should you request a VTC ALJ hearing?
27. What is an example of a problem a patient could display at a VTC ALJ hearing?
28. If no photograph was sent to the QIC and the patient will not be at the hearing, should you still request a VTC ALJ hearing?
29. Should attorneys for Part A claims ask the patient(s) to appear at the hearing?
30. You missed the reconsideration appeal deadline. What can you do?
31. An appeal mailed before the deadline reached the QIC after the deadline. What should you do?
32. The redetermination denial is wrong "on the face of the decision." What should you do?
33. You missed the deadline to submit a reconsideration appeal because of a fire at your office. What can you do?
34. Your reconsideration appeal was dismissed by the QIC. What do you have to do?
35. Why was your reconsideration appeal dismissed?
36. Your reconsideration appeal was dismissed because of missing information but you are still within the deadline to appeal. What should you do?
37. Your reconsideration appeal was dismissed because of missing information and you are past the deadline to appeal. What should you do?
38. The QIC dismissed your reconsideration appeal saying you didn't send required information—but you know you did. You are past the deadline to appeal. What should you do?
39. You are past the deadline but can prove "good cause" for a late appeal. What should you do?
40. Your ALJ appeal was denied. What should you do?
41. You missed the deadline to submit an ALJ appeal. What should you do?
42. Your ALJ appeal was dismissed. What should you do?

You opened the book to this section because you are in the middle of an appeal and you are on the edge of panic. I included this section to calm you down and to assure you the next step in your appeal is doable.

Take a deep breath and look for your question below along with the answer to that question. And please, do not rely on just these short answers. Go to the longer section in the book I refer you to and read it before you act on the next step in your appeal. You need to know what you are doing—and how to do it—before you start.

The most common Medicare appeal problems are shown in **bold** in the order they arise during the appeals process, along with a short, non-bolded answer to the problem.

1. Can you submit a claim for services provided more than a year ago?

No. You have one year to get a claim submitted after a service is provided.

2. Does Medicare provide appeal request forms for each level of appeal?

Yes. You should use the CMS-20027 form when requesting a redetermination appeal.

You should use the CMS-20033 form when requesting a reconsideration appeal.

You should use the OMHA-100 form to request an ALJ appeal.

Put the title of the claim form into the search bar (e.g., "CMS-20027") and it will come up.

3. Your initial claim was denied. What should you do?

Below is what you should do and the order in which you should do it.

4. Why was your claim denied?

First, you must be sure of the reason why the claim was denied. The Remittance Advice (RA) notice will have the denial codes that apply to your claim. You can put "Medicare Remittance Advice Denial Codes" into your Internet search bar and look up each of the denial codes on the notice. However, I would strongly advise you to purchase the book *Denial Codes Plain English Descriptions*, published by DecisionHealth and available at www.codingbooks.com. When you are appealing a claim, you need a clear understanding of the individual denial codes and the code combinations (strings of denial codes) used by Medicare.

5. Was it a clerical error, a violation of a Medicare policy billing rule, or both?

Was there a clerical error on the claim form? Or did you get a substantive denial (e.g., the service was "not medically reasonable or necessary")? Or was there both a clerical error and a substantive denial?

6. What should you do if the claim was denied because of a clerical error?

If the claim was denied because of a clerical error on the claim form, fill out a new claim form with the clerical error corrected. Then fill out a redetermination appeal form (CMS-20027). Include a copy of your denial notice and submit all three documents (the CMS-20027 form, a copy of the originally submitted claim, and a copy of the corrected claim form) to the contractor for a redetermination appeal.

7. Is it okay to ask for a reopening of the claim if you still have time to submit a redetermination appeal?

NO! NEVER ask for a reopening if you still have time to submit a redetermination appeal. See the redetermination section for an explanation of why you should ask for a redetermination instead of a reopening.

8. What if your claim was denied because of a Medicare policy billing rule?

If you received a substantive denial (e.g., "the service was not medically reasonable and necessary"), fill out the form for a redetermination appeal (CMS-20027), include a copy of your denial notice, and send both documents to the contractor as a request for a **redetermination** appeal. Don't send an explanation to the contractor detailing why the service was medically reasonable and necessary. Instead, send your "medically reasonable and necessary" explanation to the QIC for the reconsideration appeal.

9. What if the denial was due to both a clerical error and a Medicare policy billing rule?

If your original claim was denied because of a clerical error AND because the contractor claimed the service was not medically reasonable and necessary, fill out a new claim form with the clerical error correction, fill out a redetermination appeal form (CMS-20027), include a copy of your original denial, and send all three documents to the contractor with a request for a **redetermination** appeal.

See Chapter 18, "Redetermination Appeals," for more detailed information.

10. Your redetermination appeal was denied. What should you do?

You should submit a completed reconsideration appeal form (CMS-20033), plus a letter (no more than three pages) stapled to copies of all your patient care documents to the QIC. The letter stapled to your patient care documents is your letter brief. It will explain in plain English why your denied service was medically reasonable and necessary based on the clinical facts, and—if the service was not allowed according to the applicable LCD (Local Coverage Determination)—why your denied service was more effective than, was safer than, and was (hopefully) less expensive than other treatment choices.

11. Where will the judge look for support of the clinical facts in your letter?

The "clinical facts" used to support the three-page letter are based on the patient care documents you will submit as evidence (e.g., progress notes, letters, photographs, operative reports, lab results, imaging reports).

12. What will the conclusions regarding effectiveness, safety, and cost be based on?

The conclusions regarding effectiveness, safety, and cost will be based on the peer-reviewed articles and textbook sections that you will also submit as evidence to the QIC.

13. If you late-send a letter brief to the ALJ, will the ALJ consider your letter brief?

If you do **not** submit your patient care documents to the QIC, and you then submit the letter brief to the ALJ, the ALJ will **not** consider your letter brief when deciding your ALJ appeal. Why? Because the rules were changed in 2005, and the new rule says: If you fail to submit all your evidence to the QIC, you will not be allowed to submit any "new" evidence for the ALJ hearing.

14. Will the ALJ make sense out of patient care documents sent without a letter?

If you submit your patient care documents to the QIC but fail to submit a letter that ties all the evidence into a coherent package, the ALJ may not spend time sifting through your pile of patient care documents in order to make sense out of your appeal. Or, the ALJ may not understand what the patient care documents prove regarding the claim.

15. If you send the patient care documents to the QIC without a letter, can you later send a letter brief to the ALJ?

Yes! As long as the letter relies only on the patient care documents, you absolutely can send a letter explaining the patient care documents to the ALJ.

16. If you are facing the deadline for a reconsideration appeal, what should you do?

If you stumble across a denied redetermination appeal and you now have only a few days to get a reconsideration appeal request to the QIC, fill out CMS-20033 and submit it, without any accompanying evidence, to the QIC. Because the QICs never send reconsideration decisions in less than four weeks, you will have at least four weeks to send the evidence (patient care documents, articles, textbook sections, and standard of care statements) and the letter to the QIC after you submit the request for a reconsideration appeal on time. But if you fail to get the reconsideration appeal request in on time, you will have to request a reopening or an extension. Reopenings and extensions are very hard to get.

See Chapter 19a, "Submitting the Reconsideration Appeal," for more detailed information.

17. You missed the deadline to submit a redetermination appeal. What can you do?

Always ask for a reopening if the initial claim was denied because of a clerical error.

Ask for a reopening if you mailed the redetermination appeal before the 125-calendar day time limit but your reconsideration appeal did not reach the contractor until after the 125-calendar day deadline.

Ask for a reopening if the contractor's initial determination is wrong "on the face of the determination" (e.g., the applicable LCD says the service was allowed when provided but the contractor incorrectly claims the LCD did not allow the service).

Ask for an extension if you can meet the good cause requirement of "circumstances beyond your control" (e.g., fire, flood).

See Chapter 18, "Redetermination Appeals," for more detailed information.

18. If your redetermination appeal was "dismissed," what do you absolutely have to do?

You must get the dismissal reversed in order to continue with the appeal. Unless the dismissal is reversed, your appeal is dead in the water.

19. Why was your appeal dismissed?

Your appeal was dismissed because you didn't send the required information, and/or the appeal was submitted too late.

20. You have time to resubmit a dismissed redetermination appeal. What should you do?

Make the necessary corrections on the appeal request form and resubmit it.

21. Your redetermination was dismissed and you are past the time limit. What should you do?

If you are past the time limit to submit a redetermination appeal and you didn't send the required information on the appeal request form, correct the appeal request form and resubmit with a request for a reopening based on a clerical error.

22. If you are past the time limit to appeal and the contractor says you didn't send the required information but you can prove you did, what should you do?

Send the contractor a letter stating you did send the required information, staple the supporting documents to the letter, and ask for a reopening.

23. If you are past the time limit to appeal, but you can meet the good cause requirement of "circumstances beyond your control," what should you do?

Ask for an extension. See Chapter 18, "Redetermination Appeals," for more detailed information.

24. Your reconsideration appeal was denied by the QIC. What should you do?

Immediately submit a request for an ALJ appeal, using CMS form OMHA-100.

25. You submitted a photograph to the QIC. Why should you request a video teleconference (VTC) ALJ hearing?

A clinical photograph is not worth a thousand words. A clinical photograph is worth a thousand articles.

Always ask for a video teleconference ALJ hearing if the patient's physical problem was demonstrated in a photograph previously sent to the QIC. You will explain the photograph as you tell the judge the story of the patient's problem.

26. The patient is willing to appear at the hearing. Should you request a VTC ALJ hearing?

If no photograph was sent to the QIC but the patient's problem is evident just by looking at the affected body part, ask the patient to come to the video teleconference hearing. At the hearing, you will ask the patient to show the judge the deformity/problem that required the denied treatment. Obviously (or not), you **cannot** ask a patient to display a "sensitive" body part to an ALJ during a hearing.

27. What is an example of a problem a patient could display at a VTC ALJ hearing?

A diabetic patient with an ulcer on the bottom of the foot, who is willing to be present at a video teleconference ALJ hearing and is willing to show his/her foot to the ALJ, would be an example. Having that patient show the ALJ their foot problem during the hearing would be worth a *million* articles.

28. If no photograph was sent to the QIC and the patient will not be at the hearing, should you still request a VTC ALJ hearing?

You should *always* request a video teleconference ALJ hearing because you need to know if the judge is paying attention to what you are saying and/or whether the judge looks confused. In either case, you will have to ask the judge if there is a question you can help answer regarding the presentation.

29. Should attorneys for Part A claims ask the patient(s) to appear at the hearing?

Yes. If the patient's testimony will support payment of the claim, do not miss the opportunity to have the patient participate in the hearing by phone.

For example, if the Medicare patient had a transurethral prostatectomy procedure (TURP) and was hospitalized for 24 hours after surgery for adequate pain control, the patient's statement that he needed IV pain medication for the first 24 hours and that he was discharged as soon as the pain was under control is stronger evidence than any academic presentation you will make and more convincing than any expert you present during the hearing.

See Chapter 19a, "Submitting the Reconsideration Appeal," for more detailed information.

30. You missed the reconsideration appeal deadline. What can you do?

Ask for a reopening if you met the 185-calendar day time limit based on the postmarked date on the redetermination denial envelope.

31. An appeal mailed before the deadline reached the QIC after the deadline. What should you do?

Ask for a reopening. See Chapter 17, "Reopenings," for more information.

32. The redetermination denial is wrong "on the face of the decision." What should you do?

Ask the QIC for a reopening if the contractor's redetermination decision is wrong "on the face of the decision" (e.g., the applicable LCD says the service was allowed when provided but the contractor claims the LCD did not allow the service). See Chapter 17, "Reopenings," for more information.

33. You missed the deadline to submit a reconsideration appeal because of a fire at your office. What can you do?

Ask for an extension if you meet the requirement of "circumstances beyond your control" (e.g., fire, flood). See Chapter 19, "Reconsideration Appeals," for more detailed information.

34. Your reconsideration appeal was dismissed by the QIC. What do you have to do?

You must get the dismissal reversed in order to continue with the appeal.

35. Why was your reconsideration appeal dismissed?

Your appeal was dismissed because you didn't send the required information and/or the appeal was submitted too late.

36. Your reconsideration appeal was dismissed because of missing information but you are still within the deadline to appeal. What should you do?

If you are still within the time limit to appeal and you didn't send the required information on the appeal request form, correct the appeal request form and resubmit it.

37. Your reconsideration appeal was dismissed because of missing information and you are past the deadline to appeal. What should you do?

If you are past the time limit to appeal and you didn't send the required information on the appeal request form, correct the appeal request form and resubmit with a request for a reopening based on a clerical error.

38. The QIC dismissed your reconsideration appeal saying you didn't send required information—but you know you did. You are past the deadline to appeal. What should you do?

Send another copy of the originally submitted reconsideration appeal request form along with a letter stating all the required information was sent and ask for a reopening based on the QIC's error.

39. You are past the deadline but can prove "good cause" for a late appeal. What should you do?

If you are past the time limit to appeal but can prove "good cause" for a late appeal, ask for an extension.

See Chapter 19b, "Extending the Time Limit for a Reconsideration Appeal," for more detailed information.

40. Your ALJ appeal was denied. What should you do?

The only time you should appeal an ALJ decision to the Council (the Medicare Appeals Council of the Department of Health & Human Services, Departmental Appeals Board) is when you can prove, based on Medicare documents (e.g., the applicable LCD), that the wrong standard was applied, **and** if the right standard had been applied, the ALJ would have had to rule in your favor.

If the ALJ's decision was clearly wrong based on Medicare's published rules, appeal to the Council. Otherwise, don't bother.

See Chapter 20d, "Fighting the Dismissal of an ALJ Appeal," for more detailed information.

41. You missed the deadline to submit an ALJ appeal. What should you do?

If there are grounds for a reopening, ask for a reopening.

If you can meet the "good cause" requirements (circumstances beyond your control), ask the ALJ for an extension.

See Chapter 20e, "Reopening an ALJ Appeal," for more detailed information.

42. Your ALJ appeal was dismissed. What should you do?

You must get the dismissal reversed in order to continue with the appeal. Your appeal was dismissed because you didn't send the ALJ the required information and/or the ALJ appeal was submitted too late.

If you are still within the time limit to appeal and you didn't send the required information on the appeal request form, correct the appeal request form and resubmit.

If you are past the time limit to appeal and you didn't send the required information on the appeal request form, correct the appeal request form and resubmit with a request for a reopening based on a clerical error.

If you are past the time limit to appeal, and the ALJ says you didn't send the required information but you know you did, ask for a reopening based on the ALJ's error.

If you are past the time limit to appeal but you can prove "good cause" for a late appeal, ask for an extension.

See Chapter 20, "Administrative Law Judge (ALJ) Appeals," for more detailed information.

6

Hard Truths About You and Medicare

OUTLINE

1. What are the myths you tell yourself about Medicare?
2. What are the unwelcomed truths regarding these myths?
3. Here are some additional unwelcomed truths about Medicare payments.
4. Why are you making less money than another provider who does exactly what you do?
5. How much would your Medicare bottom line have to change to make a difference in your life?

1. What are the myths you tell yourself about Medicare?

a. You bill Evaluation & Management (E&M) codes of lower complexity than you should because you are afraid of being audited, and down-coding will keep you from being audited.
b. You do not bill for all the services you provide because billing for fewer services will keep you from being audited.
c. You do not appeal denied claims because you do not want to attract attention to your practice/business and, after all, "denied claims are just the cost of doing business."
d. When you were last audited by Medicare, you immediately cut the check rather than fight because you did not want the interest to accrue.

2. What are the unwelcomed truths regarding these myths?

a. You really don't know the exact requirements for each of the E&M codes you bill, so you automatically check off lower level E&M codes in order to make yourself feel more secure.
b. Not billing for all the services you provide will not protect you from being audited. It just prevents you from being paid for the services you provide. You will eventually be audited by Medicare, just as you will eventually be audited by the IRS for your personal income taxes.
c. You don't appeal denied claims because you are not sure if you should be paid for the denied services, and you are not prepared to fight through the appeals process.

d. When you get the demand letter from the Recovery Audit Contractor (RAC), you cut the check rather than fight because you are not sure whether you are entitled to payment for the disputed codes, you are not prepared to fight, and you do not want to pay the interest that accrues as the appeals process drags on.

3. Here are some additional unwelcomed truths about Medicare payments.

a. When it comes to underpayments and overpayments, Medicare pays you no interest on underpayments. But Medicare charges you 10% interest on all overpayments.
b. The RAC companies are private, for-profit companies working on a contingency fee basis; they don't get paid unless they win.
c. Medicare doesn't like or dislike you. Medicare is just underfunded by Congress. So, Medicare has tightened the payment rules and is attempting to take back all "improper payments."
d. The government has less and less money to spend on an increasing number of people receiving Medicare benefits. Who is getting caught in the middle of this financial tug-of-war ? Look in the mirror.

4. Why are you making less money than another provider who does exactly what you do?

Still unconvinced? OK, here is another unwelcomed truth. In your town there is another Medicare-contracted provider who sees the same number of patients, from the same cross-section of the population, provides almost identical services, observes all Medicare rules regarding billing, but is doing much better financially than you are. Why?

The other provider or supplier:

- Stays knowledgeable about Medicare billing rules.
- Documents and bills the correct level E&M code at each patient encounter.
- Documents and bills for every Medicare-billable service and/or supply provided.
- Remains disciplined regarding claims submissions.
- Correctly appeals and wins payment for almost all denied claims.
- Correctly appeals and wins almost all claims at issue in any Medicare audit.

5. How much would your Medicare bottom line have to change to make a difference in your life?

Think about it. A 10% difference in your take-home income every year would make a huge difference to your bottom line. Isn't it worth the effort to learn how to bill correctly, how to appeal wrongly denied claims, and how to appeal mistaken demands for repayment of overpayment? Of course it is. And no matter how experienced you are, and no matter how much you think you know about appealing denied claims and about fighting Medicare audits, you will learn at least one thing from this book that you will immediately adopt and apply. And that "one thing" will make an immediate difference to your bottom line.

7

Why You Must Fight—Even If You Are an Insurance Company Coward!

OUTLINE

1. How much money are the RACs taking back from the providers?
2. Medicare now refers to these contractors as "Recovery Auditors." Why am I using "RAC"?
3. Are the RACs paid the same way the other medical review contractors are paid?
4. When and how did the RACs start?
5. What are the contingency fee rates paid to the RACs?
6. How is a provider's response to a RAC audit viewed by the RAC?
7. What will your MAC do after you repay an overpayment demand without a fight?

1. How much money are the RACs taking back from the providers?

In 2013, the Recovery Audit Contractors (RACs) took back **$3.65 billion** from Medicare providers and suppliers. You have to know what you are doing with your billing and appeals because at $3.65 billion a year and climbing, it is not a question of whether you will be audited. It is only a question of when and how often.

2. Medicare now refers to these contractors as "Recovery Auditors." Why am I using "RAC"?

For simplicity's sake, RAC is easier to use than "recovery auditor." And the acronym RA also refers to "remittance advice."

3. Are the RACs paid the same way the other medical review contractors are paid?

No. The RACs are the *only* medical review contractors who work on a contingency fee basis. The other medical review contractors (i.e., MACs, UPICs, CERT, and SMRC) work on a cost-plus basis (allowed expenses plus a predetermined profit).

4. When and how did the RACs start?

The RACs started as an experiment during President Clinton's second term and have been successful beyond the federal government's wildest dreams. The RACs recovered the following amounts in the fiscal years 2010 through 2014. You can verify all this by searching "CMS.gov recovery audit program."

FY 2010	$92.3 million
FY 2011	$797.4 million
FY 2012	$2.3 billion
FY 2013	$3.65 billion
FY 2014	$2.39 billion

The aggregated amount recovered in overpayments from 2010 through 2014 was **$9.23 billion.**

5. What are the contingency fee rates paid to the RACs?

The RAC companies get to keep between 9.0% and 17.5% of the amount they get back from the provider, depending on the type of claim being audited. See Chapter 22, "Medicare Audits," for more information.

6. How is a provider's response to a RAC audit viewed by the RAC?

Imagine you are working at a RAC company. You know your company only makes money on a contingency fee basis and you know your company has to eat all of the costs of medical reviews and that your company **must return the contingency fee** when a provider successfully appeals a demand for return of overpayment.

Working under these rules, you send a request for medical records to two contracted providers (providers/suppliers). Both are suspected of having received overpayments for the same service(s) in the amount of $10,000 each. Your company then spends time and effort (i.e., money) to review the medical records of both providers. And based on your reviews, you tell the MAC (Medicare Administrative Contractor) to send both providers a repayment of overpayment demand for $10,000.

One provider responds by immediately paying the full amount of the demand without a fight and your company gets to keep the full contingency fee flowing from that payment. The other provider responds by appealing the demand all the way through the appeals process to an ALJ hearing—where the provider wins. Whose records will you be auditing in the near future, the provider who immediately paid without question or the provider who refused to pay and then went on to beat you in court?

If you think the RACs are not cherry-picking their targets, think again.

7. What will your MAC do after you repay the overpayment demand without a fight?

And if you think your MAC will not come after you once you pay the overpayment demand, you should also think again. Put "Medicare Internet-Only Manuals" into the search bar and select Publication #100-08 Medicare Program Integrity Manual. Click on "Chapter 8—Administrative

Actions and Statistical Sampling for Overpayment Estimates" and select "Section 8.2 Overpayment Procedures." Here is what the last paragraph in Section 8.2 says:

> Contractors have the option to request the periodic production of records or supporting documentation for a limited sample of submitted claims from providers or suppliers to which amounts were previously overpaid to ensure that the practice leading to the overpayment is not continuing. The MAC may take any appropriate remedial action described in this chapter if a provider or supplier continues to have a high level of payment error. Offer the provider a consent settlement based on the potential projected overpayment amount.

When you receive a mistaken demand for repayment of overpayment, you must fight. Otherwise, you will just be paying the playground bully over and over again.

8

Where Were We and Where Are We with Medicare Appeals?

Below, I compare Medicare appeals before 2005, when the Medicare appeals rules were changed, with Medicare appeals in 2017. Although there are more Medicare ALJs (Administrative Law Judges) and more hearing offices in 2019 than there were in 2017, the comparison remains appropriate because the changes in the Medicare rules since 2005 are greatly skewed against the providers.

Before 2005, there were 139 Medicare hearing offices, with a hearing office in every major city in the United States.

In 2017, there were four Medicare hearing offices, and one of them was administrative only.

Before 2005, there were more than a thousand ALJs available for Medicare hearings.

In 2017, there were 72 Medicare ALJs for the entire country.

Before 2005, a provider (provider or supplier) could schedule an in-person ALJ hearing at a nearby hearing office.

Now, a provider cannot have an in-person hearing without a "good cause" statement approved by the assigned ALJ, and there is little chance the supervising ALJ will approve the expense or the time for the assigned ALJ to travel to the provider's city to conduct a hearing. Therefore, the provider would have to travel to one of the hearing offices in the country for the in-person hearing—assuming the "good cause" statement is approved by the assigned ALJ.

Before 2005, a provider could submit evidence at any point in the appeals process, including submitting evidence for the first time at the ALJ hearing.

Now, the provider must submit all evidence before the reconsideration decision is published. Any new evidence submitted after the QIC decision must be accompanied by a "good cause" statement explaining the late submission. If the assigned ALJ finds the "good cause" statement to be inadequate, the late-submitted evidence will not be considered by the ALJ.

Before 2005, the provider could expect to receive the ALJ's written decision within the required 90 days after the hearing.

Now, the average written decision is received by the provider more than 500 days after the hearing—despite the same 90-day requirement.

Currently, there is a backlog of more than 1,000,000 ALJ appeals to be decided.

The Honorable Nancy Griswold, the Chief ALJ for the Office of Medicare Hearings and Appeals, has requested more ALJs and more hearing offices and has asked Congress to make the following changes in the rules for Medicare appeals:

1. All evidence must be submitted at the time of the redetermination appeal.
2. A refundable filing fee will be charged for all appeals and the filing fee will be reimbursed if the provider wins a fully favorable decision (i.e., if the provider appeals five denied codes and four of the codes are decided in favor of the provider, the filing fee will not be reimbursed).
3. If the amount at issue is less than the amount required to appeal in federal district court ($1,600), the case will be decided by an attorney and not by an ALJ.

Now, do you really think things are going to get easier?

9

Why You Must Stay on Track During the Appeals Process

OUTLINE

1. What happens once your appeal goes off track?
2. What is the theme running through the Medicare appeals process?
3. Are timely appeals with all required information "discretionary" for the reviewing party?
4. Are late appeals or appeals missing information "discretionary" for the reviewing party?
5. What is your procedural goal with every appeal?
6. Other than staying on track through the redetermination and reconsideration appeals, what is the only other requirement for a successful appeal?
7. What is the most powerful evidence you can submit to the QIC?
8. How should you authenticate photographs you want to submit to the QIC?
9. In addition to progress notes and photos, what else should you send to the QIC?
10. Where can you find a basic overview of the Medicare appeals process?
11. What happens if you miss the deadline at any level of appeal?
12. What is the "exhaustion of remedies" doctrine and how is it applied?
13. What can you do to "move the date" in your favor when you are up against a deadline?
14. Why should you always save denial envelopes?
15. Why aren't you sending your claims immediately after providing the service?
16. When is it okay to leave the office before finishing all computer entries, dictation, and super-bills?
17. Is your income tied to your actual production?
18. You leave computer entries, dictation, and super-bills for "later." What happens?
19. Why designate one person in your group/business to handle all Medicare appeals?
20. How often should you review all current appeals in your practice/business?
21. How should you structure the appeals process in your practice?
22. Why is a master Medicare appeals file doable?
23. Do you need to print all the information in the master file for each denied claim?
24. What is meant by the "date of a Medicare denial document" in a claim file?
25. Why do you need a single master computer file for each denied Medicare claim?

26. Why must you keep the envelopes associated with all Medicare appeal documents?
27. How much time do you have to get your appeal submitted at each level of appeal?
28. Why do you have to keep a calendar for all of your Medicare appeals?
29. Why should you keep an Excel spreadsheet of all your Medicare-denied claims?

You have a claim in front of you that is "somewhere" in the appeals process. But this cannot be guesswork. You have to know exactly where you are, what your best option is going forward, how much time you have, and how to take that next step in the process.

1. What happens once your appeal goes off track?

Once your claim is off track, the whole process becomes far more difficult, and this is not by accident. It's not that you can't get a time extension when you are late in responding, it's not that you can't get a dismissal reversed when you fail to submit the required information on an appeal form, and it's not that you can't get an appeal reopened long after the time limit has expired for a claim. It's just a lot harder, a lot more work, and a lot less certain you will succeed with these tasks.

2. What is the theme running through the Medicare appeals process?

The theme running through the Medicare appeals process is this: **You must stay on track.** Once you fail to submit the required information in the required period of time at any level of appeal, you have a very steep road to climb.

3. Are timely appeals with all required information "discretionary" for the reviewing party?

No. Appeals that are submitted on time and with the correct information are not "discretionary" with the reviewing party. This statement means:

a. A **Medicare Administrative Contractor** (e.g., Noridian) must respond to a timely submitted **redetermination** appeal that contains all of the required information with a "Yes, we will pay this claim" or a "No, we won't pay this claim and here are the specific reasons why."
b. A **Qualified Independent Contractor** must respond to a timely submitted **reconsideration** appeal that contains all of the required information, with a "Yes, we will pay this claim" or a "No, we won't pay this claim and here are the specific reasons why we will not pay."
c. An **Administrative Law Judge** must respond to a timely submitted **ALJ** appeal that contains all of the required information with a "Yes, I will order payment of this claim" or a "No, I will not pay this claim and here are the reasons why."
d. The **Medicare Appeals Council** (Council) must respond to a timely submitted **Council** appeal that contains all of the required information with a "Yes, we will order payment of this claim" or a "No, we will not pay this claim and here are the reasons why" or a "We are remanding this appeal back to the ALJ for another hearing based on our findings."

4. Are late appeals or appeals missing information "discretionary" for the reviewing party?

Yes. Once an appeal has gone off track, you are in serious trouble. All of the following requests are discretionary with the reviewing party: a request for a **time extension** to submit a claim, a request to get a **claim dismissal reversed**, and a request to get a **claim/appeal reopened**. This means the MAC, the QIC, the ALJ, and the Council have the discretion to kill your appeal because you made a procedural error. And all **these "discretionary" decisions are final**. They are not subject to further appeal.

5. What is your procedural goal with every appeal?

Your procedural goal is to **keep your appeal on track** and to **avoid discretionary decisions** as you work through the redetermination and reconsideration appeals toward the ALJ hearing. Staying on track forces the reviewing party to issue a substantive (yes or no) decision and allows your claim to reach the ALJ, where you stand the very best chance of winning payment. Once you are off track, you are in no-man's-land, where the reviewing party can say no and can permanently bury your appeal and any chance of payment.

6. Other than staying on track through the redetermination and reconsideration appeals, what is the only other requirement for a successful appeal?

Other than staying on track, the only other requirement for a successful appeal is to **submit all your evidence at the time you submit the QIC appeal.**

7. What is the most powerful evidence you can submit to the QIC?

If the patient's problem can be demonstrated in a photograph, and the problem is not in a "sensitive" body area, send hard copies of the images of your patient's problem.

8. How should you authenticate photographs you want to submit to the QIC?

The background for each image should be a computer-printed page with the patient's initials, the patient's Medicare number, and the date the image was taken.

All of this information should be in a font large enough to read clearly when looking at the hard copy of the photograph.

9. In addition to progress notes and photos, what else should you send to the QIC?

In addition, your "evidence" should include a classic comic book version of the patient's problem (e.g., a Krames pamphlet), a short, written explanation describing what you did and why you did it, and a peer-reviewed article or textbook section that supports your treatment. That's it. Usually, nothing else is required in order to win your Medicare payment disputes.

10. Where can you find a basic overview of the Medicare appeals process?

You will get much more out of this book if you first read *The Medicare Appeals Process: Five Levels to Protect Providers, Physicians and Other Suppliers*. This publication contains an overview of the basic rules at each level of appeal and will tell you how to use the rules to your advantage. The publication is available at http://www.cms.hhs.gov/MLNProducts/downloads/MedicareAppealsProcess.pdf.

11. What happens if you miss the deadline at any level of appeal?

Usually, once you miss an appeal deadline (statute of limitations), that claim is dead in the water. Although there are "good cause" exceptions for late appeals listed in the CFR (405.942), most late-submitted appeals will have to be written off. This is the biggest reason why you should submit your appeals immediately upon receiving the original denial, immediately upon receiving the redetermination appeal denial, and immediately upon receiving the reconsideration appeal denial. Appeal early and often.

12. What is the "exhaustion of remedies" doctrine and how is it applied?

The **Administrative Procedures Act** controls everything that happens with Medicare. The "exhaustion of remedies" doctrine, incorporated in the Administrative Procedures Act, states:

> You must complete a redetermination appeal of your denied claim before you can request a reconsideration appeal of your denied claim;
> You must complete a reconsideration appeal before you can request an ALJ (Administrative Law Judge) appeal of your denied claim;
> You must complete an ALJ appeal before you can request a Medicare Appeals Council appeal of your denied claim;
> And you must complete a Council appeal before you can request a federal district court appeal of your denied claim.

You can never, ever skip a level of appeal.

13. What can you do to "move the date" in your favor when you are up against a deadline?

It's not uncommon for the date on the redetermination or reconsideration letter to be significantly earlier than the postmarked date on the envelope containing the redetermination and/or reconsideration denial decision. **Always** staple the redetermination and reconsideration denial envelopes to the denial letters. This may protect you in the event your next appeal is deemed "untimely" based on the date of the denial letter.

Although you are allowed five days from the date of the letter for the purpose of calculating the statute of limitations for the next level of appeal, the postmarked date on the envelope may be more than a week after the date on the first page of the actual letter.

14. Why should you always save denial envelopes?

This will allow you to argue that the correct arrival date for your appeal request is **not** the date on the first page of the letter plus five days. *The correct arrival date for your appeal request is the postmarked date on the denial envelope plus five days.*

15. Why aren't you sending your claims immediately after providing the service?

It makes no sense to send insurance claims out once a week or, God forbid, once a month. All codes should be submitted to Medicare for all services within 24 hours of providing the service(s).

If your billing department isn't meeting this standard, you really, really want to know why not.

16. When is it okay to leave the office before finishing all computer entries, dictation, and super-bills?

Never! With the exception of a family emergency, you should never allow yourself to go home until you have completed all of your super-bills and have finished all of your dictation—every day.

17. Is your income tied to your actual production?

Whether you have your own practice/business or are part of a large provider group/business, some part of your reimbursement is likely tied to the amount of money you actually bring into the practice/business. And no one else can stay on top of your billings like you can because no one else is aware of the details of the services you are providing.

18. You leave computer entries, dictation, and super-bills for "later." What happens?

Leaving your dictation until some later date means your notes will be incomplete. If your progress notes are incomplete, several bad things can happen. If you fill out the super-bill at the time of the service but you don't dictate the progress note until sometime later, the super-bill will accurately reflect the services you provided but your late-dictated note may be incomplete and not contain the documentation needed to support your billing. If you delay both the dictation and the completion of the super-bill, your later-completed super-bill may not reflect all of the services provided.

Leaving your dictation and super-bills incomplete means you are leaving money on the table every day you do this.

Remember the point about the two providers in the same city who see the same number of patients and provide the same types of services, but one provider makes a lot more money than the other? Well, here we are.

19. Why designate one person in your group/business to handle all Medicare appeals?

What happens when you place two people in charge of one task and the task doesn't get done? Yup. That is exactly what we are talking about. You can and should avoid the finger-pointing that occurs when two people are given responsibility for a single task that is tedious and has to be done over and over again.

The calendar is your enemy. Placing one person in charge of all Medicare appeals gives you the best chance of avoiding late submissions.

You want to be sure the redetermination and reconsideration appeals are submitted in a timely manner. And you want to be sure the patient care documents are submitted with the reconsideration appeal request. Making one person responsible for all of this is the time-proven best way to avoid blowing a statute of limitation and is the best way to avoid "good cause" arguments for the late submission of evidence at the ALJ hearing level of appeal.

20. How often should you review all current appeals in your practice/business?

You should review all current appeals in your practice/business once a week with the one person who is overseeing the appeals in your practice/business. It won't take five minutes and you will be surprised at what hasn't been done.

21. How should you structure the appeals process in your practice?

Here is a brief outline of a structural approach for Medicare appeals, and for all other insurance claim denials as well. For that **one** compulsively organized person in your group who has accepted the task of handling **all** denied claims:

1. Every notice of denial should be stapled to the envelope it comes in—without exception.
2. Every denial should be calendared for each step in the appeal process.

3. An electronic master list of denied claims should be kept and updated every week.
4. An electronic master file should be created **for each patient** with a denied claim and each master file should contain:
    a. A **signed** copy of the initial history and physical note for that patient.
    b. A **signed** copy of the progress notes for the date of service at issue.
    c. A copy of the submitted claim form(s).
    d. A copy of each submitted appeal request.
    e. A copy of each denial response from Medicare.
    f. A **list** of the documents that apply to the denied claim, including:
        i. The name and number of the applicable Local Coverage Determination (LCD).
        ii. The "literature" (titles of articles and textbooks) cited by the LCD.
        iii. The titles of the articles that refute the LCD rule relied on by the contractor.
        iv. The name(s) and number(s) of the LCDs from other Medicare jurisdictions that support your appeal.
        v. The Medicare Manual sections cited by the QIC.

22. Why is a master Medicare appeals file doable?

Ninety percent or more of all your appeals will be for the top ten codes or combination of codes that are constantly denied in your practice/business. As you appeal each of these top ten codes over and over again, you will accumulate the current information needed to fight against the erroneous denials of these codes. And you will eliminate the out-of-date information that no longer applies.

23. Do you need to print all the information in the master file for each denied claim?

No. A single master **computer** file with all of this information will do. You do *not* have to print and keep paper copies of all the above for each denied claim/set of claims.

a. Recommendation: Get a desktop scanner. They are inexpensive, will scan 20 or more pages (double-sided) a minute, will convert each scanned set of documents into a pdf file, and the scanner will take almost no room on the desk. I use and recommend the Fujitsu ScanSnap.
b. Create an individual folder for each patient (last name, first name). All documents for each patient are labeled by date of document/title of document.
c. You want your computer file to be an accurate chronology of the events as they unfold for each claim denial.

24. What is meant by the "date of a Medicare denial document" in a claim file?

For the denial documents you receive *from* Medicare, the date of the document is **not** the date you put the document into your computer file. The date of the document is the postmarked date on the envelope containing the denial document (e.g., the envelope containing a redetermination denial notice).

25. Why do you need a single master computer file for each denied Medicare claim?

You want anyone in your group/business to be able to access any claim file and to be able to find any document in that claim file in a matter of seconds.

26. Why must you keep the envelopes associated with all Medicare appeal documents?

This is important enough to repeat. The denial letter itself may be dated much earlier than the postmark on the envelope containing the denial letter. When calculating the statute of limitations for a particular appeal level, you want to add the extra five days starting from the date on the denial envelope and not the date on the denial letter. If the calculated due date falls on a non-workday (weekend or holiday), roll the statute of limitations forward to the next work day.

27. How much time do you have to get your appeal submitted at each level of appeal?

Redetermination: The deadline for filing a request for redetermination is **125** calendar **days** from the date on the envelope containing the Medicare Summary Notice (MSN) or Remittance Advice (RA).

QIC reconsideration: The deadline for filing a request for reconsideration is **185** calendar **days** from the date on the envelope containing the notice of the redetermination.

ALJ hearing: The deadline for filing a request for an ALJ hearing is **65** calendar **days** from the date on the envelope containing the reconsideration notice.

Council review: The deadline for filing a request for review by the Medicare Appeals Council is **65** calendar **days** from the date on the envelope containing the ALJ's decision.

Judicial review: The deadline for filing for judicial review in federal court is **65** calendar **days** from the date on the envelope containing the Appeals Council's decision.

28. Why do you have to keep a calendar for all of your Medicare appeals?

Again . . . too many claims, too many dates, too easy to drop a claim.

29. Why should you keep an Excel spreadsheet of all your Medicare-denied claims?

Because you want to avoid financial death by statute of limitations.

10

Do It the Same Way Every Time

OUTLINE

1. Why should you do your appeals the same way every time?
2. Who in your office/business should you pick to track all appeals?
3. How often do you have to review your Medicare appeals spreadsheet?
4. What happens when you do not review the Medicare appeals spreadsheet once a week?
5. How often should you review the Remittance Advice notices you receive and why?
6. How long does it take to go through 20 pages of Medicare RA notices?
7. How long does it take to perfect an assembly line approach to your top 20 denied codes?
8. You remain unprepared to appeal your most commonly denied codes. What's wrong with this picture?

1. Why should you do your appeals the same way every time?

You should make your appeals like McDonald's makes food. You want to do it the same way every time, constantly looking for ways to streamline the process and to make the finished product better. Before you jump on me for this example, think about it. McDonald's isn't trying to sell gourmet food and you aren't trying to appear in front of the U.S. Supreme Court. You want your appeals to be good enough to win payment every time and you want to spend no more time than necessary to make it happen.

2. Who in your office/business should you pick to track all appeals?

You should appoint one person—and only one—in your office to be responsible for everything having to do with your Medicare appeals. Pick the obsessive-compulsive person (the one who drives you crazy with their need to be thorough) to be responsible for all Medicare appeals in your office. That one person should be responsible for updating the Medicare spreadsheet on your office computer every day and should be responsible for getting every appeal out the door in a timely fashion.

3. How often do you have to review your Medicare appeals spreadsheet?

You should review the Medicare spreadsheet with that one office person at the same time on the same day every week so you both know where you are with every claim that has been partially or completely denied. This is your money. No one else cares about it like you do.

4. What happens when you do not review the Medicare appeals spreadsheet once a week?

Appeals will inevitably slip through the cracks and you will be unable to collect the money you earned providing those lost services.

5. How often should you review the Remittance Advice notices you receive and why?

Here is one more thing you will hate me for: You should personally go through the entire stack of RA notices you receive every day, highlighting every denied or down-coded claim on every Medicare RA. You have to know everything being denied every day or a lot of appeals will get dropped. No one, other than your spouse if working in your office, will keep track of your checkbook like you will. So, you have to check on the payments every day.

6. How long does it take to go through 20 pages of Medicare RA notices?

It doesn't take more than two minutes. I know this is correct because I had a four-doctor practice and I went through all of the RAs every day for all four doctors.

7. How long does it take to perfect an assembly line approach to your top 10 denied codes?

In a few months, you will have a library of articles, textbook sections, policy guidelines, diagrams, and photographs regarding each of your top ten denied codes. And at least 90% of the time, you will be appealing these same ten codes over and over again.

8. You remain unprepared to appeal your most commonly denied codes. What's wrong with this picture?

Everything. If you find yourself unprepared to appeal a denied code that your office/business bills once a year, that's forgivable. But if you remain unprepared and unwilling to appeal the ten most commonly denied codes in your office/business . . .

11

Overview of Options Table

OUTLINE

1. How should you read and use the following "options" table?
2. The first column on the left, titled "Submitting an Appeal on Time with the Required Information at Each Level of Appeal," is the column you want to stay in for the entire appeal.
3. The second column from the left, titled "Requesting an Extension of the Time Limit to Submit an Appeal," applies when you have exceeded the time limit to submit the appeal and you have a good reason for an extension to be granted.
4. The third column from the left, titled "Fighting a Dismissal of an Appeal," refers to the sudden death dismissal.
5. The fourth column from the left, titled "Reopening a Denied Claim or Appeal," refers to what you have to do when you exceed the time limit to submit an appeal at any level of appeal and you cannot meet the "good cause" requirements for an extension.

1. How should you read and use the following "options" table?

I have included a table designed to take you through each part of the appeals process. Hopefully, you will be able to keep almost all your denied claims in the far left-hand column, proceeding smoothly from the initial denial through the redetermination appeal, through the reconsideration appeal, and on to the ALJ hearing. But sometimes bad things happen with appeals and you need to know what to do when a bad thing happens.

2. The first column on the left, titled "Submitting an Appeal on Time with the Required Information at Each Level of Appeal," is the column you want to stay in for the entire appeal.

Staying in that column means you are timely submitting your appeal at each level of appeal and your appeal documents contain all of the required information for each level of appeal.

3. The second column from the left, titled "Requesting an Extension of the Time Limit to Submit an Appeal," applies when you have exceeded the time limit to submit the appeal and you have a good reason for an extension to be granted.

Never request a time extension if you can get the appeal request form in on time. If you have not exceeded the time limit—at any level of appeal—then you have enough time to get the minimum amount of information required on the correct CMS (Centers for Medicare & Medicaid Services) appeal form to the MAC, to the QIC, to the ALJ, or to the Council. The only time you will request an extension is when you have already exceeded the time limit for submission of an appeal, and you have a "good cause" reason for an extension to be granted.

4. The third column from the left, titled "Fighting a Dismissal of an Appeal," refers to the sudden death dismissal.

If your appeal is dismissed for any reason at any level of appeal, you must get the dismissal reversed in order to continue with the appeal. Unless and until you get the dismissal reversed, your appeal is dead in the water.

5. The fourth column from the left, titled "Reopening a Denied Claim or Appeal," refers to what you have to do when you exceed the time limit to submit an appeal at any level of appeal and you cannot meet the "good cause" requirements for an extension.

A reopening for anything other than a clerical error on a claim form is a Medicare Hail Mary pass—an act of desperation that rarely works.

An Overview of the Recurring Options at the Redetermination, Reconsideration, and ALJ Levels of Appeal

Submitting an Appeal on Time with the Required Information at Each Level of Appeal	**Requesting an Extension of the Time Limit to Submit an Appeal** (based on unavoidable circumstances)	**Fighting a Dismissal of an Appeal** (that was too late or did not include required information)	**Reopening a Denied Claim or Appeal** (based on a clerical error or a clearly wrong decision)
This is the column you want to be in and stay throughout the redetermination, reconsideration, and ALJ appeals.	You are asking for an "extension" of the time to submit an appeal because you were unable to get the appeal submitted on time.	Your appeal request was dismissed because your appeal documents were submitted late and/or you did not submit the required information.	You exceeded the statute of limitations and you do **not** have a "good cause" reason to request an extension. All you can do is request a reopening.
If you are in this column, it means your appeal at each level was submitted on time and your appeal documents at each level included the information required by CMS.	You want an extension of time to submit your appeal but it is unlikely you will meet one of the **"good cause"** qualifiers.	When an appeal is dismissed, your appeal is over and your claim is dead unless you get the dismissal reversed based on **"good and sufficient cause."**	You can successfully request a reopening to correct a **clerical error** on a claim form at **any time**.
Staying in this column through the redetermination and reconsideration appeals and through the ALJ appeal request means you have satisfied all of the requirements and you are on your way to an ALJ hearing—where you have the very best chance at winning your appeal of substantive denials.	"Good cause" for an extension means "unavoidable circumstances beyond the provider's control, such as major floods, fires, tornados, and other natural catastrophes."	The phrase "good and sufficient cause" is not defined by Medicare. But the phrase tells us "good cause" is not enough to get a dismissal reversed. The additional word "sufficient" means a very high level of good cause is required in order to get a dismissal reversed.	Otherwise, you have to prove the decision by the contractor, the QIC, or the ALJ was clearly wrong "on the face of the decision." For example, if the QIC relied on a later version of the LCD that said the service in question was not covered but the LCD version in effect *when the service was provided* stated the service *was* covered—that was clearly wrong "on the face of the decision."
Submitting the worst appeal on time is better than submitting the best appeal one day late.	If the extension is denied, the only other thing you can do to keep the claim alive is to ask for a reopening.	You must get the dismissal reversed before you can get back on the appeal track with the claim. If you can't get it reversed, your appeal is dead.	If you can't get the claim/appeal reopened, your appeal is dead.

12

Your Medicare Spreadsheet

OUTLINE

1. Are you one of those providers who say: "I am too busy seeing patients to keep track of denied claims"?
2. Do you need custom software to track Medicare appeals?
3. What information should be recorded on the appeals spreadsheet?
4. When it comes to appeals, what is the difference between a denied initial claim and a demand for repayment of overpayment?
5. How can you quickly know where claims stand when you review the spreadsheet?
6. Should you erase paid claims from the spreadsheet?

1. Are you one of those providers who say: "I am too busy seeing patients to keep track of denied claims"?

Often, I will see a doctor I have known for many years at a meeting and the doctor will say something like: "I am too busy seeing patients to keep track of denied claims." I always find myself thinking in response: "Okay. When you reach the point where your overhead exceeds your payments, let me know . . ."

2. Do you need custom software to track Medicare appeals?

No. For the Medicare spreadsheet on your office computer, use an Excel spreadsheet or Google Sheets. Don't waste money paying for custom software—like I did.

3. What information should be recorded on the appeals spreadsheet?

From left to right, you will want vertical columns that contain the following basic information:

Patient's name (last, first)
Date of service
Denied code (one code per line)

Date of the first denial
Date the redetermination appeal was sent
Date the redetermination appeal was paid, denied, or dismissed
Date the reconsideration appeal was sent
Date the reconsideration appeal was paid, denied, or dismissed
Date the ALJ appeal was sent
Date the ALJ appeal was paid, denied, or dismissed

You can figure out how you want to enter the information regarding extensions, dismissals, and reopenings on the spreadsheet. For example, when you receive a dismissal, when you appeal the dismissal, when the dismissal is reversed, and when you appeal the "reversed dismissal" claim to the next level of appeal should all be entered on the spreadsheet as these events happen. The important thing is you MUST have a spreadsheet you can look at and know exactly where you are with every denied or dismissed claim.

4. When it comes to appeals, what is the difference between a denied initial claim and a demand for repayment of overpayment?

The only difference is when the denial occurs. When a claim is originally denied, Medicare refuses to pay when you send the original claim form. When a claim is the subject of a demand for repayment of overpayment, Medicare has paid the original claim but now wants the money back. In either situation, the appeals process is the same: You must go through the redetermination, reconsideration, and ALJ appeals—until the claim is paid or until the demand for repayment of overpayment is withdrawn.

You will always treat a claim that is the subject of a demand for repayment of overpayment as a "denied" claim. Your appeal of the "overpayment" claim is exactly the same as your appeal of an originally denied claim.

5. How can you quickly know where claims stand when you review the spreadsheet?

Use colors on your spreadsheet. A row with a claim that has been successfully appealed should have no color. A row with a claim that has been denied and is being appealed should have a color such as light yellow. A row with a claim that has been dismissed and the dismissal is being appealed should have another color such as light blue. A simple coloring scheme will allow you to go to the active claims immediately.

6. Should you erase paid claims from the spreadsheet?

No. Do **not** erase the paid claims from the spreadsheet. Medicare makes mistakes all the time and you may get a demand to repay the amount you have been paid on an already successfully appealed claim (a successfully appealed denial or a successfully appealed demand for repayment of overpayment). In that situation, you will respond with a letter to the demanding Medicare party stating: "The claim in question has already been decided through the appeals process and Medicare does not get three bites at the apple. Please let me know you are canceling your demand for repayment of overpayment. Otherwise, please state the legal basis for your demand."

13

"Good Cause" Does Not Mean What You Think It Means

OUTLINE

1. Is the phrase "good cause" used differently at different parts of the appeals process?
2. What does "good cause" mean for an extension?
3. What does "good and sufficient cause" mean when it comes to vacating/reversing a dismissal?
4. What are the good cause requirements for a reopening?
5. Where is good cause for a reopening defined?
6. How long does a provider have to request a reopening?
7. What does the Medicare Manual say about reopenings?

1. Is the phrase "good cause" used differently at different parts of the appeals process?

Yes. Medicare gives a common word or phrase more than one legal definition, depending on the situation, and these legal definitions have nothing to do with the common use of the word or phrase. As an example, providers/suppliers think they know what the phrase "good cause" means. But in Medicare legalese, "good cause" is given several different definitions, and each definition is applied to a separate part of the appeals process.

The "good cause" needed for an extension is different from the "good and sufficient cause" needed to reverse a dismissal, which is still different from the "good cause" needed for a reopening. The Medicare appeals pathway is full of procedural land mines. The Marx brothers should have made one more movie: *Night at the Medicare Appeal.*

2. What does "good cause" mean for an extension?

See 405.942. For an extension, the phrase **good cause** means "unavoidable circumstances beyond the provider's/supplier's control such as major floods, fires, tornados, and other natural catastrophes." And the Medicare Claims Processing Manual (MCPM), Chapter 29, Section 240.3, states:

"Contractors should **NOT** routinely find good cause when a provider/supplier submits an untimely appeal request." (Emphasis added.)

The MCPM goes on to state: "Failure of a billing company to timely submit appeals or other information is **NOT** grounds for finding good cause for late filing. The contractor does **NOT** find good cause where the provider/supplier claims that a lack of business office management skills or expertise caused the late filing." (Emphasis added.)

Medicare does not want the contractor to grant your request for an extension and Medicare will not grant your request for an extension unless God has intervened.

3. What does "good and sufficient cause" mean when it comes to vacating/reversing a dismissal?

See 405.952, 405.972, 405.1004, and 405.1052. Medicare says a simple clerical error on a claim form is always a "good and sufficient cause" to vacate a dismissal. Interestingly, the phrase "good and sufficient cause" is not defined by CMS/Medicare. This gives the contractor, the QIC, and the ALJ more ways to decide against you.

In addition, the "good *and* sufficient cause" phrase implies there are *two separate requirements* to vacate a dismissal. First, you must meet the 405.986 "good cause" requirements. Second, your 405.986 reasons must be "sufficient." This means your 405.986 argument has to be so significant that it would be clearly unreasonable for the contractor, the QIC, or the ALJ not to vacate the dismissal.

If you ask a contractor, a QIC, or an ALJ to vacate a dismissal for any reason other than a simple clerical error, your evidence must be very clear and sufficient enough to overcome your failure to submit the appeal on time.

Besides simple clerical error, there are other "good and sufficient cause" reasons listed in the 42 CFR: "There is evidence that was not considered, and that evidence may result in a different conclusion" and "The evidence that was considered clearly shows on its face that an obvious error was made."

Remember, you are in a situation where you missed the deadline to submit the appeal, Medicare wants your appeal to go away, and the subjective decision by a contractor, a QIC, or an ALJ that you fail to show "good and sufficient cause" to vacate a dismissal is final.

If you are appealing a dismissal at the reconsideration or ALJ level of appeal, hopefully you have already submitted the patient care documents that contain the evidence proving "an obvious error was made." Again, Medicare is looking for any excuse to deny payment.

4. What are the good cause requirements for a reopening?

See Sections 405.980, 405.986, and the MCPM, Chapter 34, Section 10.6.2. A party may request a contractor reopen its initial determination *at any time* to correct a **clerical error** on which the determination was based.

A party may request a contractor reopen its initial determination or redetermination *within one year* from the date of the initial determination or redetermination **for any reason.**

A party may request a contractor reopen its initial determination or redetermination *within four years* from the date of the initial determination or redetermination **for good cause** in accordance with Section 405.986.

5. Where is good cause for a reopening defined?

Good cause for a reopening is defined in 405.986: "There is good cause for reopening when there is evidence that was not considered and that evidence may result in a different conclusion or the evidence that was considered clearly shows on its face that an obvious error was made."

6. How long does a provider have to request a reopening?

A provider may request the QIC, ALJ, or MAC reopen a claim within **180 days** (actually, 185 days) of the QIC, ALJ, or MAC decision for **good cause** in accordance with **405.986.**

7. What does the Medicare Manual say about reopenings?

See the **Medicare Claims Processing Manual, Chapter 34, Section 10.6.2:**

> While a contractor can reopen to correct an unfavorable determination, CMS does **NOT** expect that a contractor would regularly grant these requests, especially for older claims where the claims history is not readily available. Both the contractor and the provider/supplier have a reasonable expectation of administrative finality in the processing of their claims. Additionally, administrative efficiency and the ability of a Medicare contractor to continue vital functions (i.e., process Medicare claims and process appeal requests) require that contractors grant such requests rarely. (Emphasis added)

14

Table of Good Cause for Obtaining Extensions, Vacating Dismissals, and Reopening Claims

OUTLINE

1. When are extensions granted for good cause?
2. What is "good and sufficient cause" to vacate a redetermination dismissal?
3. What is "good and sufficient cause" to vacate a reconsideration dismissal?

1. When are extensions granted for good cause?

Extensions may be granted for "good cause" if:

a. You sent the appeal request before the due date but the appeal request did not get to the contractor, the QIC, or the ALJ until after the due date, or
b. You did not send the appeal request on time to the contractor, the QIC, or the ALJ until after the due date because of circumstances beyond your control (e.g., fire or flood).

2. What is "good and sufficient cause" to vacate a redetermination dismissal?

See 405.952. "Good and sufficient cause" for a **contractor** to vacate a dismissal of a redetermination appeal, see 405.952, includes the following:

- The contractor says you are not a proper party, but you can prove under 405.906(b) that you are.
- The contractor says your redetermination request did not "substantially comply" with 405.944, but you can prove that it did.
- You can prove the error on the request for redetermination—that resulted in the dismissal—was only a clerical error.

- The contractor says your appeal was too late but you can prove "circumstances beyond your control."
- The contractor says there was no initial determination on the claim but you can prove there was because you have the Remittance Advice notice for the initial claim.

3. What is "good and sufficient cause" to vacate a reconsideration dismissal?

See 405.972. "Good and sufficient cause" for a QIC to vacate a dismissal of a reconsideration appeal, see 405.972, includes the following:

a. The QIC says you are not a proper party, but you can prove under 405.906(b) that you are.
b. The contractor says your redetermination request did not "substantially comply" with 405.964(a) and (b), but you can prove that it did.
c. You can prove the error on the request for reconsideration—that resulted in the dismissal—was only a clerical error.
d. The QIC says you failed to file the reconsideration appeal request on time according to 405.962, but you can prove you mailed the appeal within 185 calendar days of the postmarked date on the envelope containing the redetermination denial.
e. The QIC says you failed to file the request on time for reconsideration of a contractor's dismissal of a redetermination request according to 405.974(b)(1). But you can prove you mailed the request for reconsideration of the contractor's dismissal of your redetermination request within 65 calendar days of the postmarked date on the envelope containing the contractor's dismissal of your request for a redetermination appeal.
f. The QIC says your reconsideration appeal was too late but you can prove "circumstances beyond your control."
g. The QIC says there was no redetermination appeal decision but you can prove there was because you have the redetermination denial letter.

Extensions	Vacating Dismissals	Reopenings
You missed the deadline to submit an appeal and you are asking for additional time.	Your appeal has been dismissed because it was too late and/or did not have the required information.	Your claim or appeal was denied and you do not have "good cause" for an extension.
If you are granted the extension, you can submit the appeal.	You have to get the dismissal reversed to continue your appeal.	Your only option is to ask for a reopening.
You think you have **"good cause"** under 405.942 to ask the contractor, the QIC, or the ALJ to grant an extension of the time limit to submit your appeal.	You think you have **"good and sufficient cause"** to ask the contractor under 405.952, the QIC under 405.972, or the ALJ under 405.1004 and 405.1052 to vacate the dismissal.	You think you have **"good cause"** under 405.980 and 405.986 to ask the contractor, the QIC, or the ALJ to reopen the claim or appeal.
There is **no stated time limit** to request an extension—but CMS does not want to give you more time to submit your appeals.	You have **six months** after your appeal has been dismissed to request a contractor, a QIC, or an ALJ to vacate the dismissal.	You can request a reopening for a clerical error at **any time**. You can ask the contractor to reopen an initial decision or redetermination within **one year** for any reason; the contractor to reopen an initial decision or redetermination within **four years** for "good cause" in accordance with 405.986; the QIC, ALJ, or MAC to reopen an appeal within **180 days** based on 405.986 "good cause."
"Good cause" for an extension: The records were accidentally lost or destroyed (e.g., while the practice/business was being moved to another location). **You sent the request on time but it did not get there until after the deadline.** This one actually works. You did not send the appeal request on time due to circumstances beyond your control (e.g., fire or flood).	**"Good and sufficient cause"** for a **contractor**, a QIC, or an ALJ to vacate a dismissal: The appeal request form error was a clerical error. Medicare incorrectly says you are not a proper party, under 405.906(b). Medicare incorrectly says the appeal did not "substantially comply" with 405.944. Medicare says you appealed too late, but the appeal was mailed before the deadline. Medicare says you appealed too late, but you can prove "circumstances beyond your control." Medicare incorrectly says "no initial determination."	You can successfully request a reopening to correct a **clerical error** on a claim form at any time. Otherwise, for a reopening, you must prove the denial was clearly wrong "on the face of the decision" (42 CFR 405.986). For example, if the QIC relied on a later version of the LCD that said the service was not covered, but the LCD version in effect *when the service was provided* says the service was covered—that would be an example of a decision that is clearly wrong "on the face of the decision."
If the **extension is denied**, your only other option is to **ask for a reopening**.	If you cannot get the **dismissal vacated**, your appeal is dead.	If you cannot get the claim **reopened**, your appeal is dead.

15

Extensions

OUTLINE

1. When can you ask for an extension?
2. When will you be granted an extension?
3. Generally, when should you ask for an extension instead of a reopening?
4. When you miss the redetermination deadline, how can you get an extension?
5. When you miss the reconsideration deadline, how can you get an extension?
6. When you miss the ALJ deadline, how can you get an extension?

1. When can you ask for an extension?

You can ask for an extension when you miss the deadline for the next available level of appeal, but you must have a "good cause" reason for the late submission.

2. When will you be granted an extension?

You will only be granted an extension if you can prove the patient's records were lost or damaged due to an accident outside of your control (e.g., flood or fire).

3. Generally, when should you ask for an extension instead of a reopening?

When you exceed the time limit to submit an appeal, you will always ask for a *reopening* if the denial was based on a simple clerical error, or you can prove the denial was based on an error by the contractor, the QIC, or the ALJ.

If there was no clerical error, and you cannot prove the denial was based on an error by the contractor, the QIC, or the ALJ, you will ask for an *extension*—if the reason you are late is because the patient's records were lost or destroyed.

4. When you miss the redetermination deadline, how can you get an extension?

See 405.942. The provider/supplier must show "good cause" for an extension of the time to submit a redetermination appeal. Examples of good cause include but are not limited to the following situations: The patient's records were destroyed or damaged by fire or other accidental cause, or in my opinion—if the patient's records were lost.

But how many times do you think you can use "the records were lost" excuse? This is similar to the "I lost my homework" excuse.

5. When you miss the reconsideration deadline, how can you get an extension?

See 405.962. The provider/supplier must show the same good cause reasons as for a redetermination extension.

6. When you miss the ALJ deadline, how can you get an extension?

See 405.1014. The provider/supplier must show the same good cause reasons as for a redetermination extension.

16

Dismissals

OUTLINE

1. Is a dismissal a denial of payment?
2. When an appeal is dismissed, what happens to the claim?
3. Why are appeals dismissed?
4. How can you avoid dismissals?
5. How can you get the redetermination appeal form?
6. How can you get the reconsideration appeal form?
7. How can you get the ALJ appeal form?
8. After you receive a denial, how soon should you submit your next-level appeal?
9. Why is it so important to appeal to the next level as soon as you receive a denial at any level?
10. What huge advantage comes with appealing early?
11. The MAC or the QIC refuses to look at an incorrectly dismissed appeal. What can you do?
12. CMS's Regional Office refuses to look at an incorrectly dismissed appeal. What can you do?
13. How dangerous are dismissals?
14. Your redetermination appeal was dismissed by the MAC. How did that happen?
15. Why does a MAC dismiss a redetermination appeal request?
16. The MAC says you are not a proper party to request a redetermination appeal. What does that mean?
17. How should you respond when the MAC says you are not a proper party?
18. The MAC says your redetermination appeal failed to substantially comply with 405.944. What does that mean?
19. Which item is most frequently missing on the redetermination appeal?
20. The MAC incorrectly states your redetermination appeal failed to "substantially comply with 405.944." What can you do?
21. The MAC says you filed the redetermination appeal late. What does that mean?
22. Is the time limit to submit a redetermination appeal 120 days?
23. When will the MAC accept a late-submitted redetermination appeal and reverse the dismissal?
24. What is the Medicare definition of "good and sufficient cause"?

25. A provider must prove "good and sufficient cause" to get a dismissal vacated. How is it possible there is no Medicare definition of "good and sufficient cause"?
26. Is there a partial definition of the phrase "good and sufficient cause"?
27. Which 405.942 "good cause" reason to vacate a dismissal actually works?
28. Why should you be afraid of the phrase "good and sufficient cause"?
29. What if you have "good and sufficient cause" but the MAC or QIC refuses to vacate the dismissal?
30. Will a clerical error always save an appeal that has been dismissed by a contractor?
31. Your reconsideration appeal was dismissed. How did that happen?
32. What are the reasons QICs dismiss a reconsideration appeal request?
33. The QIC dismisses your appeal, saying you are not a proper party to request a reconsideration appeal. What does that mean?
34. How should you respond to the QIC?
35. The QIC says you failed to substantially comply with 405.964. What does that mean?
36. Which items are most frequently missing on the reconsideration appeal?
37. How should you respond when the QIC says your appeal failed to substantially comply with 405.964?
38. Your ALJ appeal was dismissed. How did that happen?
39. Why are ALJ hearing requests dismissed before the hearing is scheduled?
40. What is the time limit to request an ALJ hearing?
41. When will an ALJ accept a late-submitted appeal and reverse the dismissal?
42. How does an ALJ determine if there is "good cause" for a late filing?
43. How do you get all the way to an ALJ hearing and not meet the Amount In Controversy (AIC) requirement?
44. What should you write when you want to include less than $170 in claims in a future ALJ hearing scheduled for other claims?
45. Why are ALJ hearing requests dismissed after the hearing is scheduled?
46. You were a hearing no-show, did not contact the ALJ, and did not explain why. How did this happen and what should you do?
47. Does an ALJ remember a provider who schedules a hearing, misses the hearing, and then fails to explain why?
48. The ALJ sends you a notice asking why you did not appear but you do not respond. When and how does this happen and what should you do?
49. How important are the ALJs to your Medicare appeals?
50. What happens to a denied claim before and after the ALJ appeal?
51. Why should you always be willing to lose the ALJ decision rather than lie to the ALJ?
52. What is the result of failing to appear and then failing to explain why?
53. What is the question you should ask yourself when you lie to an ALJ or you fail to show for a hearing without explaining why?

1. Is a dismissal a denial of payment?

No. A dismissal is **not** a denial of payment. A dismissal is a **denial of your right to continue the appeal** of a claim that was denied and has now been dismissed for technical reasons during the appeals process.

2. When an appeal is dismissed, what happens to the claim?

When a claim appeal is dismissed—whether by the contractor, by the QIC, or by the ALJ—that claim is **off** the appeals track. Unless and until you get the dismissal vacated (reversed), that claim is dead in the water.

3. Why are appeals dismissed?

Appeals are dismissed when the contractor, the QIC, or the ALJ concludes you are not a proper party to the dispute, the appeal form you submitted did not include all the required information, and/or your appeal was submitted too late.

4. How can you avoid dismissals?

First, **use the forms provided by Medicare** for the redetermination, reconsideration, and ALJ levels of appeal. And second, get your appeals in early.

5. How can you get the redetermination appeal form?

The redetermination appeal form can be downloaded by putting **CMS-20027** in the search bar.

6. How can you get the reconsideration appeal form?

The reconsideration appeal form can be downloaded by putting **CMS-20033** in the search bar.

7. How can you get the ALJ appeal form?

The ALJ appeal form can be downloaded by putting **OMHA-100** in the search bar.

8. After you receive a denial, how soon should you submit your next-level appeal?

As soon as you get a denial, at any level, you should immediately appeal to the next higher level of appeal. It is a mistake to "wait" until you have a large number of denied claims to appeal them all at once.

9. Why is it so important to appeal to the next level as soon as you receive denial at any level?

Medicare has designed the appeals process to eliminate the claims with any technical errors. The sooner you appeal an initial claim denial, a redetermination appeal denial, or a reconsideration appeal denial, the more time you have to move through the Medicare appeals process on the way to the ALJ appeal. And because you will make many mistakes during the appeals process, you want to give yourself as much time as possible to successfully correct your mistakes as you fight for payment.

10. What huge advantage comes with appealing early?

Appealing early allows you to avoid appeal-crushing requests for extensions, reversals of dismissals, and reopenings.

11. The MAC or the QIC refuses to look at an incorrectly dismissed appeal. What can you do?

When a provider can prove the MAC or the QIC has incorrectly dismissed an appeal based on the provider's previously submitted documents, the provider should contact the CMS Regional Office for help. Here is the link to the web page that will take you to your CMS Regional Office (RO).

When you are on your RO web page, scroll down to the "Division of Financial Management and Fee for Service Operations" section to find the person you should contact. https://www.cms.gov/About-CMS/Agency-Information/RegionalOffices/index.html

12. CMS's Regional Office refuses to look at an incorrectly dismissed appeal. What can you do?

As a last resort, if the CMS Regional Office will not help, you can submit your complaint to the Medicare Fee-For-Service Appeals office at MedicareFFSAppeals@cms.hhs.gov.

13. How dangerous are dismissals?

A dismissal is Medicare's equivalent of quicksand. Unless you get out quickly, your claim has no chance of surviving.

DISMISSAL BY A MEDICARE ADMINISTRATIVE CONTRACTOR (MAC)

14. Your redetermination appeal was dismissed by the MAC. How did that happen?

You provided a medically reasonable and necessary service to a Medicare patient.
You submitted a claim to the contractor within one year of providing the service.
The contractor denied payment of the claim.
You submitted a redetermination appeal to the contractor.
The contractor dismissed your redetermination appeal.

15. Why does a MAC dismiss a redetermination appeal request?

See 405.952—Withdrawal or dismissal of a request for a redetermination.

The contractor claims the provider/supplier is **not a proper party**, under 405.906, to request a redetermination appeal.

The contractor claims the provider/supplier **failed to make out a valid request** for redetermination that complies with 405.944.

The contractor claims the provider/supplier **failed to file** the redetermination appeal request **on time** in accordance with 405.942.

An additional but uncommon possibility—the contractor claims an initial determination on the claim has not yet been issued.

16. The MAC says you are not a proper party to request a redetermination appeal. What does that mean?

It means the contractor mistakenly thinks you are not a contracted Medicare provider/supplier and/or the contractor thinks you did not accept assignment for the service in question.

17. How should you respond when the MAC says you are not a proper party?

Send a letter to the contractor that says:

I am a contracted Medicare provider/supplier. I am enclosing a copy of the originally submitted claim form that includes all the required information: my provider number, my acceptance of assignment, the specific CPT [Current Procedural Terminology] code services provided to

Medicare beneficiary, (first, last), and the date of service (month/day/year). Under 42 CFR 450.906, I am a proper party to this redetermination appeal. Please vacate the dismissal of my redetermination appeal and issue a redetermination decision.

18. The MAC says your redetermination appeal failed to substantially comply with 405.944. What does that mean?

It means the contractor thinks you did not provide all the information required in 405.944, which states a request for redetermination appeal must contain the following: the beneficiary's name, the Medicare health insurance claim number, the specific service(s) and/or item(s) for which the redetermination is being requested, the specific date(s) of service, and the name and signature of the doctor.

19. Which item is most frequently missing on the redetermination appeal?

It is the actual signature of the provider/supplier that is most frequently missing. Remember, stamped signatures are not allowed.

20. The MAC incorrectly states your redetermination appeal failed to "substantially comply with 405.944." What can you do?

If the **contractor is correct** and your original redetermination appeal request **did not contain** all the required information for a redetermination appeal, **and** if it is **less than six months** from the date you received the contractor's notice of dismissal, submit a request to the contractor to reverse the dismissal based on a corrected appeal form.

Send a corrected CMS-20027 form along with a letter to the contractor that says:

I apologize for the clerical error on the previously submitted redetermination appeal request form. I am enclosing a corrected copy of the originally submitted CMS-20027 form, which accurately includes the beneficiary's name, the Medicare health insurance claim number, the specific service(s) and/or item(s) for which the redetermination is being requested, and the specific date(s) of service, along with my name and signature. Please vacate the dismissal and issue a redetermination decision on this claim.

If the **contractor is wrong** and your original redetermination appeal request contained all the necessary information for a redetermination appeal, **and it is less than 60 days** from the date you received the contractor's notice of dismissal, submit a request to the QIC for reconsideration of the contractor's dismissal (405.974). You will almost always get a fairer review by the next higher level of appeal.

Send a letter to the QIC that says:

I am enclosing a copy of the originally submitted CMS-20027, redetermination appeal request form. The original appeal form accurately included all of the 405.944 required information: the beneficiary's name, the Medicare health insurance claim number, the specific service(s) and/or item(s) for which the redetermination was being requested, and the specific date(s) of service, along with my name and signature. Under 405.974, please vacate the dismissal and return the case to the contractor for a redetermination decision.

If **the contractor is wrong** and your original redetermination appeal request contained all the necessary information for a redetermination appeal, **and it is more than 60 days but less than six months** from the date you received the contractor's notice of dismissal, submit a request to the **contractor** to vacate the dismissal.

Send a letter to the **contractor** that says:

I am enclosing a copy of the originally submitted CMS-20027, redetermination appeal request form. The original appeal form accurately included all the 405.944 required information: the beneficiary's name, the Medicare health insurance claim number, the specific service(s) and/or item(s) for which the redetermination was being requested, the specific date(s) of service, and my name and signature. Under 405.952, please vacate the dismissal and issue a redetermination decision.

If **the contractor is wrong** and your original redetermination appeal request contained all the necessary information for a redetermination appeal, **even if it is more than six months** from the date you received the contractor's notice of dismissal, submit a request to the **contractor** to reverse the dismissal.

Send a letter to the contractor that says:

I am enclosing a copy of the originally submitted CMS-20027, redetermination appeal request form along with a copy of your notice of dismissal. My original appeal form accurately included all of the required information: the beneficiary's name, the Medicare health insurance claim number, the specific service(s) and/or item(s) for which the redetermination was being requested, the specific date(s) of service, and my name and signature.

Although I am sending this request more than six months after I received your notice of dismissal, there is good and sufficient cause to vacate the dismissal because [name of contractor] was 100% responsible for this incorrect dismissal. Please vacate the dismissal now and please issue a redetermination decision.

21. The MAC says you filed the redetermination appeal late. What does that mean?

It means the contractor did not receive your redetermination appeal within the time limit.

22. Is the time limit to submit a redetermination appeal 120 days?

No. 405.942(a) says your request for a redetermination appeal must reach the contractor within 120 calendar days from the date you received the initial claim denial. But 405.942(a)(1) says the date of receipt of the initial claim denial will be presumed to be 5 calendar days after the date of the notice of initial determination. So, you get **120 days plus 5 days after the postmarked date** on the envelope containing the initial denial. And if the 125th day falls on a weekend or holiday, the provider/supplier can move the calculated due date forward to the next workday: Keep all denial envelopes!

23. When will the MAC accept a late-submitted redetermination appeal and reverse the dismissal?

The contractor will vacate the dismissal of a late-submitted redetermination appeal request when you can establish "good and sufficient cause" for acceptance of the late submission.

24. What is the Medicare definition of "good and sufficient cause"?

Guess what? There is no Medicare definition of "good and sufficient cause."

25. A provider must prove "good and sufficient cause" to get a dismissal vacated. How is it possible there is no Medicare definition of "good and sufficient cause"?

Medicare did not define "good and sufficient cause" because Medicare wanted to give the contractor, the QIC, and the ALJ room to make the subjective decision whether to reverse the dismissal of your appeal.

26. Is there a partial definition of the phrase "good and sufficient cause"?

Although there is no Medicare definition of "good and sufficient cause," the definition for this phrase at least partially defaults to the definition of "good cause" in 405.942.

Section 405.942 says the contractor will consider the following **factors** when deciding whether a provider/supplier has "good cause" for missing the deadline to submit a redetermination appeal request: The circumstances that kept the provider/supplier from making the request on time, whether the contractor's actions misled the provider/supplier, and whether there was any physical or mental reason that prevented the provider/supplier from filing on time.

Section 405.942 includes the following statement and **examples of good cause:**

> Examples of circumstances when good cause may be found to exist include, **but are not limited to,** the following situations: The provider/supplier had a serious illness, there was a death or serious illness in the provider's/supplier's family, important records were destroyed or damaged by fire or other accidental cause, the contractor gave the provider/supplier the wrong information, the provider/supplier did not get notice of the determination, and the provider/supplier sent the request for a redetermination appeal within the time limit but the request did not reach the contractor until after the time limit.

27. Which 405.942 "good cause" reason to vacate a dismissal actually works?

A contractor must vacate a dismissal when the provider/supplier sends the request for a redetermination appeal within the time limit but the request does not reach the contractor until after the time limit.

28. Why should you be afraid of the phrase "good and sufficient cause"?

Do not underestimate the significance of the word "sufficient" in the phrase "good and sufficient cause." There is no Medicare definition of "good and sufficient cause," which gives the contractor, the QIC, and the ALJ discretion to make a subjective decision against you.

Medicare wants the contractor, the QIC, and the ALJ to dismiss as many appeals as possible. Unless you have very strong evidence supporting the reason for your late appeal, the contractor, the QIC, or the ALJ will rule against you.

29. What if you have "good and sufficient cause" but the MAC or QIC refuses to vacate the dismissal?

In the rare case where your evidence supporting the reason for the late appeal is very strong but the contractor or the QIC refuses to vacate the dismissal, I would advise you to contact the Medicare appeals section at CMS and ask them to intercede. In my experience, if you can provide the documents that objectively support "good and sufficient cause," CMS will step in and contact the contractor or the QIC.

However, don't bother asking CMS to step in when an ALJ refuses to reverse a dismissal. Medicare ALJs are "independent" from CMS, and the Medicare Appeals Council always supports a negative payment decision from an ALJ whenever the law allows it.

30. Will a clerical error always save an appeal that has been dismissed by a contractor?

Yes. A minor clerical error on the redetermination appeal request form is always "good and sufficient cause" for the contractor to vacate a dismissal—even when the redetermination appeal is late.

DISMISSALS BY QICs

31. Your reconsideration appeal was dismissed. How did that happen?

You provided a medically reasonable and necessary service to a Medicare patient.
You submitted a claim to the contractor within one year of providing the service.
The contractor denied payment of the claim.
You submitted a redetermination appeal to the contractor.
The contractor denied your redetermination appeal.
You submitted a reconsideration appeal to the QIC.
The QIC dismissed your appeal.

32. What are the reasons QICs dismiss a reconsideration appeal request?

See 405.972—Withdrawal or dismissal of a request for reconsideration.

The QIC claims the provider/supplier is not a proper party, under 405.906(b), to request a reconsideration appeal.
The QIC claims the provider/supplier failed to make out a valid request for reconsideration that "substantially complies" with 405.964.
The QIC claims the provider/supplier failed to file the reconsideration appeal request on time in accordance with 405.962.
The QIC claims the provider/supplier failed to file the request for reconsideration of a contractor's dismissal of a redetermination request on time in accordance with 405.974.
The QIC claims the contractor has not yet issued a redetermination decision.

33. The QIC dismisses your appeal, saying you are not a proper party to request a reconsideration appeal. What does that mean?

It means the QIC mistakenly thinks you are not a contracted Medicare provider/supplier and/or the QIC thinks you did not accept assignment for the service at issue.

34. How should you respond to the QIC?

Send a letter to the QIC that says:

I am a participating Medicare provider/supplier and I billed for the services at issue on an assigned basis. Along with a copy of your letter dismissing my appeal, I am enclosing a copy of the originally submitted claim form. Please vacate your dismissal of my reconsideration appeal and issue a reconsideration decision.

35. The QIC says you failed to substantially comply with 405.964. What does that mean?

The QIC thinks you did not provide all the information required in 405.964, which states a request for a reconsideration appeal must contain the following: the beneficiary's name, the Medicare health insurance claim number, the specific service(s) and/or item(s) for which the reconsideration is being requested, the specific date(s) of service, the name and signature of the provider/supplier, and the name of the contractor that made the redetermination.

36. Which items are most frequently missing on the reconsideration appeal?

The **signature** of the provider/supplier and the **name of the contractor** that made the redetermination decision are the most frequently missing items.

37. How should you respond when the QIC says your appeal failed to substantially comply with 405.964?

First, consider which of these three possibilities you fall into:

a. The QIC is **correct**—the QIC appeal form lacks some information, and it is **less than six months** since you received the redetermination denial notice from the contractor.
b. The QIC is **wrong**—your QIC appeal request contained all the necessary information, and it is **less than 60 days** since you received the redetermination denial notice from the contractor.
c. The QIC is **wrong**—your QIC appeal request contained all the necessary information, and it is **more than 60 days but less than six months** since you received the redetermination denial notice from the contractor.

If the **QIC is correct** and your original reconsideration appeal request **did not contain** all the required information for a reconsideration appeal, **and if it is less than six months** from the date you received the QIC's notice of dismissal, submit a request to the QIC to reverse the dismissal along with a corrected appeal form.

Send a letter to the **QIC** that says:

I apologize for the clerical error on the previously submitted reconsideration appeal request form. I am enclosing a corrected copy of the originally submitted CMS-20033 form, which accurately includes the beneficiary's name, the Medicare health insurance claim number, the specific service(s) and/or item(s) for which the reconsideration is being requested, the specific date(s) of service, my name and signature, and the name of the contractor that made the redetermination. Please vacate the dismissal and issue a reconsideration decision on this claim.

If the **QIC is wrong** and your original reconsideration appeal request contained all the necessary information for a reconsideration appeal, **and if it is less than 60 days** from the date you received the QIC's notice of dismissal, submit a request to the ALJ for reconsideration of the QIC's dismissal (405.1004). You will almost always get a fairer review by the next higher level of appeal.

Send a letter to the **ALJ** that says:

I am enclosing a copy of the originally submitted CMS-20033, reconsideration appeal request form. The original appeal form accurately included all of the required information: the beneficiary's name, the Medicare health insurance claim number, the specific service(s) and/or item(s) for which the reconsideration was being requested and the specific date(s) of service, my name and signature, and the name of the contractor that made the redetermination. Please vacate the dismissal and return the case to the QIC for a reconsideration decision.

If **the QIC is wrong** and your original reconsideration appeal request contained all the necessary information for a reconsideration appeal, **and if it is more than 60 days but less than six months** from the date you received the QIC's notice of dismissal, submit a request to the QIC to reverse the dismissal.

Send a letter to the QIC that says:

I am enclosing a copy of the originally submitted CMS-20033, reconsideration appeal request form. The original appeal form accurately included all of the required information: the beneficiary's name, the Medicare health insurance claim number, the specific service(s) and/or item(s) for which the reconsideration was being requested, the specific date(s) of service, my name and signature, and the name of the contractor that made the redetermination. Please vacate the dismissal and issue a reconsideration decision.

DISMISSALS BY ALJs

38. Your ALJ appeal was dismissed. How did that happen?

You provided a medically reasonable and necessary service to a Medicare patient.
You submitted a claim to the contractor within one year of providing the service.
The contractor denied payment of the claim.
You submitted a redetermination appeal to the contractor.
The contractor denied your redetermination appeal.
You submitted a reconsideration appeal to the QIC.
The QIC denied your reconsideration appeal.
You submitted an ALJ appeal to the ALJ.
The ALJ *dismissed* your ALJ appeal.

See 405.1002—Right to an ALJ hearing; 405.1052—Dismissal of a request for a hearing before an ALJ.

39. Why are ALJ hearing requests dismissed before the hearing is scheduled?

An ALJ hearing request is dismissed **before the hearing is scheduled** when the ALJ thinks the provider/supplier violated one or more of the requirements under 405.1002:

The provider's/supplier's request for an ALJ hearing must be received by the ALJ within 60 calendar days of the date on the envelope containing the QIC reconsideration denial. 405.1002.

The provider/supplier did not request a hearing within the stated period of time and the ALJ has not found good cause for extending the deadline, as provided in 405.1014.

The provider/supplier does not meet the $170 amount in controversy requirement under 405.1006.

40. What is the time limit to request an ALJ hearing?

405.1002(a)(1) says your request for an ALJ appeal must reach the ALJ office within 60 calendar days after receipt of the notice of the QIC's reconsideration. But 405.1002(a)(3) says the date of receipt of the reconsideration will be presumed to be 5 calendar days after the date of the reconsideration. So, you get **60 days plus 5 days after the postmarked date** on the envelope containing the reconsideration denial. And if the 65th day falls on a weekend or holiday, the provider/supplier can move the calculated due date forward to the next workday. Keep all denial envelopes!

41. When will an ALJ accept a late-submitted appeal and reverse the dismissal?

An ALJ will vacate the dismissal of a late-submitted ALJ appeal request when you can establish "good cause" for acceptance of the late submission.

42. How does an ALJ determine if there is "good cause" for a late filing?

The ALJ will use the standards in 405.942(b)(2) and 405.942(b)(3) to determine whether there is "good cause" for a late filing.

43. How do you get all the way to an ALJ hearing and not meet the Amount In Controversy (AIC) requirement?

The amount in controversy becomes an issue when a group of claims is appealed and there is a partial positive payment decision by the contractor and/or the QIC.

However, because you are smart enough to constantly appeal all the Medicare denials you receive, it is likely you will be able to combine the less than $170 in outstanding claims with future claims in your ongoing stream of appeals. And in my opinion, you can and should fashion a "good cause" argument for the ALJ, even when the less than $170 in outstanding claims exceeds the 60-day time limit.

But with the exception of an "amount in controversy" problem following a partially favorable contractor/QIC determination, every other reason for an ALJ dismissal of an appeal is a practice management disaster. You are not going to be paid for the denied services and you have wasted a considerable amount of time and effort guiding the claim(s) through the redetermination and reconsideration appeals.

44. What should you write when you want to include less than $170 in claims in a future ALJ hearing scheduled for other claims?

I would write something like this:

> *Dear Judge [last name],*
>
> *I am scheduled to appear before you on [date] for a hearing. I am writing this letter to ask you to find good cause to additionally include [a claim/a group of claims] in our hearing scheduled for [date].*
>
> *These additional claims were originally part of a larger group of claims. But because of partial positive decision(s) by [the contractor and/or the QIC], the remaining amount in controversy from that appeal is less than $170.*
>
> *Although more than 60 days have passed since the QIC decision, these remaining claim(s) were for medically reasonable and necessary services and these claim(s) would have qualified for an ALJ hearing if the amount had met the $170 amount in controversy requirement. Significantly, Medicare is not prejudiced in any way by including this/these claim(s) in our upcoming hearing scheduled for [date].*
>
> *I am enclosing copies of the redetermination and reconsideration decision letters.*
>
> *Thank you for considering this good cause request to include these claims in our upcoming hearing.*

45. Why are ALJ hearing requests dismissed after the hearing is scheduled?

An ALJ hearing request is dismissed **after a hearing is scheduled** under 405.1052 when:

The provider/supplier does not appear at the time and place of hearing and does not contact the ALJ hearing office within ten calendar days or does not provide good cause for not appearing.

The ALJ sends a notice asking why the provider/supplier did not appear and the provider/supplier does not respond to the ALJ's notice within ten calendar days or does not provide good cause for the failure to appear.

46. You were a hearing no-show, did not contact the ALJ, and did not explain why. How did this happen and what should you do?

ALJ hearings require too many notices for a provider/supplier to be unaware of a hearing.

Your office requested the hearing. The ALJ sent you a "Notice of Hearing" letter approximately three weeks before the hearing (see 405.1022). The letter included the type of hearing (by telephone or by video teleconference), the exact issues to be decided, a request for detailed information regarding any witnesses who were to appear on your behalf, how you could change the time or place of the hearing, and a warning that a failure to appear at the hearing may result in a dismissal of your case.

The "Notice of Hearing" letter also included a demand from the ALJ for the provider/supplier to sign and send written confirmation to the ALJ's office, confirming receipt of the ALJ letter and acceptance of the terms of the hearing.

Let's say you responded to the "Notice of Hearing" letter and you told the ALJ, in your response letter, that you accepted the terms of the hearing (the time and type of hearing and the issues to be decided). But then you failed to show up for the hearing and you failed to contact the ALJ with a good cause explanation for your failure to appear. Your appeal will of course be dismissed. But the dismissal of the hearing is the least of your problems.

47. Does an ALJ remember a provider who schedules a hearing, misses the hearing, and then fails to explain why?

Are you kidding? The Medicare ALJs have brutal caseloads and cannot afford to waste hours of prehearing preparation and at least an hour set aside for the hearing itself. You will absolutely be remembered and you will probably be spoken of when the ALJs have lunch together.

48. The ALJ sends you a notice asking why you did not appear but you do not respond. When and how does this happen and what should you do?

You must send the ALJ a letter humbly apologizing for your failure to appear and your failure to provide "good cause" for the non-appearance.

If you think the ALJs don't talk to each other about providers/suppliers who are rude enough to schedule a hearing, fail to appear at the hearing, and then fail to explain why they didn't appear, you would be wrong. This is similar to a patient scheduling surgery and then doesn't show up at the hospital and doesn't respond to phone calls from your office asking why they didn't show up. The critical difference, of course, is that while you can choose not to see that patient again, it is likely other claims you will be appealing will be assigned to the same ALJ.

49. How important are the ALJs to your Medicare appeals?

Unless a Medicare payment is denied because of a simple clerical error on a claim form, it is unlikely you will be awarded payment on that claim until you get to the ALJ hearing. **The ALJ represents your first and last chance at a neutral third-party decision on denied claims.**

50. What happens to a denied claim before and after the ALJ appeal?

In response to the redetermination appeal request, the contractor will sustain an initial claim denial of payment for anything other than a clerical error.

In response to the reconsideration appeal request, the QIC will sustain the contractor's redetermination denial almost every time.

If you lose the ALJ decision, the Medicare Appeals Council will only rule in your favor when there is a clear error of law on the ALJ's part (e.g., the applicable LCD allowed the denied service and the ALJ denied payment based on an out-of-date LCD).

51. Why should you always be willing to lose the ALJ decision rather than lie to the ALJ?

You must maintain the integrity of your reputation with the ALJs. You must never, ever lie to an ALJ. Once the ALJ tags you as a liar, it is unlikely you will ever be able to repair that relationship.

52. What is the result of failing to appear and then failing to explain why?

If you fail to show for the ALJ hearing and your excuse for missing the hearing does not meet "good cause" requirements—or worse, you don't even bother to explain why you missed the hearing—you will have embarrassed yourself and disrespected the ALJ.

53. What is the question you should ask yourself when you lie to an ALJ or you fail to show for a hearing without explaining why?

What are my chances for success the next time I have a hearing in front of that judge?

17

Reopenings

OUTLINE

1. What is a reopening?
2. How is a reopening by Medicare different from a reopening initiated by a provider?
3. Where can you find information on reopenings?
4. When will you ask for a reopening?
5. If you still have time to submit a redetermination appeal, when or why should you ask for a reopening?
6. If you still have time to submit a reconsideration appeal, when or why should you ask for a reopening?
7. Is there anything you can request in a reopening that you cannot request in an appeal?
8. Why should you always avoid asking for a reopening if there is still time to appeal?
9. When will a reopening get a denied claim or appeal back on the appeals track?
10. How does CMS define "clerical errors"?
11. What should you send when you request a reopening based on a clerical error?
12. Why not phone the contractor and request a reopening?
13. Why is it confusing when CMS mistakenly denies a claim/appeal as a "duplicate"?
14. What should you send when requesting a reopening of a mistaken "duplicate"?
15. Does CMS include the failure to bill for items or services as a clerical error?
16. What should you do if you discover items or services were not billed?
17. What if you discover services you provided 13 months earlier were never billed?
18. How does Medicare justify the one-year time limit to bill for services?
19. What does the CFR say regarding "good cause" for a reopening?
20. In plain English, how is the first part of 405.986 [405.986(a)(1)] applied?
21. Is the 405.986(a)(1) "good cause for reopening" section ever applied in favor of a provider?
22. In plain English, how is the second part of 405.986 [405.986(a)(2)] applied?
23. Is a provider's request for a reopening an appeal?
24. What is the functional difference between an appeal and a reopening?
25. When and on what basis can an initial determination or a redetermination be reopened?
26. How much time does a provider have to ask a QIC, an ALJ, an attorney adjudicator, or the Council to reopen a decision?
27. What does the Medicare Claims Processing Manual (MCPM) say about provider reopenings?

1. What is a reopening?

A reopening is a second look at a claim to determine whether the original payment or denial was correct.

2. How is a reopening by Medicare different from a reopening initiated by a provider?

For a Medicare contractor, a reopening is a corrective action taken to claw back money from a provider when a medical review reveals a possible overpayment—after payment has been made.

For a provider, a reopening is a remedial action taken to get a denied initial claim or a denied appeal back on the appeals track when the provider waits too long to directly appeal the denial.

It should be no surprise that Medicare uses reopenings far more frequently and far more successfully than do providers.

3. Where can you find information on reopenings?

See the 42 CFR Sections 405.980–405.986, the Internet-Only Manual 100-04 (Medicare Claims Processing Manual), Chapters 29 and 34, and the Medicare Learning Network (MLN) article MM 4147.

4. When will you ask for a reopening?

As a provider, you will ask for a reopening **only** when you miss the deadline for an appeal.

5. If you still have time to submit a redetermination appeal, when or why should you ask for a reopening?

You wouldn't. If you are still **within** the 120-day time limit for a redetermination appeal, you will **never** ask for a reopening. You will always ask for a redetermination.

6. If you still have time to submit a reconsideration appeal, when or why should you ask for a reopening?

You wouldn't. If you are still **within** the 180-day time limit for a reconsideration appeal, you will **never** ask for a reopening. You will always ask for a reconsideration.

7. Is there anything you can request in a reopening that you cannot request in an appeal?

No. Whatever you are asking for in a reopening request, you can ask for in an appeal as long as the time limit for submission of the appeal has not expired.

8. Why should you always avoid asking for a reopening if there is still time to appeal?

If you submit an appeal and the contractor or QIC **denies** the appeal, you can always continue to the next level of appeal.

But if you submit a request for a reopening while there is still time to appeal and the contractor or the QIC denies the reopening, you may run out of time to appeal by the time you get the reopening denial. And that reopening decision is final.

Never, ever ask for a reopening if there is still time to appeal!

9. When will a reopening get a denied claim or appeal back on the appeals track?

A reopening request by a provider will succeed when:

a. The provider makes a **clerical error** on a claim form.
b. The claim is denied as a "**duplicate**" but the claim is not a duplicate.
c. There is **good cause** in accordance with Section 405.986(a)(2) to reopen the claim.

10. How does CMS define "clerical errors"?

CMS defines clerical errors on claim forms as:

a. Mathematical or computational mistakes by the provider.
b. Inaccurate data entry.
c. Claims incorrectly denied as duplicates.

11. What should you send when you request a reopening based on a clerical error?

You should attach a copy of the original claim form, a copy of the corrected claim form, a copy of the supporting progress notes, and a copy of the claim/appeal denial all stapled to the reopening request (e.g., Noridian's redetermination/reopening form).

12. Why not phone the contractor and request a reopening?

Given the choice, you should **never** do any part of an appeal by phone. Once a claim has been denied, you want your appeal to be documented at every step in the process. As an example, if you are a Noridian provider, use the Noridian redetermination/reopening form instead of asking for a reopening through the Noridian phone portal.

13. Why is it confusing when CMS mistakenly denies a claim/appeal as a "duplicate"?

When CMS classifies the mistaken denial of a claim/appeal as a duplicate, CMS calls this a "clerical error." See 405.980(a)(3) and the Medicare Claims Processing Manual, Chapter 34, Section 10.4.

A mistaken denial of a claim as a "duplicate" is an error made by Medicare (by the contractor, the QIC, or the ALJ). This is confusing because all the other (mathematical, computational, and data entry) clerical errors are errors made by the provider.

14. What should you send when requesting a reopening of a mistaken "duplicate"?

Send a letter to the contractor, QIC, or ALJ requesting a reopening based on the fact that the claim or appeal denied as a "duplicate" was not a duplicate. Attach a copy of the original claim form and a copy of the mistaken denial.

15. Does CMS include the failure to bill for items or services as a clerical error?

No. CMS says clerical errors do **not** include the failure to bill for items or services. CMS states a reopening shall **not** be granted to add items or services that were not previously billed.

16. What should you do if you discover items or services were not billed?

If it has been less than a year since the item was dispensed or the service was provided, submit a new claim.

17. What if you discover services you provided 13 months earlier were never billed?

You are out of luck. For example, if you performed bilateral surgical procedures but the claim was submitted for the procedure on only one extremity and 366 days have passed since the service was provided, a reopening will not be granted to submit a claim for the procedure on the second extremity.

18. How does Medicare justify the one-year time limit to bill for services?

Medicare claims this is fair based on a need for "finality and claims processing efficiency."

19. What does the CFR say regarding "good cause" for a reopening?

42 CFR Section 405.986 says:

> Establishing good cause. Good cause may be established when:
>
> There is new and material evidence that—
>
> Was not available or known at the time of the determination or decision, and
>
> May result in a different conclusion, or
>
> The evidence that was considered in making the determination or decision clearly shows on its face that an obvious error was made at the time of the determination or decision.

20. In plain English, how is the first part of 405.986 [405.986(a)(1)] applied?

405.986(a)(1) is applied as a tool by the Medicare contractor to enforce a demand for repayment of overpayment.

405.986(a)(1) says a contractor can take back payment from a provider when there is new and material evidence the contractor did not have when the initial claim or the redetermination appeal was paid and based on the new and material evidence, payment was made in error.

For example, when a contractor or a RAC finds a provider is billing higher complexity E&M codes with unusual frequency, the contractor can demand copies of the provider's medical records supporting those billed and paid E&M codes. If review of the provider's medical records does not support the higher complexity E&M codes, the contractor can reopen the claims and demand a repayment of overpayment.

21. Is the 405.986(a)(1) "good cause for reopening" section ever applied in favor of a provider?

Not that I know of.

22. In plain English, how is the second part of 405.986 [405.986(a)(2)] applied?

405.986(a)(2) can be used by the contractor to demand repayment of overpayment from the provider.

If a RAC discovers a contractor has been issuing inappropriate payments to providers for a specific code or service based on an obvious error, the contractor can use 405.986(a)(2) to reopen the inappropriately paid claims and demand repayment. However, 405.986(a)(2) can also be used by the provider to demand payment of a mistaken denial.

For example, if the LCD policy in effect at the time the service was provided supported payment but the contractor denied payment based on an out-of-date LCD policy, the provider would have good cause to demand a reopening and payment of that claim.

23. Is a provider's request for a reopening an appeal?

No. A request for a reopening is **not** an appeal. A request for a reopening is an attempt to preserve your right to appeal after you have waited too long to appeal.

24. What is the functional difference between an appeal and a reopening?

When you submit an *appeal* to the contractor, to the QIC, or to the ALJ, you are asking to be paid.

When you submit a request for a *reopening*, you are asking permission to continue your appeal of a denied claim or a denied appeal that is dead in the water because you missed the deadline to appeal.

As a provider, if you are successful in reopening a denied claim or appeal, you will then be able to continue with the appeal.

25. When and on what basis can an initial determination or a redetermination be reopened?

A provider can ask a contractor to reopen an **initial determination or a redetermination** within **one year** of the initial determination or a redetermination **for any reason.** See Section 405.980(c)(1).

A provider can ask a contractor to reopen an **initial determination or a redetermination** within **four years** of the initial determination or a redetermination for **good cause** in accordance with **Section 405.986.** See Section 405.980(c)(1).

A provider can ask a contractor to reopen an **initial determination** ***at any time*** for the purpose of correcting a clerical error (responsible for the denial). See Section 405.980(c)(1).

Does this mean a provider can ask a contractor to reopen a claim two years after the claim has been denied if the denial was due to a clerical error on the originally submitted claim form? Theoretically, yes. But how many times have you discovered a two-year-old denial was based on a clerical error on the originally submitted claim form?

26. How much time does a provider have to ask a QIC, an ALJ, an attorney adjudicator, or the Council to reopen a decision?

A provider may ask **a QIC, an ALJ, an attorney adjudicator, or the Council** to reopen their decision within **180 days** from the date of the decision for **good cause** in accordance with **Section 405.986.**

27. What does the Medicare Claims Processing Manual (MCPM) say about provider reopenings?

The MCPM, Chapter 34, Section 10.6.2 says:

> While a contractor can reopen to correct an unfavorable determination, CMS does **not** expect that a contractor would regularly grant these requests, especially for older claims where the claims history is not readily available. Both the contractor and the provider/supplier have a reasonable expectation to administrative finality in the processing of their claims. Additionally, administrative efficiency and the ability of a Medicare contractor to continue vital functions (i.e., process Medicare claims and process appeal requests) require that contractors grant such requests rarely. (Emphasis added.)

18

Redetermination Appeals

18a

The Goal of a Redetermination Appeal
42 CFR Sections 405.904–405.958

OUTLINE

1. What is the most important goal for a redetermination appeal?
2. When will a redetermination appeal succeed?

1. What is the most important goal for a redetermination appeal?

The most important goal of a redetermination appeal is to make sure the Medicare contractor has a "correct" copy of the claim form—accurate in every regard. In particular, you want to make sure **all of the diagnosis and treatment codes are correctly entered** on the claim form.

2. When will a redetermination appeal succeed?

When you have a claim that is denied because of a clerical error on the originally submitted claim form, you have a very good chance of being paid at the redetermination level of appeal.

18b

Submitting the Redetermination Appeal

OUTLINE

1. What happened?
2. What Medicare form will you use for the redetermination appeal?
3. When will you win and when will you lose a redetermination appeal?
4. How long do you have to submit a redetermination appeal?
5. When is a redetermination appeal considered "filed" with a contractor?
6. What if you can't get your redetermination appeals submitted on time?
7. What should you expect with redetermination appeals?
8. Who makes the redetermination appeal decision whether to pay you?
9. Where do you send the request for a redetermination appeal?
10. Why did the contractor deny payment?
11. What is the most important information on the Remittance Advice form?
12. Where can you find out exactly what the RA denial codes mean?
13. Is there a no-cost source of information that explains in plain English why the claim was denied?
14. Are the denial notices sent to the provider and the patient the same?
15. What evidence should you submit with a redetermination appeal request?
16. If payment was denied because of a data entry error, what should you submit?
17. What are examples of minor data entry error(s) on the originally submitted claim?
18. What if two mutually exclusive codes were for services provided by two different providers?
19. Why should you ask for a redetermination when the denial is due to a data entry error?
20. What are you trying to avoid by asking for a redetermination instead of a reopening?
21. When a denial is not based on a clerical error, what should you send?
22. Why not send copies of the patient care documents proving you should be paid?
23. Why not submit everything at the time of the redetermination appeal?
24. Do you have to send documents more than once when you appeal a denied claim?
25. What should you do if you find mistakes on the initial Remittance Advice?
26. If a claim is denied based on medical necessity, why not go to a QIC appeal immediately?
27. Can a contractor accept a data entry correction and then deny payment for a new reason?
28. Why not wait and submit all the "evidence" when you ask for an ALJ hearing?
29. What do you do if the contractor dismisses your redetermination appeal?

1. What happened?

You were denied payment by the contractor.

2. What Medicare form will you use for the redetermination appeal?

You will fill out the CMS form for a redetermination appeal (**CMS-20027**). Search **CMS-20027** and that form comes right up.

3. When will you win and when will you lose a redetermination appeal?

You will almost always win a redetermination appeal if the denial was based on a clerical error. However, if the denial was based on a Medicare billing "rule," it is unlikely you will win payment before the ALJ level of appeal.

4. How long do you have to submit a redetermination appeal?

See 42 CFR Section 405.942. You get **120 calendar days** after the postmarked date on the envelope containing the initial determination, **plus 5 days.** And if the calculated "due" date falls on a Saturday, Sunday, legal holiday, or any other nonwork day, the required filing deadline is the next working day. Keep the envelope the denial came in!

5. When is a redetermination appeal considered "filed" with a contractor?

The MCPM, Chapter 29, Section 310.2 "Time Limit for Filing a Request for Redetermination" says the date an appeal is considered filed is the date the contractor receives the appeal in the corporate mailroom, or via facsimile, or via the secure Internet portal/application.

When the filing deadline for a redetermination ends on a Saturday, Sunday, federal legal holiday, or any other nonwork day, the contractor shall apply a rollover period that extends the filing deadline to the next working day.

6. What if you can't get your redetermination appeals submitted on time?

But you can. The only thing you have to do is to get a single page CMS-20027 form submitted on time. Your financial security depends on paying attention to the appeals when your claims are wrongly denied.

7. What should you expect with redetermination appeals?

Not much. The only time you will prevail at the first level of appeal is when you have a clerical error on the claim form that can be "claim corrected."

8. Who makes the redetermination appeal decision whether to pay you?

A clerk working for the contractor, with a limited number of "pull-down" options on the computer screen, makes the determination whether to pay or deny your redetermination appeal.

9. Where do you send the request for a redetermination appeal?

See 42 CFR Section 405.944. A request for a redetermination appeal is sent to the contractor that issued the initial determination. The mailing address for the redetermination appeal will be on the initial determination RA (Remittance Advice).

10. Why did the contractor deny payment?

Once you know the exact reason(s) why the payment was denied, you will know what to send with the redetermination appeal, and most of the time, you will know what to send with the reconsideration appeal.

11. What is the most important information on the Remittance Advice form?

See 405.921. The Remittance Advice (RA) was formerly known as the Explanation of Medicare Benefits (EOMB). Section 405.921 states: "The notice of initial determination (RA) sent to a provider/supplier must contain all applicable claim adjustment reasons. The remark codes on the RA explain the contractor's determination (denial)."

The **remark codes** are the most important information on the RA. They tell you why your payment was denied.

12. Where can you find out exactly what the RA denial codes mean?

You may have a difficult time figuring out what all the Remittance Advice and denial codes applied to a single billed code actually mean. You are not alone. This process is not intuitive and a provider should never assume she knows why a claim was denied and, therefore, does not have to look up the denial codes.

Buy the book *Denial Codes Plain English Descriptions* published by DecisionHealth, available at www.codingbooks.com.

Alternatively, see the Medicare Claims Processing Manual, Chapter 22, "Remittance Advice," Section 60—Remittance Advice Codes. Then go to the Washington Publishing Company website at www.wpc-edi.com for the lists of Remittance Advice Remark Codes (RARCs) and Claims Adjustment Reason Codes (CARCs). There are approximately 950 RARC codes and 350 CARC codes currently listed and defined on the wpc-edi.com website—and the list is growing.

13. Is there a no-cost source of information that explains in plain English why the claim was denied?

Yes! Your patient/client also receives a copy of the payment denial. Ask the patient/client to send you a copy of the denial they received. The denial notice sent to the patient takes all the guesswork out of the reasons for the denial.

14. Are the denial notices sent to the provider and the patient the same?

See 405.921(a) and 405.921(b). The denial notice letter sent to the patient (Medicare beneficiary) must explain, in plain English, why the claim was denied. See 405.921(a). In contrast, the notice to the provider/supplier contains the reason(s) for denial written in codes.

Section 405.921(a) may be capsulized as follows: "The notice of initial determination sent to the beneficiary must be written in a manner calculated to be understood by the beneficiary and must contain the reasons for the determination, including whether a local medical review policy, a local coverage determination, or national coverage determination was applied."

15. What evidence should you submit with a redetermination appeal request?

See 405.946. It depends on why the claim was denied. If it was denied based on a "data entry error" on the claim form, you will submit one thing, but if the claim was denied because the service was "not medically reasonable and necessary," you will submit something else.

16. If payment was denied because of a data entry error, what should you submit?

You should submit a completed CMS-20027 redetermination appeal request form, a one-page letter that includes the reason payment was denied and how that data entry error on the original claim form has been corrected on the new claim form you are submitting with the appeal.

17. What are examples of minor data entry error(s) on the originally submitted claim?

All of the following are considered "minor clerical errors": Mathematical or computational mistakes, transposed procedure or diagnostic codes, inaccurate data entry, misapplication of a fee schedule, computer errors, denial of claims as duplicates, which the party believes were incorrectly identified as a duplicate, and incorrect data items, such as provider number, use of a modifier, or date of service. See the Medicare Claims Processing Manual, Chapter 34, Section 10.4, "Reopenings Based on Clerical or Minor Errors and Omissions."

18. What if two mutually exclusive codes were for services provided by two different providers?

A less obvious example, but something that happens in group practices: Two procedure codes on the same claim form are mutually exclusive if the services are performed by the same physician on the same day. However, if the services were provided by two different physicians in your group, and the identity of each provider is listed next to each procedure code, you can avoid the denial.

19. Why should you ask for a redetermination when the denial is due to a data entry error?

Unless you have already exceeded the 125-day time limit to submit a redetermination appeal, you will never, ever ask for a reopening. You will always ask for a redetermination. Here's why: If you ask for a reopening and the contractor accepts the correction of the minor clerical error on the claim form but then denies payment for some other reason, you may run out of time to request a redetermination.

But if you ask for a redetermination in a timely manner and the contractor denies payment for **any** reason, you are entitled to a redetermination appeal decision.

If the contractor agrees with the minor clerical error correction but then denies payment based on a substantive reason, the contractor must issue a redetermination denial, and that gives you 180 days to submit a request for a reconsideration appeal.

The only time you will use a reopening request is when you have exceeded the 125-day statute of limitation for submitting a redetermination appeal.

20. What are you trying to avoid by asking for a redetermination instead of a reopening?

You submit a new claim to the contractor.

1. The contractor denies payment based on a "clerical error" on the claim form.
2. Sometime later in the 125-day time period allowed for a redetermination request, you resubmit a corrected claim form with a request for a reopening.
3. The contractor agrees with the corrected clerical error but now denies payment of the same claim for a new and different reason (e.g., "lack of medical necessity").

4. By the time you get the "medical necessity" denial from the contractor, you have exceeded the 125-day time period for a redetermination appeal.
5. Now, you either have to get an extension from the contractor or you have to resubmit the same claim to the contractor and win a reopening decision.

If you had asked for a redetermination the first time you resubmitted the claim with the corrected clerical error, the contractor would have been required to treat the request as a redetermination. And even though the contractor will deny payment, that denial would be a completed redetermination appeal, enabling you to move to the next level of appeal—the QIC reconsideration appeal.

21. When a denial is not based on a clerical error, what should you send?

For anything other than a claim form with a corrected, minor clerical error, don't bother sending any "evidence" to the contractor for the redetermination. Just enter a statement on the CMS-20027 form that "the service was medically reasonable and necessary and should be paid." You will provide all of your "evidence" when you submit the reconsideration appeal.

Submit the redetermination appeal **on time** and with **all of the required information** on the form!

22. Why not send copies of the patient care documents proving you should be paid?

Here are the reasons why you only want to send a completed CMS form 20027 (redetermination appeal request form) when payment is denied because the service was "not medically reasonable and necessary."

a. The redetermination decision is issued by the contractor who denied payment on the original claim, and that contractor is unlikely to rule against itself on anything other than data entry errors.
b. Medical necessity denials are infrequently reversed at the redetermination level of appeal.
c. You will need to submit a letter brief to the QIC for the reconsideration appeal. The letter brief will explain what you did, why you did it, and why that service was correct. You will attach all of the patient care documents along with articles, textbook sections, and standard-of-care statements to the letter brief as evidence.
d. Medicare does not allow appeal documents to be submitted by email. You have to send all the documents you want to submit at each level of appeal by fax or by regular mail.
e. The redetermination folks are good at losing documents.

23. Why not submit everything at the time of the redetermination appeal?

The contractors lose documents and you do not want to find yourself in front of the ALJ only to find out the judge does not have everything you previously submitted.

24. Do you have to send documents more than once when you appeal a denied claim?

No. Once you submit a document at any point in the appeals process, you do not have to submit that document again. In fact, Medicare does not want duplicate copies of documents sent for appeals. All documents submitted have to be included in the claim file, and duplicates just make the appeal process that much harder and that much more labor-intensive for Medicare.

Medicare is obligated to forward all submitted documents to each succeeding level of appeal. See Medicare Claims Processing Manual, Chapter 29, "Appeals of Claims Decisions," Sections 320.3–320.5.

25. What should you do if you find mistakes on the initial Remittance Advice?

If the initial RA denying payment of a claim contains errors made by the contractor (e.g., date[s] of service), make a copy of the RA, highlight the RA error(s) on the copy, attach the highlighted RA copy to your **redetermination** appeal request, and begin your redetermination appeal with a sentence that details the errors on the RA.

Although this may seem very obvious, you *must* go back and make sure the claim you initially submitted did not contain the same error(s) that appear on the RA.

26. If a claim is denied based on medical necessity, why not go to a QIC appeal immediately?

You can't. You are never allowed to skip a level of appeal. The "exhaustion of remedies" doctrine is an administrative law doctrine that requires the timely appeal of all your denied claims in the exact correct order of appeal every time: from the redetermination appeal to the reconsideration appeal to the ALJ appeal.

27. Can a contractor accept a data entry correction and then deny payment for a new reason?

Yes. In fact, at each level of appeal, the denial of payment may be sustained for completely new and different reasons not cited previously.

28. Why not wait and submit all the "evidence" when you ask for an ALJ hearing?

You are not allowed to do this. As of March 2005, any evidence you want the ALJ to consider must be submitted when you request a reconsideration appeal. The time to submit **all** of your evidence is when you request a reconsideration (QIC) appeal.

As a sign of where we are going with Medicare appeals, the Chief ALJ has asked Congress to change the rule regarding the submission of evidence, requesting that all evidence be submitted at the time of the redetermination appeal because this would "improve the efficiency of the appeals process." Congress has not yet acted on this request.

29. What do you do if the contractor dismisses your redetermination appeal?

See Chapter 18d, "Fighting the Dismissal of a Redetermination Appeal."

18c

Extending the Time Limit for a Redetermination Appeal

OUTLINE

1. Should you ask for an extension instead of requesting a redetermination?
2. What bad things happen when you put off your appeal?
3. Can you submit a redetermination appeal as quickly as you can submit a request for an extension?
4. Why is the worst appeal submitted on time better than the best appeal one day late?
5. What is the most common reason for an extension request?
6. How long do you have to submit a request for an extension after you miss the 125-day deadline?
7. Can you meet the "good cause" requirements for an extension?
8. What is Medicare's exact view on extensions?
9. What "good cause" reason for an extension actually works?

1. Should you ask for an extension instead of requesting a redetermination?

No! Your initial claim was denied and you **still have enough time** to get your redetermination appeal to the contractor within the 125-day time limit (120 calendar days plus 5 calendar days from the postmarked date on the Remittance Advice envelope containing the initial determination). See 405.942. Resist the temptation to procrastinate.

2. What bad things happen when you put off your appeal?

The decision to grant an extension is "discretionary" (optional) for the contractor, and three very bad facts will inevitably flow from your "I will get to it later" response:

First, the contractor will deny your request for an extension because you will **not** meet the "good cause" requirement for "circumstances beyond your control." See below.

Second, the claim for your otherwise timely and competently provided, medically "reasonable and necessary" service is dead in the water.

Third, the contractor's decision is **final.**

3. Can you submit a redetermination appeal as quickly as you can submit a request for an extension?

Yes! If you have time to submit a request for an extension before the 125-day time limit has expired, you have time to submit a *redetermination* request *form*. Download CMS-20027 (the Medicare *redetermination* request *form*) from the Internet, fill it out, and send it by proof-of-delivery, overnight mail to the contractor.

4. Why is the worst appeal submitted on time better than the best appeal one day late?

Medicare is going to deny payment for your services whenever possible. You must stay on track and avoid all discretionary decisions by Medicare. Period.

And you can ALWAYS supplement your appeal request with additional documents after you get the basic appeal form, with all the necessary information, submitted on time.

5. What is the most common reason for an extension request?

Here is the most common reason. **You missed the deadline (125 days) to submit** a redetermination appeal. As a result, you want an extension of the time limit to submit your redetermination appeal.

6. How long do you have to submit a request for an extension after you miss the 125-day deadline?

Surprisingly, Medicare gives no time limit for the submission of an extension request. But Medicare does not want to grant requests for extensions, so the longer you wait, the less likely the extension will be granted.

7. Can you meet the "good cause" requirements for an extension?

Probably not. The 405.942 "good cause" requirements for an extension are discussed at greater length in the Medicare Claims Processing Manual (MCPM), Chapter 29, Section 240.3: "**Good cause**" for an extension means "unavoidable circumstances beyond the physician's control, such as major floods, fires, tornados, and other natural catastrophes."

8. What is Medicare's exact view on extensions?

Significantly, the MCPM also states: "Contractors should **not** routinely find good cause when a physician (i.e., provider/supplier) submits an untimely appeal request. A billing company failing to timely submit appeals or other information is **not** grounds for finding good cause for late filing. The contractor does **not** find good cause where the physician claims a lack of business office skills caused the late filing." (Emphasis added.)

If you are thinking an apology to the contractor for missing the deadline, along with the explanation that the denied claim was accidentally buried under some paperwork in the office will meet the "good cause" requirement for an extension—think again.

9. What "good cause" reason for an extension actually works?

When you send a request for a redetermination appeal before the 125-day deadline but the request doesn't reach the contractor until after the deadline, that is a good cause reason for an extension.

Keep all denial envelopes! They are crucial for "dates" and you will have to submit a photocopy of the denial envelope that clearly shows the postmarked date if this is the basis for your extension request.

Finally, you must send all requests for extensions by proof-of-delivery mail so you can prove the request for the extension was sent before the 125-day time limit expired.

18d

Fighting the Dismissal of a Redetermination Appeal

OUTLINE

1. What happened?
2. Why was your redetermination appeal dismissed?
3. What does 405.944 require for a redetermination request?
4. How does CMS calculate the time for submitting a redetermination request?
5. What is the significance of a dismissal?
6. Should you appeal the dismissed redetermination appeal to the contractor (MAC) or to the QIC?
7. Why appeal a dismissed redetermination appeal to the QIC and not to the contractor?
8. How much time do you have to appeal a dismissed redetermination appeal?
9. How much time do you have to appeal a dismissed redetermination appeal to the QIC?
10. How should you treat the dismissal of a redetermination appeal?
11. When a MAC reverses a dismissal for "good and sufficient cause," what does that mean?
12. What are the practical points regarding a MAC's decision to reverse a dismissal?

1. What happened?

Your redetermination appeal has been dismissed by the contractor. See 405.952.

2. Why was your redetermination appeal dismissed?

Your redetermination appeal was dismissed because:

a. You failed to submit a redetermination request that **substantially complied** with 405.944, and/or
b. You failed to submit the redetermination request **on time.** See 405.942.

3. What does 405.944 require for a redetermination request?

Section 405.944 states you must include all the following when you send your request for a redetermination: the beneficiary's name, the Medicare health insurance claim number, the specific service(s) and/or item(s) for which the redetermination is being requested, the specific date(s) of the service, and the name and signature of the party (you) or the representative of the party.

4. How does CMS calculate the time for submitting a redetermination request?

CMS calculates the time for submitting a redetermination request as follows. See 405.942.

a. A redetermination must be filed within **120 calendar days** from the date you received the notice of the initial determination.
b. The date of receipt of the initial determination will be presumed to be **5 calendar days** after the date of the notice of initial determination unless there is evidence to the contrary.

You have 125 calendar days from the date on the envelope containing the notice of the initial determination to get your redetermination appeal to the contractor.

Save the envelopes containing all denials and appeal determinations. The postmarked date on the envelope containing the initial denial may be over a week later than the date on the actual denial letter. In that case, you get to calculate the 125 calendar days starting from the date on the envelope containing the denial letter, rather than having to rely on the date written on the denial letter as long as you kept the envelope!

5. What is the significance of a dismissal?

A "dismissed" claim is dead in the water and your appeal is finished unless you get the contractor to reverse the dismissal (405.952[d]) or you get the QIC to modify or reverse the dismissal (405.974[b]).

6. Should you appeal the dismissed redetermination appeal to the contractor (MAC) or to the QIC?

If it is less than **60 days** from the date of the notice of dismissal of the redetermination appeal, you should appeal the dismissal to the QIC.

7. Why appeal a dismissed redetermination appeal to the QIC and not to the contractor?

As a general rule, you always want to appeal a negative decision to the next higher authority. It is unlikely you will get the authority that issued the negative decision (in this case, the contractor) to reverse itself. No one likes to admit they were wrong. It is far more likely you will get the QIC to modify or reverse the contractor's dismissal. The QIC is emotionally unattached to the lower decision.

8. How much time do you have to appeal a dismissed redetermination appeal?

Medicare gives you **six months** from the date of the notice of dismissal to appeal the dismissal (of the redetermination appeal) to the contractor.

9. How much time do you have to appeal a dismissed redetermination appeal to the QIC?

Medicare gives you only **60 days** from the date of the notice of dismissal of the redetermination appeal to appeal the dismissal to the QIC.

10. How should you treat the dismissal of a redetermination appeal?

Treat the dismissal of the redetermination appeal as an **emergency**. Appeal the contractor's dismissal to the QIC immediately. Getting the QIC to reverse or modify the contractor's dismissal of your request for a redetermination is addressed in 405.974(b) as follows:

Reconsideration of a contractor's dismissal of a redetermination request

1. A party to a contractor's dismissal of a request for redetermination has the right to have the dismissal reviewed by a QIC if the party files a written request for review of the dismissal with the QIC within **60 calendar days** after receipt of the contractor's notice of dismissal.

  a. The date of receipt of the contractor's notice of dismissal is presumed to be 5 **calendar days** after the date of notice of the dismissal unless there is evidence to the contrary (This is how you actually get 65 days instead of 60 days).
  b. For purposes of meeting the 60-calendar day filing deadline, the request is considered as filed on the date it is received by the QIC.
2. If the QIC determines that the contractor's dismissal was in error, it vacates the dismissal and remands the case to the contractor for a redetermination.
3. A **QIC's reconsideration** of a contractor's dismissal of a redetermination request is **binding** and not subject to further review.

11. When a MAC reverses a dismissal for "good and sufficient cause," what does that mean?

If you miss the 65 calendar-day deadline, you will have to appeal the dismissal to the contractor instead of to the QIC. The contractor may reverse (vacate) its dismissal of your redetermination request within **six months** from the date of the notice of dismissal if you can prove there is "good and sufficient cause" to reverse the decision.

It is important to note the phrase "good and sufficient cause" is not defined by Medicare. But you can assume Medicare is telling the contractor there has to be a really good reason to reverse a dismissal.

12. What are the practical points regarding a MAC's decision to reverse a dismissal?

1. The word "may" means vacating the dismissal is "discretionary" (optional) for the contractor.
2. Because 405.952(d) states the time period is "within six months from the date of the notice of dismissal," you have room to argue the issue of time. Hopefully, you won't have to because you will get the request to "vacate" (reverse) the dismissal to the contractor immediately.
3. Arguments to the contractor include all of the following:
   a. "My redetermination request **substantially** complied with the requirements cited in 405.944. Specifically, my request included (at least) three of the following four requirements:
      i. The beneficiary's name
      ii. The Medicare health insurance claim number
      iii. Specific service(s) and/or item(s) for which the redetermination is being requested and the specific date(s) of the service, and
      iv. The name and signature of the party (you) or the representative of the party."
      The most common 405.944 mistake is the absence of the provider's signature on the redetermination request. Rubber-stamped signatures are not allowed.
   b. Tell the contractor: "We are resubmitting another request for redetermination that includes my signature. I apologize for the clerical error on the previously submitted request. Please vacate the dismissal of this claim." Or,
   c. "I apologize for failing to submit the request for redetermination on time. Unfortunately the office computer was stolen/a fire destroyed the records/we had a flood and lost the file containing our appeal documents/my billing person ran off to Syria to join ISIS and took all of our appeal files with her, etc. These circumstances were outside of my control and I am therefore respectfully asking you to vacate the dismissal of this appeal."

18e

Reopening an Initial Determination and Reopening a Redetermination Appeal

OUTLINE

1. Where can you find out about Medicare reopenings?
2. When should you ask for a redetermination reopening versus a reconsideration extension?
3. When can you ask to reopen an *initial* determination and reopen a *re*determination?
4. What are the 405.986 requirements for a "good cause reopening"?
5. How much time do you have to reopen an initial determination to correct a clerical error?
6. Can you attack a denial based on a clerical error at any level of appeal?
7. What are the differences between a redetermination and an initial decision reopening?

1. Where can you find out about Medicare reopenings?

Put Medicare Claims Processing Manual, Chapter 34, "Reopening and Revision of Claim Determinations and Decisions," Section 10.4 into the Internet search bar and that section will come right up. Also see 405.980–405.986.

2. When should you ask for a redetermination reopening versus a reconsideration extension?

Most commonly, you will be asking the contractor to **reopen** the redetermination decision because you missed the 185-calendar day deadline (405.962) to submit a reconsideration appeal and you cannot meet the "circumstances beyond your control" requirement for an extension. The only way you can keep the claim alive and headed for an ALJ hearing is by getting the denied initial determination or the denied redetermination appeal reopened.

Now for the bad news: Unless the reopening request is based on a clerical error on the initial claim or a clerical error on the redetermination appeal, it is unlikely you will be successful in getting the contractor to reopen the claim.

3. When can you ask to reopen an *initial* determination and reopen a *re*determination?

Under 405.980(c), here are the time frames and requirements for reopening an initial determination and reopening a redetermination:

- A party may request that a contractor reopen its initial determination or redetermination within **one year** from the date of the initial determination or redetermination **for any reason.**

Other than a clerical error on the initial claim, the correction of which would allow for payment, I can't think of another circumstance that would allow for a successful reopening "for any reason" within one year.

A party may request that a contractor reopen its initial determination or redetermination within four years from the date of the initial determination or redetermination for good cause in accordance with Section 405.986.

4. What are the 405.986 requirements for a "good cause reopening"?

Section 405.986 says:

> Establishing good cause. Good cause may be established when:
> There is **new** and **material** evidence that—
> Was **not available or known** at the time of the determination or decision, and
> **May result in a different conclusion,** or
> The evidence that was considered in making the determination or decision clearly shows on its face that **an obvious error** was made at the time of the determination or decision.
> A change in substantive law or interpretative policy is **not** a basis for reopening an initial decision or redetermination.

Other than the incorrect application of an LCD policy, I can't think of another circumstance that would allow for a successful reopening within four years from the date of the initial determination or redetermination for good cause.

5. How much time do you have to reopen an initial determination to correct a clerical error?

A party may request a contractor reopen its **initial determination** at **any time** for the purpose of correcting a clerical error on which that determination was based.

6. Can you attack a denial based on a clerical error at any level of appeal?

Yes! Any denial based on clerical error can be attacked at any level of appeal.

7. What are the differences between a redetermination and an initial decision reopening?

a. Even though Medicare says you should request a reopening instead of a redetermination if your original claim was denied due to a minor, clerical, data entry error, do **not** submit a reopening request unless you have already exceeded the time limit for a redetermination appeal.
b. When you still have time to submit the initial appeal as a redetermination request, you have nothing to gain and everything to lose if you submit your initial appeal as a reopening request instead of as a request for a redetermination appeal.

c. If you submit a request for a redetermination appeal, the contractor can process your request as a redetermination and either pay or deny the claim, or can process your request as a reopening and pay the claim.
d. If you submit a request for a redetermination appeal, the contractor cannot process your request as a reopening and then deny the reopening and, therefore, deny payment.
e. If the contractor processes your request as a **redetermination** and denies the claim, you are then able to submit a request for a reconsideration appeal.
f. If you submit a request for a **reopening** and the contractor accepts the corrected clerical error but also sustains the initial denial for another reason, you can then submit a redetermination request *only* if time has not run out for a redetermination appeal. 405.980(a)(3).
g. However, if you have already exceeded the time limit for a redetermination request, a reopening is the only way you can keep that appeal alive.
h. Under limited circumstances, a reopening request is a very potent weapon to use when you exceed the time limits for a redetermination, reconsideration, and an ALJ appeal request.
i. If payment was denied because you entered the wrong diagnosis code, the wrong procedure code, or the wrong modifier, use a reopening request to breathe life back into the claim, even if the statute of limitations (SOL) has run out.
j. What should you do if you find mistakes on the initial Remittance Advice received from the Medicare contractor? Although this may seem very obvious, you *must* go back and make sure the claim you initially submitted did not contain the same error(s).
k. Assuming you made entry errors on the originally submitted claim and those entry errors gave rise to the denial, you will submit a corrected claim form along with a short narrative explaining what was corrected when you submit the redetermination appeal request and the corrected claim form.
l. Assuming you made no entry errors on the originally submitted claim, but the Remittance Advice (RA) contains errors you think were responsible for the denial, you will submit a copy of your originally submitted claim form along with a narrative explaining how and why the RA errors are inconsistent with what you submitted on the original claim form.
m. Again: Do not submit a reopening request for an initially submitted claim unless you have already exceeded the time limit for a redetermination. A reopening request may eat up the time for a redetermination appeal. See 405.927 and 405.980(a)(3).
n. Finally, send all redetermination requests immediately after you receive the initial denial!

18f

Table for Redetermination Appeals

OUTLINE

1. What does the statement "the worst appeal submitted on time is better than the best appeal submitted one day late" mean?

Submitting the Redetermination Appeal Request	Extending the Time Limit for a Redetermination Appeal	Fighting the Dismissal of a Redetermination Appeal	Reopening a Redetermination Appeal
You timely submitted a claim to the contractor (within one year of the date of service). The contractor sent you a Remittance Advice denying payment. You then timely submitted a redetermination appeal request (within 120 days of the date of receipt of the RA).	You find yourself right up against the 120-day time limit to submit a redetermination appeal. You are tempted to ask the contractor for more time to submit the appeal documents. **Don't ever do this.** Granting an extension is optional for the contractor. If the contractor denies the request for an extension, the only thing you can do is to request a reopening. Unless the reopening is based on clerical error, your appeal is over, and you will not be paid for the service(s) you are appealing.	The redetermination appeal was dismissed because: 1. The appeal did not include the required information, and/or 2. The appeal was received by the contractor more than 120 days after you received the initial claim denial.	Unless the initial claim contained a clerical error that was the basis for the denial, it is unlikely you will get the contractor to reopen the claim.
Unless the original claim was denied because of a minor claim entry error that you can correct and resubmit, the contractor will most likely deny payment of the redetermination appeal.	**Do not request an extension if you have time to submit a redetermination appeal.** Download, print, and fill out CMS-20027 immediately. Then mail the appeal request by overnight delivery.		
You will timely submit a reconsideration appeal request to the QIC within 180 days of receiving the redetermination denial.	The worst appeal submitted on time is better than the best appeal submitted one day late.	You must get the dismissal reversed before you can continue with the appeal.	You want to get paid, but the contractor does not want to pay you and the contractor will use any technical advantage to avoid paying you.

1. What does the statement "the worst appeal submitted on time is better than the best appeal submitted one day late" mean?

No matter how badly written/incomplete your appeal documents are, if those documents are submitted within the required time limit for the next level of appeal, those documents will keep your appeal on track and will allow you to continue your appeal.

No matter how clever and well written your appeal documents are, if those documents are submitted even **one day late** for the next level of appeal, those documents may **not** keep your appeal on track and may **not** allow you to continue your appeal.

19

Reconsideration Appeals

19a

Submitting the Reconsideration Appeal
42 CFR Sections 405.960–405.978

OUTLINE

1. How did you get to the reconsideration appeal?
2. What is the address of the QIC where you will send the reconsideration appeal request?
3. How long do you have to submit a reconsideration appeal request?
4. How does CMS calculate the date you received the redetermination denial notice?
5. What if the appeal is mailed within 185 days but reaches the QIC after 185 days?
6. Your appeal was mailed more than 180 days after the date on the redetermination denial letter. What should you write?
7. What happens if the 185th day falls on a weekend or holiday?
8. What if you can't mail an appeal to the QIC within 185 days after the redetermination denial?
9. Has Medicare created a form to request a reconsideration appeal?
10. What is the single most important fact about the reconsideration appeal?
11. What does Medicare's 2005 rule on evidence actually say?
12. Why did Medicare change the rule on the submission of evidence?
13. Should payment for medical services revolve around rules of evidence?
14. Why should providers be allowed to submit evidence at any time during an appeal?
15. What outcome should you expect from a reconsideration appeal?
16. Why is this actually a good thing?

17. Why not go to an ALJ appeal right away?
18. How many different codes are you actually appealing?
19. How should you organize the appeal documents on your computer?

1. How did you get to the reconsideration appeal?

You timely submitted the initial claim to the Medicare contractor for payment.
You were denied payment by the contractor.
You timely submitted a redetermination appeal to the contractor.
The contractor denied the redetermination appeal.

2. What is the address of the QIC where you will send the reconsideration appeal request?

The address of the QIC is located at the end of the notice of redetermination.

3. How long do you have to submit a reconsideration appeal request?

A reconsideration appeal must be submitted to the QIC within **185 calendar days** (405.962) of the postmarked date on the envelope containing the notice of redetermination.

4. How does CMS calculate the date you received the redetermination denial notice?

Section 405.962(a)(1) says the date you received the redetermination denial will be presumed to be five calendar days after the date on the redetermination denial letter unless there is evidence to the contrary.

Your "evidence to the contrary" is **the postmarked date on the envelope** containing the redetermination denial. For example, if the date on the denial letter is September 5, and the postmarked date on the envelope containing the denial letter is September 12, you get 185 days after September 12 to get the reconsideration appeal to the QIC.

5. What if the appeal is mailed within 185 days but reaches the QIC after 185 days?

Here is what the Medicare Claims Processing Manual, Chapter 29, "Appeals of Claims Decisions," Section 320.2—Time Limit for Filing a Request for a Reconsideration says about this exact question:

> If a party (a provider) has mailed the request for reconsideration to (the QIC) in good faith within the time limit, and the request did not reach the appropriate QIC until after the time period to file a request expired, the QIC considers the request as timely filed.

6. Your appeal was mailed more than 180 days after the date on the redetermination denial letter. What should you write?

We will use the above dates of September 5 on the letter and September 12 on the postmarked envelope. In addition to the reconsideration appeal form (see below), you will write the following on your office letterhead and staple it to the reconsideration appeal form.

Attention QIC:

The actual redetermination denial letter has the date of September 5.

However, the envelope containing the redetermination denial letter was postmarked September 12. A copy of that envelope is enclosed.

Therefore, the date of notice for the redetermination denial letter is September 12.

In addition, 42 CFR Section 405.962(a)(1) states (in part): "The date of receipt of the redetermination will be presumed to be five calendar days after the date of the notice of redetermination."

As a result, the calculated date of receipt of the redetermination is September 17.

My reconsideration appeal was mailed within 185 days after September 17. A copy of the proof of mailing date is enclosed.

The MCPM, Chapter 29, Section 320.2 states: "If a party (a provider) has mailed the request for reconsideration to (the QIC) in good faith within the time limit and the request did not reach the appropriate QIC until after the time period to file a request expired, the QIC considers the request as timely filed."

Based on 42 CFR Section 405.962(a)(1) and the MCPM, Chapter 29, Section 320.2, the reconsideration request was timely filed. Please issue a reconsideration decision for this appeal.

7. What happens if the 185th day falls on a weekend or holiday?

If the calculated date (185 days after the postmarked date) falls on a weekend or a *federal* holiday, you can roll the date forward to the next business day.

8. What if you can't mail an appeal to the QIC within 185 days after the redetermination denial?

This is your business and your livelihood. You cannot afford to give away all the services that go unpaid as a result of mistaken denials.

9. Has Medicare created a form to request a reconsideration appeal?

Yes. CMS created the **CMS-20033** form for you to fill out and submit for a reconsideration appeal. Search CMS-20033 and the form comes right up.

10. What is the single most important fact about the reconsideration appeal?

Here is the most critical piece of information regarding the reconsideration appeal: All the evidence you will want the ALJ to consider must be submitted to the QIC before the QIC issues its written decision.

Even if you have to submit the CMS-20033 form without any accompanying evidence in order to meet the 185-day deadline, you can still submit your evidence later.

Get that CMS-20033 form in on time!

11. What does Medicare's 2005 rule on evidence actually say?

Here is Medicare's 2005 rule on submitting evidence. Section 405.966, "Evidence to be submitted with the reconsideration request," states:

When filing a request for reconsideration, you should present evidence and allegations of fact or law related to the issue in dispute and explain why you disagree with the initial determination and the redetermination.

- Any **missing documentation** identified in the notice of redetermination must be submitted with your request for reconsideration.
- Absent **good cause**, failure to submit all evidence, including any documentation requested in the notice of redetermination, **PRECLUDES (disqualifies)** subsequent consideration of that evidence [by the ALJ]. (Emphasis added.)

12. Why did Medicare change the rule on the submission of evidence?

CMS/Medicare and OMHA (Office of Medicare Hearings and Appeals) say the requirement to submit all your evidence to the QIC for the reconsideration appeal is based on a need for "judicial efficiency." I think the rule was changed because the providers were winning too many ALJ decisions.

13. Should payment for medical services revolve around rules of evidence?

I don't think so. Providing medical services to Medicare beneficiaries should be about providing medical services and not about fighting complex rules of evidence.

14. Why should providers be allowed to submit evidence at any time during an appeal?

I think the providers/suppliers should be allowed to provide relevant evidence favoring payment at any stage of the appeals process because Medicare is never prejudiced by seeking the correct answer to the question: Was the service medically reasonable and necessary? If the answer is yes, the provider should be paid. Otherwise, the appeals process will eventually turn into complex civil litigation and the providers will never be paid for denied claims—except when the denial is due to a clerical error.

15. What outcome should you expect from a reconsideration appeal?

You should expect to lose at the reconsideration level of appeal. The QICs make a huge amount of money by doing little more than parroting back the contractor's redetermination denial reasons and by adding a paragraph or two from a pull-down menu.

16. Why is this actually a good thing?

It is not unusual to receive QIC decisions with citations to Medicare Manual rules that have nothing to do with the issues in the dispute. As a result, you must look up every rule cited in the QIC decision and you should pray the QIC author has included extraneous material ripe for presentation to the ALJ.

17. Why not go to an ALJ appeal right away?

You are not allowed to. Medicare follows the rules in the Administrative Procedures Act (APA), including the "exhaustion of remedies" doctrine, which says: You must complete each level of appeal before you are allowed to go to the next higher level of appeal. In plain English, you have to complete the redetermination appeal before you are allowed to submit a reconsideration appeal and you have to complete the reconsideration appeal before you are allowed to submit an ALJ appeal. In addition, your appeals must always be submitted within the stated time requirement at each level of appeal and your appeal requests must include all of the required information.

Congratulations! Although you will probably **not** be paid as a result of your reconsideration appeal, you are on the path to the ALJ appeal, where you stand the best chance of winning.

18. How many different codes are you actually appealing?

This is important enough to repeat. There are no more than **ten** codes that make up the majority of the codes in your practice/business being denied by Medicare. You should maintain and constantly renew your library of supporting documents for those ten codes.

19. How should you organize the appeal documents on your computer?

The appeal documents should be entered/scanned into your computer the same way every time. I hope I have your attention now because this item is incredibly boring to read but incredibly important to understand and implement.

You can enter the documents in your computer however you want to, but you must do it the same way every time. Why? Anyone working on Medicare appeals in your office should be able to find any document in a particular patient's appeal file on your office computer in far less than a minute.

Here are my recommendations:

Keep a Medicare appeals master file on your computer desktop: For each patient with a claim that is being appealed, use the following subject headings for filing of the documents that apply to that claim.

- Last name, first name of patient, and the patient's Medicare number
- Date of service (DOS) and procedure code(s) at issue
- Date of initial claim submitted
- Date of contractor's denial
- Date of progress note, procedure report, imaging studies, etc.
- Date redetermination appeal request form (CMS-20027) was sent
- Date contractor's redetermination denial was sent
- Date reconsideration appeal request form (CMS-20033) was sent
- Date of QIC denial
- Date ALJ appeal request form (OMHA-100 and OMHA-100A) was sent

By entering all patients alphabetically, in a single file and by last name, you can immediately find the patient you are looking for. By making the date of service at issue the first subfile under the patient's last name, even if there are 20 separate dates of service at issue for a single patient, all the appeals are logically separated and easily found. You want to set up the files in a way that makes the search for any document easy and instinctive.

All dates in a Medicare patient appeal file should be entered as 00-00-0000 (month-day-year). However you choose to enter the dates on your computer, do it the same way every time and always include the year. Some appeals drag on and you need to be clear on the dates.

19b

Extending the Time Limit for a Reconsideration Appeal

OUTLINE

1. What happened?
2. What good cause requirements will you have to meet to qualify for an extension?
3. What does the QIC consider for an extension request?
4. What is an example of something that worked but is not included in the 405.942 "good cause" considerations?
5. If an extension should be granted, should you push until CMS says no?
6. What is the one excuse for an extension that you must avoid?
7. If you can request an extension before the 185-day deadline, can you submit a *reconsideration* request *on time*?
8. What is the difference between submitting the worst appeal request on time and submitting the best appeal request one day late?

1. What happened?

Your redetermination appeal was denied. You want to appeal the redetermination denial but **you have exceeded the 185-day time limit** (405.962) to submit a reconsideration appeal.

2. What good cause requirements will you have to meet to qualify for an extension?

You can submit the request for an extension to the QIC, but you will have to meet the 405.942(b)(2) and (b)(3) "good cause" requirements in order to qualify for an extension of the time limit that will result in a definite (pay or no pay) reconsideration decision by the QIC.

3. What does the QIC consider for an extension request?

The 405.942(b)(2) and (b)(3) "good cause" considerations by the QIC include, **but are not limited to,** the following:

- Whether the contractor misled the provider in the redetermination appeal process
- Whether the provider was too ill to contact the QIC
- Whether the provider had a death or serious illness in his or her immediate family

- Whether the provider's records regarding the appeal were destroyed or damaged by fire or other accidental cause
- Whether the provider did not receive notice of the redetermination decision
- Whether the provider sent the request for the reconsideration appeal to the QIC in good faith within the time limit, but the request did not reach the QIC until after the time period to file the request expired

4. What is an example of something that worked but is not included in the 405.942 "good cause" considerations?

Several years ago, I was representing a radiation oncology group that had a full-time in-house biller. Unfortunately, the biller had a nervous breakdown, and despite five previous years of competent billing performance, the biller started sending all appeals, including the reconsideration appeals, to the Medicare contractor's address. By the time the radiation oncologists were aware of what was happening, a significant number of reconsideration appeals had been sent to the wrong address and the time limit to submit QIC appeals had expired.

When I sent a letter to the QIC explaining all of this, I attached a declaration signed by the registered nurse who worked at the radiation oncology center. The nurse had professionally interacted with the biller on several occasions while the biller was having severe emotional problems and the nurse was able to sign, under penalty of perjury, a declaration stating the biller had health problems that interfered with her ability to do her job. The QIC rejected the explanation as adequate consideration for an extension. So, I contacted the CMS appeals department and, after reviewing the letter sent to the QIC, CMS told the QIC to grant the requested extension. The QIC granted the extension and then issued a reconsideration denial for *all* of the involved claims. I then requested an ALJ hearing and the ALJ ruled in favor of the radiation oncology group for every one of the claims involved in the extension.

5. If an extension should be granted, should you push until CMS says no?

Yes. However, you must bear in mind that the "good cause" requirements for a time extension can be reduced to a single statement: **Any delay must be caused by circumstances outside of your control.**

You will only meet the good cause requirements for an extension once or twice in your practice/business lifetime. For this reason, you never want to be in the position of having to send a request for an extension of the time limit to submit a reconsideration appeal. You must appeal on time.

6. What is the one excuse for an extension that you must avoid?

I am referring to the provider who knows so little about the appeals process that the provider thinks you can just ask for an extension and it will be granted. Even worse, **that provider may still have enough time** to get the reconsideration appeal to the QIC within the **185**-day time limit (180 days plus 5 days from the postmark date on the envelope containing the redetermination denial). But our provider is a felony procrastinator and wants to procrastinate a little longer, thinking she will ask the QIC to extend the time limit to submit her appeal documents, and the QIC will say "sure."

DON'T EVER DO THIS!

The decision to grant an extension is **discretionary** for the QIC and two very bad facts will flow from the "I will get to it later" response. First, the QIC will deny the request for an extension because the "good cause" requirement of circumstances beyond the provider's control will not be met. As a result, the claim for (otherwise timely and competently provided, medically reasonable and necessary) services will be dead in the water. Second, the QIC's decision is final.

7. If you can request an extension before the 185-day deadline, can you submit a *reconsideration* request *on time*?

Yes. Download **CMS-20033** (the Medicare *reconsideration* request *form*) from the Internet, fill it out, and send it with proof of delivery, by overnight mail to the QIC. Even if the QIC gets the appeal form after the time has run out, as long as the appeal was mailed before the time limit expired, the QIC is required to accept the appeal request. See 405.962(b) and then 405.942(b)(2)(vi).

8. What is the difference between submitting the worst appeal request on time and submitting the best appeal request one day late?

The worst appeal request submitted on time frequently works. The best appeal request submitted one day late almost never works.

You can ALWAYS supplement your QIC appeal request documents after you get the reconsideration appeal request form in on time!

By contrast, you will almost never salvage a late appeal request. Why? Because Medicare is looking for any excuse to deny payment and your failure to submit the reconsideration appeal on time allows Medicare to avoid payment of your claim.

You must stay on track and avoid the discretionary decisions by people who decide whether you are going to get paid and who do NOT want to pay you! It's not personal. Medicare just does not have the money.

19c

Fighting the Dismissal of a Reconsideration Appeal

OUTLINE

1. Why was your reconsideration appeal dismissed?
2. How many options do you have when your reconsideration appeal is dismissed?
3. How much time do you have to appeal a reconsideration dismissal to the QIC as opposed to the ALJ?
4. Will the QIC or an ALJ more fairly review your dismissal?
5. When and to whom should you appeal a reconsideration dismissal?
6. Does Medicare think they can rely on providers being lazy?
7. Does Medicare have a form for an ALJ review of a dismissal by the QIC?
8. Is the information in this book intended for non-participating providers?
9. What should you send to the ALJ when you are appealing a QIC's dismissal?
10. When appealing a QIC's dismissal, what could a letter to the ALJ look like?
11. If you can prove the QIC appeal was timely, what could a letter to the ALJ look like?
12. When a QIC appeal is submitted late due to circumstances outside of your control, what could a letter to the ALJ look like?
13. When it's too late to protest to the ALJ and only the QIC can vacate the dismissal, what rules apply to the QIC's review?
14. What common 405.964 mistakes result in dismissal of a QIC appeal?
15. What are examples of "good and sufficient cause" to vacate a QIC dismissal?
16. Is it easy to meet "good and sufficient cause" to vacate a QIC dismissal?
17. What is the takeaway regarding the QIC dismissal of a reconsideration appeal?

1. Why was your reconsideration appeal dismissed?

Your reconsideration appeal was "dismissed" by the QIC because you didn't provide **all** the necessary information and/or you didn't get your QIC/reconsideration appeal in **on time.**

2. How many options do you have when your reconsideration appeal is dismissed?

You only have one option. You must get the "dismissal" reversed before you can continue appealing the denied claim. A "dismissed" claim is dead in the water and your appeal is finished unless you get the QIC to vacate the dismissal (405.972(d)), or you get the ALJ to reverse the dismissal (405.1004).

3. How much time do you have to appeal a reconsideration dismissal to the QIC as opposed to the ALJ?

It should come as no surprise that Medicare has created a **procedural trap** for the unwary when it comes to protesting a QIC "dismissal." You can take up to **six months** to get your protest of the dismissal to the same QIC that dismissed the claim. But you only have **60 days** to get your protest of the QIC's dismissal to an ALJ.

4. Will the QIC or an ALJ more fairly review your dismissal?

I hope your answer was "ALJ" because you are far more likely to get a competent and fair review by an ALJ who has not previously seen the claim as opposed to the QIC that originally dismissed your claim.

5. When and to whom should you appeal a reconsideration dismissal?

Be smart and send your dismissal appeal to the ALJ immediately. The notice of dismissal from the QIC will include the address for the ALJ office where you will send the protest of the dismissal.

6. Does Medicare think they can rely on providers being lazy?

Absolutely, yes! And once again, Medicare is right. A lot of claims die when QICs issue claim dismissals because the provider waits so long that the dismissal can only be appealed to the QIC and/or the frustrated provider just gives up on the appeal.

When the QIC dismisses a reconsideration appeal, protest the QIC dismissal to the **ALJ** office listed in the dismissal letter within **60 days** of receiving the dismissal.

7. Does Medicare have a form for an ALJ review of a dismissal by the QIC?

Yes. Download and print Medicare form **HHS-725** (Request for ALJ to Review Dismissal by the QIC).

There is one tricky part on the HHS-725 form. At the bottom of "page 1 of 3," you are asked the question: **Did the beneficiary assign his or her appeal rights to you as the provider/supplier?** Check the box that says **No.**

You are **not** appealing for the patient. You are appealing for **yourself** as the participating Medicare provider/supplier. Search Medicare form **CMS-20031** and you will see why you **must** check the box that says No.

8. Is the information in this book intended for non-participating providers?

No. The information in this book is intended only for participating Medicare providers.

If you don't want to use the Medicare HHS-725 form, here is what you must include in your letter to the ALJ (the most common missing information is in bold):

- The beneficiary's name
- The patient's Medicare health insurance claim number
- The specific service(s) and/or item(s) for which the redetermination was requested and the specific date(s) of the service(s)
- **The name and signature of the party** (you) or the representative of the party (your attorney)
- **The name of the contractor** that issued the **redetermination** denial

If you are sending a letter rather than using the Medicare form, list these required items in bullet form at the beginning of your letter.

9. What should you send to the ALJ when you are appealing a QIC's dismissal?

Your completed HHS-725 form, or your letter to the ALJ, should be sent with copies of your original reconsideration appeal request and the QIC notice of dismissal.

10. When appealing a QIC's dismissal, what could a letter to the ALJ look like?

Date

From: Last, First,

Provider or Supplier designation (degree or name of business)

Office address:

Medicare provider number:

Tax ID number:

To: The ALJ office address included in the notice of dismissal from the QIC

Re: A request for an ALJ reversal of a reconsideration dismissal by (name of QIC), QIC appeal number ______________________

Beneficiary's name (last, first):

Beneficiary's Medicare health insurance claim number:

The specific service(s) and/or item(s) for which the reconsideration was requested and the specific date(s) of the service(s):

The name of the contractor that made the redetermination decision:

(Because you will not know the name of the ALJ your case will be assigned to, start the letter to the ALJ office [below the bulleted items above] with the greeting "Your Honor.")

Your Honor,

This appeal was dismissed by the QIC because necessary information was not included in the originally submitted appeal request and/or the appeal request was not submitted on time.

Please, if your appeal was dismissed for only one of these two possible reasons, do **not** list both reasons in your letter to the ALJ. That kind of sloppiness makes the ALJ think you are sending a **form letter** and like it or not, that is a subliminal message you do not want to send.

When I submitted the reconsideration request, I failed to include [list whatever you failed to include]. Otherwise, I substantially complied with the 42 CFR 405.964(a) and (b) reconsideration appeal requirements.

The 405.964(a) and (b) requirements include the beneficiary's name, the beneficiary's Medicare health insurance claim number, the specific service(s) and/or item(s) for which the reconsideration was requested and the specific date(s) of the service(s), your signature, and the name of the contractor that made the redetermination decision. You will put whichever requirement was missing in the sentence above. Most commonly, the QIC appeal request did not contain the actual signature of the doctor and/or the name of the contractor that made the redetermination decision.

11. If you can prove the QIC appeal was timely, what could a letter to the ALJ look like?

The QIC appeal was submitted on time. Enclosed is a copy of the postmarked envelope that contained the redetermination denial from the contractor. The dismissal notice states my QIC appeal was received on__________. However, the USPS proof of delivery mail statement (see enclosed copy) says the QIC received my appeal on ________. Therefore, the QIC received my appeal within 185 days after the date of the notice of redetermination, as allowed in 405.962.

Save the envelopes containing all denials and appeal determinations. Frequently, the postmarked date on the envelope containing the redetermination denial may be a week or more later than the date on the redetermination denial letter. In that case, you get to calculate the 185 calendar days starting from **the date on the envelope** containing the denial letter, rather than having to rely on the date written on the denial letter—as long as you kept the envelope!

12. When a QIC appeal is submitted late due to circumstances outside of your control, what could a letter to the ALJ look like?

The QIC appeal was submitted late due to circumstances outside of my control. Specifically . . .

Give the ALJ enough details about why the submission of the appeal was late but do not include any argument about the claim itself. This request to the ALJ to reverse the QIC's dismissal should only be about the dismissal.

13. When it's too late to protest to the ALJ and only the QIC can vacate the dismissal, what rules apply to the QIC's review?

The QIC **may** vacate (reverse) its dismissal of your reconsideration request within **six months** from the date of the notice of dismissal if you can prove there is "good and sufficient" cause to vacate the decision. The word "may" means vacating the dismissal is **discretionary** for the QIC.

14. What common 405.964 mistakes result in dismissal of a QIC appeal?

The most common 405.964 mistakes are the absence of the doctor's signature and/or the name of the contractor that made the redetermination. Here is what you will say in your letter to the QIC:

I am resubmitting another request for reconsideration that includes my signature. I apologize for the clerical error on the previous request. Please vacate the dismissal of this claim.

and/or

I apologize for failing to submit the name of the contractor that made the redetermination. The redetermination decision was made by [name of contractor].

15. What are examples of "good and sufficient cause" to vacate a QIC dismissal?

Examples of good and sufficient cause to vacate the QIC dismissal decision would include any of the following: "Unfortunately, the office computer was stolen/a fire destroyed the records/we had a flood and lost the file containing our appeal documents/my billing person ran off to Syria to join ISIS and took all of our appeal files with her, etc. These circumstances were outside of my control and I am therefore respectfully asking you to vacate the dismissal of this appeal."

16. Is it easy to meet "good and sufficient cause" to vacate a QIC dismissal?

You will almost **never** meet the requirements for good and sufficient cause to vacate the QIC dismissal because ordinary billing negligence does not meet the requirements.

17. What is the takeaway regarding the QIC dismissal of a reconsideration appeal?

The takeaway: You should protest the dismissal to the ALJ within 60 days of the dismissal.

19d

Reopening a Reconsideration Appeal

OUTLINE

1. What happened?
2. Why is reopening a reconsideration appeal so difficult?
3. What are the requirements for reopening a reconsideration decision?
4. What is an example of "new and material evidence—not available or known" at the time of the determination or decision that could have resulted in a different conclusion?
5. What would be an obvious error on the face of the decision at the time of the QIC decision?
6. What is meant by "a change in substantive law or interpretative policy is not a basis for reopening an initial decision or redetermination"?
7. What is the result of getting the reconsideration appeal reopened?

1. What happened?

You probably missed the 185-calendar day deadline. See 405.962 for submitting a reconsideration appeal.

2. Why is reopening a reconsideration appeal so difficult?

You will have to meet the 405.986 good cause reasons for reopening, and the QIC's decision will be final and binding—not subject to further appeal. You really don't want to be here.

Unless the reopening request is based on a clerical error on the initial claim or a clerical error on the redetermination appeal, it is unlikely you will be successful in getting the QIC to reopen the claim.

3. What are the requirements for reopening a reconsideration decision?

Under 405.980(e), here is the time frame and the requirements for reopening a reconsideration decision:

> A party may request that a QIC reopen its reconsideration within 185 calendar days from the date of the reconsideration for good cause in accordance with 405.986:
>
> **§405.986 Good cause for reopening**
>
> Establishing good cause. Good cause may be established when:
>
> There is **new** and **material** evidence that—

Was **not available or known** at the time of the determination or decision; and
May result in a different conclusion; or
The evidence that was considered in making the determination or decision clearly shows on its face that **an obvious error** was made at the time of the determination or decision.
A change in substantive law or interpretative policy is **not** a basis for reopening an initial decision or redetermination. (Emphasis added.)

4. What is an example of "new and material evidence—not available or known" at the time of the determination or decision that could have resulted in a different conclusion?

I cannot think of an example where there was "new and material evidence" that was "not available or known" at the time of the determination or decision and that may have resulted in a different conclusion.

5. What would be an obvious error on the face of the decision at the time of the QIC decision?

An obvious error on the face of the decision would include a situation where the LCD (Local Coverage Determinations) in effect at the time of the service specifically supported the service in question and the QIC mistakenly thought the LCD said otherwise.

6. What is meant by "a change in substantive law or interpretative policy is not a basis for reopening an initial decision or redetermination"?

A change in substantive law or interpretative policy would include a situation where the LCD in effect said no when the service was provided, but a later version of the same LCD said yes.

A later change in substantive law or interpretative policy is **not** going to get your appeal reopened.

7. What is the result of getting the reconsideration appeal reopened?

If you do succeed in getting the reconsideration appeal reopened, you are back on track to appeal the claim to the ALJ.

19e

The Letter Brief

OUTLINE

1. What is a letter brief?
2. What is the goal of a letter brief?
3. What should the letter brief say?
4. What are the key questions you must answer in every letter brief?
5. Who is the target audience for the letter brief?
6. I will use the pronoun "her" when referring to the ALJ.
7. What documents will you attach to the letter?
8. Should you attach *every* patient care document to the letter?
9. How does the letter brief help you get paid?
10. Whose point of view should you take as you write the letter brief?
11. Why are you sending the letter brief to the QIC instead of to the ALJ?
12. Why does it make the most sense to submit the letter brief to the QIC?
13. Will an overworked ALJ team organize and analyze unorganized documents?
14. What can the letter brief do for you that you can't do any other way?
15. Do ALJs issue favorable "on the record" decisions just based on letter briefs?
16. Do ALJs issue favorable "on the record" decisions without letter briefs?
17. Why will the ALJ consider your letter brief to be a miracle?
18. Make it easy for the ALJ and avoid ALJ denials based on ignorance.
19. The letter brief is one of two "loopholes" available in the appeals process.
20. Is it ever okay to not send a letter brief?
21. What is the ALJ's response to no letter brief explaining why you should be paid?
22. Does your letter say what you want it to say?
23. If you are a terrible writer, how can you convince the judge to award payment?
24. How academic should your letter brief be?
25. Why should the letter portion of your letter brief be less than three pages?
26. Can the letter portion of your letter brief be only one page?
27. You will lose the ALJ appeal if the ALJ finds these things in your documents.
28. What progress note "crime" will not be forgiven by the ALJ?
29. Do not underestimate the ALJ's lack of medical knowledge.
30. How is the letter brief tied to your fear of Medicare?
31. How does the letter brief affect your presentation during the hearing?

32. How is your brief related to your answers during the hearing?
33. What should you do if the QIC adds new denial reasons in the QIC decision?
34. How should the second letter brief be written?
35. Why should you be able to submit your reconsideration appeals on time?
36. How long do you have to submit a reconsideration appeal request?
37. If you are pressed for time, can you just submit the reconsideration appeal form?
38. Will an ALJ award payment just based on a clever legal argument?
39. Why are clinical photographs always your strongest evidence?
40. Will you have to authenticate the photos in the letter brief?
41. How do you authenticate clinical photographs?
42. What happens if you don't authenticate photographs for the judge?
43. Can you ask the patient to participate in the ALJ hearing?
44. Can you submit late-taken photos of the patient to the ALJ?
45. Once the judge looks at the photos, can the judge un-ring that bell?
46. What argument should you make to get late-submitted photos accepted?
47. How should you take and store photos for hearings?
48. How can you use photos when the denied service is "included" in another service?
49. How is the letter brief and oral argument related to books for children?
50. How can you distinguish separate services without photographs?
51. What is considered "new evidence" at the time of an ALJ hearing?
52. What does Medicare say about "new evidence" at the time of an ALJ hearing?
53. How does Medicare define "good cause" for new evidence at the ALJ hearing?
54. With the backlog of cases, how will the ALJs respond to "new evidence"?
55. What is not "new evidence" at the time of an ALJ hearing?
56. Are you missing something that may kill your appeal?
57. How can you find out why your claim was denied?
58. What happens when you role-play as the contractor during your analysis?
59. How will the redetermination denial affect the judge's questions at the hearing?
60. What should you do with a vulnerable point in your argument?
61. Will the stated denial reasons always tell you what you have to prove to the ALJ?
62. What are the common denial reasons and what do you have to prove for each?
63. When required information is missing, how do you argue denied E&M codes?
64. Is an LCD policy binding on an ALJ?
65. What is the practical effect of the "substantial deference" rule?
66. Does "substantial deference" affect your burden of proof?
67. What are the differences between "substantive" denials and "procedural" denials?
68. When are you most likely to win a procedural denial and a substantive denial?
69. If you sent your patient care documents to the QIC, can you send a letter brief to the ALJ?
70. Will you be notified when your contractor sends the ALJ a position paper?
71. The contractor sends a position paper to the ALJ but not to you. What should you do?
72. Uh-oh . . . what if you cannot find support for the service you provided?
73. You can always submit a Medicare document. What is a "Medicare document"?
74. What are "non-Medicare documents" and when should they be submitted?
75. What are the Medicare Internet-Only Manuals?

76. Which of the Medicare Internet-Only Manuals explain the rules regarding LCDs?
77. Can you use the Medicare Program Integrity Manual (MPIM) on LCDs to your advantage?
78. What is the strongest evidence for LCD policies and how will you use this?
79. What is the second strongest evidence for LCD policies?
80. What is the third strongest evidence for LCD policies?
81. What is the most common substantive reason used by Medicare to deny payment?
82. What does the phrase "not medically reasonable and necessary" mean?
83. Where does the phrase "medically reasonable and necessary" come from?
84. Is there a list of requirements for "medically reasonable and necessary"?
85. What "documents" should you have in front of you before you start writing?
86. If you know a service will be denied, what statement should you incorporate in the progress note?
87. What should you send with the CMS-20033 reconsideration appeal request form?
88. How should you organize the letter brief?
89. Where do you find the address for the QIC you are sending your letter brief to?
90. How should you format the letter portion of the letter brief?
91. How should you organize the first page of the letter brief?
92. How many claims can you appeal in a single letter brief?
93. How should you organize hundreds of codes in a single letter brief?
94. How does the number of codes being appealed affect the number of pages in a letter brief?
95. What kind of "demographic" table do you need, and where should it be placed?
96. Do you have to send copies of cited "Medicare" documents as attachments?
97. Do you have to send copies of the "non-Medicare documents" as attachments to the letter brief (to the QIC)?
98. How do you organize the documents that share a single attachment number?
99. How do you identify the attachment number and page numbers of the attachments?
100. How can you send a diagram and a simple explanation of the patient's problem?
101. Can you send your digital images of the patient to the QIC in an email?
102. What determines the number of attachments you will send with the letter brief?
103. What should be the order of the documents you attach to your letter brief?
104. How should you arrange the "patient care documents" attached to the letter brief?
105. How should you arrange "journal articles" attached to the letter brief?
106. How should you arrange "textbook sections" attached to the letter brief?
107. How should you arrange standard-of-care statements attached to the letter brief?
108. What should you do if the LCD did not allow the service?
109. How should you number the pages in your letter brief?
110. Must you prove you **sent** a copy of the request for the ALJ appeal to each patient?
111. Must you prove each patient **received** a copy of your request for an ALJ appeal?
112. Do you have to send a copy of the letter brief to each of the patients?
113. What is the least expensive way to prove you sent a copy of the ALJ appeal request to each patient?
114. How do you avoid HIPAA violations when using the OMHA-100A form?
115. How should you fill out Section 7 on the OMHA-100 form?
116. What is the best way to describe the problem, what you did, and why it was correct?
117. What should you write when you did not meet some MAC requirements for a service?

118. What should you write when the service is prohibited in the contractor's LCD?
119. What can you do when your contractor says "no" but another contractor says "yes"?
120. What should you do if an applicable, older LCD says "no" but the current LCD says "yes"?
121. What can you do when a claim is denied as "not medically reasonable and necessary"?
122. What must you prove when a claim is denied as "experimental/investigational"?
123. Will you be surprised when a claim is denied as "experimental or investigational"?
124. What can you do when a critical term such as "experimental or investigational" is not defined by Medicare?
125. Can you use the Anthem BC BS definition of "investigational"?
126. How would you use Anthem's definition of "investigational"?
127. What do you tell the ALJ when the "vendor" assured you Medicare would pay?
128. What if the vendor actually signed a piece of paper assuring Medicare payment?
129. An example of a vendor's magic show: the selling of platelet-rich plasma (PRP) for the repair of ruptured tendons around the ankle.
130. How should you decide whether to cite and include a document?
131. Should you rely on common sense when you are writing the letter brief?
132. What are the contractor's strongest arguments against payment?
133. Where do you include the contractor's arguments in your letter brief?
134. What do you do with a weakness in the contractor's argument against payment?
135. What do you do with a weakness in your argument for payment?
136. What do you do with a questionable weakness in an argument?
137. You didn't send a letter brief to the QIC. Can you send a letter brief to the ALJ?
138. If you send a letter brief to the ALJ, do you have to send copies to the patients?
139. Will the ALJ accept your letter brief under these facts?
140. Does your letter say what you want it to say and will the ALJ understand it?
141. What should you do if you can't find support for the denied service?
142. Did you present your strongest evidence first?
143. Other than the QIC, who else do you have to send the letter brief to?
144. How much emotion should you include in your letter brief?
145. What should you do if the QIC raises new arguments in the reconsideration decision?
146. What if you forgot to include an important piece of evidence in the letter sent to the QIC?
147. Does any of this apply to you if your medical group does all your billing and appeals?
148. If you don't want to write letter briefs and do ALJ hearings, what should you do?

In addition to the Code of Federal Regulations (CFR) sections, the following is based on my experience prosecuting thousands of denied Medicare codes for payment and litigating for a broad cross-section of providers in front of a diverse group of Administrative Law Judges (ALJs). While I did not write "in my experience" or "in my opinion" at the beginning of the answer to each of the following questions, you should assume one of those phrases applies.

1. What is a letter brief?

For our purpose of appealing denied Medicare claims, we will define a "letter brief" as an informal legal brief written to convince the ALJ to order payment of your denied claim.

2. What is the goal of a letter brief?

The goal of the letter brief is to get you paid for the denied service. You need to write what the ALJ needs to read in order to award payment of the denied claim.

3. What should the letter brief say?

Reduced to its simplest form, the letter brief should explain what you did, why you did it, why that treatment was correct, and why the contractor's denial reasons are wrong.

4. What are the key questions you must answer in every letter brief?

In the fewest number of pages possible, here are the questions you must answer in the letter brief for the judge to rule in your favor. The judge will not award payment if the judge does not know and understand the answers to these questions:

a. **In lay terms, what kind of problem does the patient have?** The ALJ must have a basic understanding of the patient's problem in order to rule in your favor.
b. **Why did the problem require treatment?** Do not take this question for granted. You must convince the judge the patient's problem needed to be treated.
c. **What service/supply did you provide for the patient's problem?** Keep it simple and state exactly why the denied service/supply was the best and most logical choice for the patient.
d. **How do you know that treatment was the correct thing to do?** What medical authorities support what you did? Provide copies of those authorities as attachments to the letter brief.
e. **Why is each denial reason offered by the contractor in the redetermination denial letter wrong?** No matter how silly the contractor's reasons may be, you have to address and dismantle each denial reason.

Your letter to the QIC should be as brief as possible, but the letter must address all of the above questions. Most importantly, your letter must be in plain English and must be understandable to a layperson.

5. Who is the target audience for the letter brief?

The target audience for the letter brief is always the ALJ team. Each ALJ usually has two staff attorneys along with a paralegal and/or legal secretary assisting her. These people make up the "ALJ team."

One of the staff attorneys will review your documents before turning them over to the ALJ, and it is reasonable to think the ALJ will want to hear the staff attorney's opinion regarding your letter brief.

Everything you do during the appeals process should be done with the ALJ team in mind as your target audience.

6. I will use the pronoun "her" when referring to the ALJ.

It is too cumbersome to use the pronouns "him/her" when referring to an ALJ. I will just use the pronoun "her" with the understanding an ALJ may be a man or a woman. Currently, I think both sexes are equally represented in the group of federal Medicare ALJs.

7. What documents will you attach to the letter?

The documents attached (stapled) to the letter will include copies of patient photographs, patient care documents (progress notes, consultation letters, lab and imaging study reports, operative reports, pathology reports, etc.), peer-reviewed journal articles, textbook sections, and standard-of-care statements published by authoritative professional organizations that represent your specialty/business.

8. Should you attach *every* patient care document to the letter?

No. Only attach the documents that will support payment of the denied claim. If a multicolored document in the patient's chart is attractive but won't help you get paid, don't attach it to the letter.

You won't help yourself by boring the judge or her staff attorney. Attach only those documents that will serve as bricks in your wall of evidence supporting payment of the denied claim.

9. How does the letter brief help you get paid?

The letter gives the ALJ an explanation of your arguments in favor of payment and an easy-to-follow road map through all of your evidence (the stapled attachments). As a result of the letter brief, the judge will be familiar with your evidence when the hearing starts, so you can use your actual hearing time to tell the patient's "story."

During the hearing, when the judge asks you a question about your treatment of the patient, you will answer the question and will tell the judge which patient care documents or policy statement attached to the letter brief support your answer.

You will need a list of the attachments IN LARGE BLOCK PRINT in front of you so you can find the patient care documents or policy statement very quickly.

10. Whose point of view should you take as you write the letter brief?

Take the point of view of the judge as you write the letter brief. As an ALJ, what would convince you to award payment? I think the answer is easy. You would want to be certain the denied treatment was medically reasonable and necessary, and you would want to know all of the contractor's denial reasons were wrong or, for good reason, should not be applied to the claims at issue.

11. Why are you sending the letter brief to the QIC instead of to the ALJ?

You have to. In 2005, Medicare changed the rules regarding appeals of denied claims. The most important change was the new rule stating all evidence has to be submitted when the second-level (reconsideration) appeal is requested. See 42 CFR Section 405.966.

12. Why does it make the most sense to submit the letter brief to the QIC?

You already know the answer. The letter brief should be submitted when you submit your patient care documents. And your patient care documents must be submitted when you request the reconsideration appeal. Without the letter, there will be nothing to tie your patient care documents together so the reader can make sense of them.

13. Will an overworked ALJ team organize and analyze unorganized documents?

Without a letter that cites the attached documents, it is unlikely the overworked ALJ or her even more overworked attorney advisor will spend time they don't have organizing and analyzing your documents.

The letter portion of your letter brief is the "treasure map" that enables the ALJ to follow your arguments—based on your organized patient care documents, articles, textbook sections, and standard-of-care documents that you are attaching as evidence.

14. What can the letter brief do for you that you can't do any other way?

The letter brief allows you to speak to the judge without interruption or opposition and allows you to frame the payment dispute for her.

15. Do ALJs issue favorable "on the record" decisions just based on letter briefs?

Absolutely, yes! See 405.1000. A well-written letter may convince the judge to rule in your favor before the hearing even takes place. But even if your letter brief does not result in payment without a hearing, you can get the judge to walk into the hearing already biased in your favor and already primed to hear your story.

16. Do ALJs issue favorable "on the record" decisions without letter briefs?

Yes. Even without letter briefs, ALJs issue favorable "on the record" decisions. So, is it reasonable to think a well-written letter brief—that clearly explains the issues and convincingly argues the denied treatment was medically reasonable and necessary—will tip the scales in favor of an "on the record" decision? Of course it is.

17. Why will the ALJ consider your letter brief to be a miracle?

Most providers who send evidence to the QIC for the reconsideration appeal just copy the patient's chart and send everything without organizing anything. And after the QIC denies the reconsideration appeal, the entire claim file is forwarded to the ALJ's office when the ALJ appeal is requested.

Your letter brief will be nothing short of a miracle to the ALJ team—like a glass of water to a person wandering in the desert. Why? Because your letter brief will give the judge a clear view of your arguments with immediate access to all of the supporting documents attached as evidence.

18. Make it easy for the ALJ and avoid ALJ denials based on ignorance.

Whatever you can do to make the ALJ's job easier, do it. Although many appeals are decided on issues that leave no room for argument, just as many appeals can be decided either way. If there is anything you can do that will help the judge understand the dispute and decide in your favor, you should do it.

On the flip side, when a judge does not understand the medicine and/or is unaware of the medical authorities supporting the provided treatment, she will likely rely on the denial rationale offered by the Medicare contractor and the QIC.

When you submit a short letter brief that clearly explains the medicine, details why you should be paid, and includes photographs and authoritative documents as attachments that support your arguments, the judge will not deny your appeal out of ignorance.

Make it easy for the judge to decide in your favor.

19. The letter brief is one of two "loopholes" available in the appeals process.

Other than the "proposed decision" you send along with the request for an ALJ appeal (see the chapter on ALJ appeals), the letter brief is the only other procedural "loophole" in the entire Medicare appeals process that works entirely in your favor. The letter brief lets you tell your story the way you want to tell it, without interruption or opposition.

20. Is it ever okay to not send a letter brief?

No. You work too hard to walk away from these denials. Even a one-page letter brief allows you to frame your arguments for the judge in a voice that is persuasive and in a light most favorable to your version of the dispute. Suck it up and get it done.

21. What is the ALJ's response to no letter brief explaining why you should be paid?

You are asking the ALJ to go out on a limb and order payment after the contractor and the QIC have already said "no." If you were the ALJ, would you go out on that limb for a provider who can't be bothered to explain in a short letter why the claim should be paid? I don't think I would.

22. Does your letter say what you want it to say?

Have someone with no medical education read your letter and then have that person tell you what the letter says. If that person gets it, the ALJ will get it. If that person does not understand what you have written, it is likely the ALJ will not understand what you have written either.

23. If you are a terrible writer, how can you convince the judge to award payment?

If you can write a progress note, you can write a letter brief to an ALJ. The ALJ doesn't care if your style stinks. The ALJ just wants the answers to the five basic questions: what was wrong with the patient, why did the problem require treatment, what did you do for the patient, how do you know it was the correct thing to do, and why are the MAC denial reasons wrong? No matter how much or how little talent you have as a writer, you can do this by always following the same approach. This will eliminate your anxiety and will allow you to get the job done in the shortest period of time.

You have to be able to tell this story like you would tell it to a patient, with the goal of having the patient understand the story *the very first time* you tell it. Why? Because it is likely the judge will only read your letter brief once.

24. How academic should your letter brief be?

Do not provide the judge with an academic essay. Just tell her what was wrong with the patient, why the patient's problem needed to be treated, what the treatment consisted of, how you know that was the right thing to do, and why the contractor's denial reasons are wrong. Sorry for the repetition, but if these five questions are the only thing you get out of this book, your time and money will have been well spent.

Speaking of the medical authorities that support what you did, use one or two authoritative policy statements, articles, or textbook sections. Do **not** list 50 articles, with 5 of them in another language just because you can.

Do not get fancy. Stay with plain English. The three-page (or less) letter should be written without any terms of art. For example, the diabetic patient did not have diabetic angiopathy with arteriosclerosis obliterans of the dorsalis pedis and posterior tibial arteries. Instead, the patient had diabetic vascular disease with blockage of the major arteries bringing blood into the foot.

Keep it simple. Use very short sentences. The goal is not to impress the ALJ with your writing ability or your knowledge of medicine. The goal is to make the ALJ understand your answers to the five key questions so you will get paid.

25. Why should the letter portion of your letter brief be less than three pages?

The ALJ will **always** read a three-page brief. The ALJ will **never** read a 30-page brief. And if you understand why the service was denied, you should be able to explain in one or two sentences why the denied service should be paid.

Okay, sometimes an ALJ will read a 30-page brief. But you should have compelling reasons for a longer brief over a shorter one.

26. Can the letter portion of your letter brief be only one page?

Yes! If you can prove the service was medically reasonable and necessary and can prove the denial rationale was wrong in one or two paragraphs, that is exactly what you should do.

ABOUT THE ALJ AND THE LETTER BRIEF

27. You will lose the ALJ appeal if the ALJ finds these things in your documents.

The ALJ may know very little about the patient's medical problem, but ALJs are experts when it comes to reviewing documents. If your documents regarding the service at issue are not legible, were not written at the time the service was provided, do not support the diagnosis (International Classification of Diseases [ICD]-10) code(s) on the claim form, or do not support the CPT and/or HCPCS (Healthcare Common Procedure Coding System) II codes on the claim form, you are going to lose.

28. What progress note "crime" will not be forgiven by the ALJ?

Here is the crime: You dictate an initial history and physical (H&P)/patient encounter note that is adequate in every regard. However, you then cut and paste that initial H&P note and use it in its entirety for every subsequent progress note for the patient, changing only a word or two here or there.

Without reading another "fact" in the case, that ALJ is going to rule against you, and she probably should.

You were far more credible when you were handwriting your notes. Do not cut and paste large portions of the initial H&P note into your subsequent progress notes.

29. Do not underestimate the ALJ's lack of medical knowledge.

You must not underestimate the ALJ's lack of medical knowledge when you (1) write the letter brief, (2) as you make your oral presentation during the hearing, and (3) while you are answering the judge's questions during the hearing. Everything you write and say has to be understood by the judge and has to make sense.

The judge knows as much about medicine as you (Medicare providers) know about the law, which is to say, nothing. But if the judge does not understand why you did what you did, there is no chance you are going to get paid. You should write it and say it to the ALJ the same way you would write it and explain it to a patient.

30. How is the letter brief tied to your fear of Medicare?

Your fear of Medicare stops you from billing for the appropriate level of complexity E&M codes and stops you from billing for all of the procedure/supply codes you are entitled to bill.

The first step in eliminating your fear of Medicare is knowing all of the codes you are entitled to bill and knowing how to use the modifiers that will qualify you for payment of the very small universe of E&M, procedure, and supply codes you bill every day.

The second step is making sure all of the appropriate codes are submitted to Medicare for each patient encounter.

The third step is knowing how to fight when payment is mistakenly denied and having the confidence to fight all the way through an ALJ hearing, if necessary.

Otherwise, you will continue to choose incorrect lower level of complexity E&M codes and you will avoid billing for all the procedure/supply codes you are entitled to bill—out of fear.

The letter brief will give you the courage needed to fight mistaken denials during the ALJ hearing. And, having seen this many times, once you win your first ALJ hearing, you will find yourself addicted to the knowledge that you can fight back and win when a denial is in error.

31. How does the letter brief affect your presentation during the hearing?

The judge will read your letter brief before the hearing and will already know the facts of your case. As a result, the letter brief enables you to concentrate on telling your patient's story during the hearing rather than wasting hearing time on a list of medical facts.

Sun Tzu, an attorney who represented Medicare providers in 500 BC, wrote in *The Art of War*: "All battles are won or lost before the battle takes place and all Medicare ALJ hearings are won or lost before the hearing takes place." Sun was right! Make it easy for the judge to rule in your favor. The brief allows you to tell your story in a way that is organized, easy to understand, and persuasive.

32. How is your brief related to your answers during the hearing?

The ALJ will never let you ramble on and on during a hearing. Writing the brief will force you to organize your thoughts, which will result in shorter, more effective answers during the hearing.

33. What should you do if the QIC adds new denial reasons in the QIC decision?

If the QIC denial letter contains new denial reasons that were not offered by the contractor in the redetermination denial letter, you must send the ALJ a second letter brief that addresses just the new QIC denial reasons.

34. How should the second letter brief be written?

The second letter brief should be written in the same format as the first letter brief. However, the only issues you will address in the body of the second letter will be the **new denial reasons** that were offered for the first time in the QIC decision letter.

Do not anger the judge by forcing her to reread what you wrote in the letter brief sent to the QIC. Worse, do not make the judge stop reading your second letter brief as soon as she realizes you are repeating yourself.

35. Why should you be able to submit your reconsideration appeals on time?

Usually, you will be fighting for payment of the ten codes that are most commonly denied payment in your practice/business. It will be the same fight over and over again. You should have a library of reconsideration appeal documents on your office computer that you can use for each of these commonly denied codes.

36. How long do you have to submit a reconsideration appeal request?

You have to submit the reconsideration appeal to the QIC within **185 calendar days** of the postmarked date on the envelope containing the notice of redetermination. See 405.962(a)(1).

Everybody wants to argue about the 185 days, as opposed to the 180 days noted in the code section, so let me explain. The language in this code section states you have 180 calendar days after you receive the redetermination denial to get your appeal request to the QIC. But the same code section also states the date of receipt of the redetermination denial will be assumed to be 5 calendar days after the date of the notice of redetermination. In other words, the 180-day clock does not start running until the fifth day after the postmarked date on the envelope containing the redetermination denial.

In addition, if you mail the request for the reconsideration appeal within the 185 calendar days, you can always make the argument that you met the 405.962(b)(3) good cause requirements cited in 405.942(b)(2) and (b)(3)—so your appeal was timely. In other words, you will argue: "I mailed it within the 185 days. It just didn't get there on time."

37. If you are pressed for time, can you just submit the reconsideration appeal form?

Yes! You have at least four weeks after you send the CMS-20033 appeal form to get your letter brief to the QIC. As long as you get the letter brief to the QIC before the QIC publishes its decision, the QIC has to consider your letter brief and the brief has to be included in the appeal file sent to the ALJ. See 405.966(a)(2).

When was the last time you received a reconsideration decision within four weeks of sending the request for a reconsideration appeal? The answer is "never." And four weeks should be plenty of time to collect additional evidence, write your letter brief, and send it all to the QIC.

38. Will an ALJ award payment just based on a clever legal argument?

No. An ALJ will never award payment based on a clever legal argument if the ALJ is not convinced the denied service was medically reasonable and necessary.

39. Why are clinical photographs always your strongest evidence?

A clinical photograph is worth a thousand articles. If the patient's underlying problem can be captured in a photo, take pictures and submit them along with the request for the reconsideration (QIC) appeal.

Describing the patient's problem in words when you can show the patient's problem in a photograph is like describing the *Mona Lisa* instead of showing someone the painting.

Don't rely on a progress note written in medical jargon to describe the patient's problem. Grab the judge's attention with a graphic photo and keep her attention with a short story in understandable English that explains the patient's problem and the denied treatment that was medically reasonable and necessary.

40. Will you have to authenticate the photos in the letter brief?

Yes. You will have to authenticate/prove the photos you send are images of the patient whose claim is at issue and you will have to prove when the images were taken.

41. How do you authenticate clinical photographs?

The easiest way to authenticate a clinical photograph is by including the necessary information within the imaging field when the picture is taken.

Use your office computer to print the patient's initials, the patient's Medicare number, and the date, in size 36 font (or larger) on a letter-sized piece of paper. Use that piece of paper as the background for each picture you take of the patient and check to make sure the identifying information clearly shows in the images after you take the pictures.

42. What happens if you don't authenticate photographs for the judge?

Unless the patient is at the hearing, the judge will probably not accept the submitted photographs as "evidence."

43. Can you ask the patient to participate in the ALJ hearing?

Of course you can. In fact, the patient's presence at the hearing will probably increase your chance of winning payment.

Having the patient sitting next to you during the video teleconference ALJ hearing changes the dynamic of the hearing. Now the ALJ is looking at a real person who needed care rather than looking at a pile of documents. And if the patient is willing to show the judge the affected body part during the hearing and is willing to answer the judge's questions as to symptoms and treatment, you are almost assured of payment.

44. Can you submit late-taken photos of the patient to the ALJ?

Maybe. If the patient has a chronic condition so the judge knows the late-taken photographs accurately reflected the patient's problem on the date of service at issue, and you were smart enough to "authenticate" the photos when they were taken, the judge may allow them to be entered into the record.

The worst thing that happens is that the judge will not accept the photos as evidence for the hearing.

45. Once the judge looks at the photos, can the judge un-ring that bell?

No. And the human response is to look at the photos. Once the judge looks at the photos, nothing can un-ring that bell.

46. What argument should you make to get late-submitted photos accepted?

You should consider saying something like this to the judge:

> *Your Honor, these photos are incorporated by descriptive reference in the patient's progress notes that were previously submitted in this appeal. Therefore, these photos are not "new evidence" and should be accepted by the Court for this appeal.*

47. How should you take and store photos for hearings?

Use your smartphone to take the digital images and send the images to a cloud email address. The digital images (later converted to hard copies that you will send to the QIC) will probably be more important to the judge than the rest of your testimony, and probably more important than the rest of your prehearing letter brief.

However, do not waste time or money converting digital images to hard copy images unless the claim is denied.

48. How can you use photos when the denied service is "included" in another service?

If the patient's problem, and what you do for that problem, can be captured in photographs, then those photographs will always be your strongest evidence for payment. Here is an example of a simple billing problem ripe for photographic presentation to an ALJ:

Suppose you perform matricectomy procedures at both the tibial and fibular borders of the same left hallux nail (both edges of the left big toenail are surgically, permanently removed). You are probably thinking Medicare will pay for the first matricectomy procedure and will deny payment for the second matricectomy procedure, and there is nothing you can do about it. I would argue otherwise, and advise using something like the following explanation in your letter brief to the QIC:

> *The MAC paid the 11750-TA code for the tibial border matricectomy of the left great toenail and denied the 11750-TA-59 code for the fibular border matricectomy of the left great toenail. Both matricectomy procedures were performed on [first, last name of beneficiary] on the same day.*
>
> *The 11750 CPT code is defined as: "Excision of nail and nail matrix, partial or complete (e.g., ingrown or deformed nail), for permanent removal." This definition describes the excision of nail and nail matrix from one* ***contiguous*** *surgical site, whether part or all of the nail and nail matrix is removed. This 11750 definition does not address the clinical situation where separate excisions of nail and nail matrix are performed at each nail border, leaving the central portion of nail, nail matrix, and nail bed intact.*
>
> *The -59 modifier is described in the "Appendix A—Modifiers" section of the CPT Manual as follows:*
>
> > ***59 Distinct Procedural Service:*** *Under certain circumstances, it may be necessary to indicate that a procedure or service was distinct or independent from other non-E/M services performed on the same day. Modifier 59 is used to identify procedures/services, other than E/M services, that are not normally reported together but are appropriate under the circumstances. Documentation must support a different session,* ***different*** *procedure or* ***surgery, different site*** *or organ system,* ***separate*** *incision/****excision, separate lesion****, or separate injury not ordinarily encountered or performed on the same day by the same individual.* (Emphasis added.)
>
> *Usually, either the medial (tibial) or lateral (fibular) border of a nail requires a matricectomy procedure. It is unusual for both the tibial and the fibular borders of the same toenail to require matricectomy procedures at the same time, but it does happen. And based on the CPT Manual description regarding the use of the -59 modifier, we have* ***different surgeries*** *performed at* ***different sites****, with* ***separate excisions*** *for* ***separate lesions****, on the same toe, on the same day.*
>
> *The "separateness" of the surgical (matricectomy) procedures is supported by all of the following clinical facts:*
>
> 1. *Two separate partial avulsion procedures were performed, first at the tibial border and then at the fibular border of the same nail plate.* (Show the photographs of each avulsion.)
> 2. *A matricectomy procedure was then performed at each surgical site.* (Show the photographs of each matricectomy procedure.)
> 3. *You cannot get to the second surgical site from the first surgical site because you have a wide zone of nail plate along with the underlying skin of the nail bed separating the two surgical sites.* (Show an end-on view of the toe that demonstrates the intact nail plate separating the two surgical sites.)
> 4. *You can get a postoperative infection at one surgical procedure site that does not involve the other surgical procedure site.* (Because infection following a matricectomy procedure is not uncommon, take advantage of the opportunity to photograph this

exact occurrence when it presents so you will have a clinical example photograph you can show the ALJs.)

5. *You can have a recurrence of the problem (ingrown toenail) at one surgical procedure site while the other surgical procedure is a complete success.* (Unfortunately, recurrence is also not uncommon. When it occurs, photograph it so you can show this to the ALJ as you are making the argument for the separateness of the two matricectomy procedures.)

The denied 11750-TA-59 code for the fibular border matricectomy of the left great toenail should be paid because the two surgical procedures were identifiably separate and the -59 modifier was appropriately used to show the separateness of the procedures.

That takes care of what you will write in the letter brief. Now, what will you tell the ALJ? First, you should assume the ALJ has read your letter brief. As a result, you will **not** want to repeat the same sentences the judge already read in your letter brief.

And because you are smart enough to know you will **always be denied** payment for the second matricectomy procedure performed on the same toe on the same day, you will keep a hard copy set of digital images that demonstrate tibial and fibular border matricectomy procedures performed on the same toe as well as hard copies of post-op infection at one surgical site and recurrence at one surgical site available for use in letter briefs. You only have to take this set of images once. You will keep the original images on your smartphone and you will keep five sets of hard copies of these images in your desk for future appeals of this same problem. You will submit one set of these images to the QIC, as part of your letter brief, with your request for the reconsideration appeal.

Here is how I would present this issue to the ALJ:

Your Honor, the images submitted to the QIC represent the matricectomy procedures performed on [first, last name of beneficiary's] left great toe. Although these images are not of this patient's toe, the images demonstrate the exact same procedures performed at the same time, for the same problem (infected, ingrown tibial and fibular borders of a great toenail).

First, the great toe was locally anesthetized for the two surgical procedures. If you imagine the patient's toe on cross-section as a circle, and you convert that circle to a square, we have to anesthetize the nerve at each corner of the square in order to make the surgeries painless. In addition, Your Honor, if you squeeze the skin on your thumb as I am (turn your hand around so the judge can see what you are doing), *you can see the hourglass appearance of your thumb. Where the hourglass is most concave is where we deposit the anesthetic solution because that is where the largest subcutaneous space is available for a pain-free injection. Where the hourglass is most convex, at the level of the joint prominence, is where we do not want to inject the anesthetic solution because that is where the smallest subcutaneous space is available and where an injection of local anesthetic would be most painful.* (Do not miss an opportunity to engage the judge!)

The next images demonstrate the surgical scrub of the foot and the placement of a tourniquet at the base of the toe. The tourniquet is used to prevent blood flow into the surgical sites while the chemical (phenol) is applied to destroy the nail-forming tissue. We want to avoid dilution of the phenol as it is applied to the nail forming tissue (the nail matrix). So we are using the tourniquet to give the phenol time to act.

The next images demonstrate the surgical removal of the tibial border of the nail, back to and including that portion of the nail plate growing from under the skin of the proximal nail fold.

The next images demonstrate the surgical removal of the fibular border of the nail, back to and including that portion of the nail plate growing from under the skin of the proximal nail fold.

Then, you see the application of the phenol to the tibial border as the first surgical site and then the application of the phenol to the fibular border as the second surgical site.

Significantly, the central portion of the nail plate between the two surgical sites, the underlying nail bed, and the associated skin of the proximal nail fold are not violated during these two separate surgical procedures.

The next images demonstrate the application of the surgical dressing materials to each site and then to the entire toe.

In addition, the following images demonstrate a postoperative infection at one of the two matricectomy sites on a toe and recurrence at one of the two sites.

Your Honor, the letter brief submitted to the QIC and the images reviewed today support the conclusion that the -59 modifier requirements have been met for payment of the second matricectomy procedure. I am respectfully requesting the court to order payment of the denied 11750-TA-59 code for the fibular border matricectomy of the left great toenail.

Why am I advising you to present all of this to the judge?

You want the judge to step into the story and then into the room when you performed the matricectomy procedures. You want the judge to experience what you did and why you did it. You want the judge to objectively and personally understand why the denial of payment for the second surgical procedure is unsupportable based on the 59 modifier conditions being met, unreasonable based on the obvious "separateness" of the procedures, and yes, "unfair" based on the judge constructively being there and seeing what you did.

The images will keep the judge's attention. The short statements accompanying the images will enable the judge to understand what you are saying and why you deserve to be paid. Do not underestimate the power of a story coupled with clinical photographs!

49. How is the letter brief and oral argument related to books for children?

Before you learned how to read, your parents read books to you that had big pictures and just a few words on each page. Why? Because you couldn't read, you needed big pictures and short explanations in order to hold your attention and enable you to understand the story. Well, if the ALJ doesn't know the medicine involved in the dispute, you better use big pictures and short explanations if you want to get paid.

For those of you who mistakenly think I am demeaning the ALJs, consider the following question: Is there a difference in your level of attention at a medical meeting where a nationally acclaimed surgeon is lecturing on a surgical procedure and is just using slides with words only, as opposed to the same surgeon lecturing on the same surgery but using clinical slides that illustrate each portion of the procedure? Of course there is.

Judges are no different. You will be most successful in keeping the judge's attention and enabling her to understand what you did for the patient if you can show her big pictures and explain each picture in just a few words.

50. How can you distinguish separate services without photographs?

Make sure you are incorporating an explanation in your progress note as to how and why the services are separate.

If you are frequently providing the same two services at the same time, you should take the time to research and write a paragraph that explains why the services are separate, and the paragraph should cite recognized authorities that support the "separateness" of the services. You want to keep that paragraph handy when you are dictating your progress notes.

A good example would be the established diabetic patient who returns with a deep plantar ulcer complicated by cellulitis. You know in advance that the MAC will deny payment of the E&M code billed with the wound debridement code and that the MAC will claim the E&M was included in the debridement code. In this situation, you should dictate something like the following into the patient's progress note:

> *This patient required a 99215 E&M service in addition to the code submitted for debridement of the ulcer because the E&M service required for this patient's limb-threatening/life-threatening problem far exceeded the E&M included in any wound debridement code. Similarly, the 99215 Clinical Examples in Appendix C of the CPT Manual includes the example of an "Office visit for an established diabetic patient with a cellulitic deep plantar abscess and history of previous forefoot amputation of the contralateral side. (Podiatry Surgery)."*

Whether your patient had a "history of previous forefoot amputation of the contralateral side" is irrelevant. What matters is that the patient's current problem is serious enough to warrant the 99215 E&M service. The expert committee of physicians who write the clinical examples in Appendix C of the CPT Manual know a 99215 E&M service is required in this clinical situation and they want you to know this as well.

51. What is considered "new evidence" at the time of an ALJ hearing?

If Medicare did **not** write it, or if Medicare did **not** rely on it to determine a Medicare coverage policy, then the document in question will be considered "new evidence" at the time of the hearing.

Assuming you just submit a CMS-20033 reconsideration appeal request form and nothing else, what would be considered "**new evidence**" at the ALJ hearing? All of your patient records, photographs, procedure reports, lab reports, letters about the patient exchanged with other treating doctors, journal articles, textbook chapters, and standard of care statements would be considered "new evidence."

52. What does Medicare say about "new evidence" at the time of an ALJ hearing?

Medicare says new evidence will **not** be admitted and/or considered by the ALJ—no matter how convincing that evidence may be—unless you can prove to the ALJ that you have "good cause" for the late submission. See 405.966(a)(2).

53. How does Medicare define "good cause" for new evidence at the ALJ hearing?

Medicare doesn't define it. Why not? Because Medicare does not want to define it. This way the ALJ can make an individual decision, but that is not always a bad thing.

In my experience, many of the ALJs have bent over backward to find a reason to admit late-submitted evidence, especially when the ALJ thought that evidence would and should determine the outcome of the case.

54. With the backlog of cases, how will the ALJs respond to "new evidence"?

The work pressure on the Medicare ALJs is spiraling out of control as a result of the huge backlog of ALJ appeals. As a result, the past looks better than the future for any provider who wants to submit late evidence to an ALJ.

55. What is not "new evidence" at the time of an ALJ hearing?

If Medicare wrote it or relied on it to determine a Medicare coverage policy, that document is never "new evidence" and that document can always be presented, for the first time, at the ALJ hearing.

This means you can present any of the articles or textbook sections cited in the applicable LCD at the time of your hearing. Because many Medicare contractors use the same old articles year after year to support out-of-date coverage policies in their newer versions of the same LCD, you may have a powerful argument that the contractor's "current" LCD policy does not reflect the current standard of care.

ABOUT THE DENIAL AND THE LETTER BRIEF

56. Are you missing something that may kill your appeal?

Yes! Your Medicare contractor makes the original determination on your claim and the same Medicare contractor decides the outcome of your redetermination appeal. If you think a denial reason offered by your contractor in the Remittance Advice (RA) and repeated in the redetermination denial letter makes no sense, chances are you are missing something.

Make no assumptions. You must know for sure why your claim was originally denied. You have to understand what the denial codes on the original Remittance Advice notice mean and then you have to apply those definitions to the code at issue.

57. How can you find out why your claim was denied?

Purchase the book *Denial Codes Plain English Descriptions*, published by DecisionHealth and available at www.codingbooks.com. The individual Medicare denial codes and the Medicare denial code combinations are explained in detail and in plain English.

In the alternative, you can ask the patient to send you a copy of the letter the patient received explaining the denial. While the Medicare contractor sends you a denial explanation using denial codes—see 405.921(b)(2)(iii)—that same contractor has to send the patient an explanation (in plain English) designed to be understood by a layperson. See 405.921(a)(1).

Last but not least, pretend you are the contractor. Use the denial codes on the RA, and use the explanation in the redetermination denial letters (the one you received and the one the patient received) to reverse-engineer the denial of your claim. Be aggressive as you role-play. Tear your claim apart, looking for reasons to deny payment.

Make no assumptions. You must look up and understand every denial code in the RA and every Medicare Manual section cited in the redetermination denial letter, and you have to apply those denial code definitions and Medicare Manual sections to the code at issue—as though you were the contractor.

58. What happens when you role-play as the contractor during your analysis?

At first, you will be surprised how frequently you missed a big piece of the contractor's denial rationale. But soon, you will be doing this role-switching regularly because it works. And don't feel bad. One of the most common errors made by lawyers is the sin of telling yourself your version of the story so many times you not only believe it, you are actually unable to see your opponent's counterarguments until it is too late.

Once you know exactly why the claim was denied, you have to think: What are my most effective arguments against the denial and what is my strongest evidence supporting those arguments? The answers to these questions will determine how you will write the letter brief.

59. How will the redetermination denial affect the judge's questions at the hearing?

The redetermination denial reasons are the 600-pound gorilla in the hearing room because the judge is going to key her questions on the redetermination denial reasons. You must neutralize the redetermination denial reasons in your letter brief, and you must be competently conversational with the redetermination denial reasons during the hearing.

Based on the denial codes and based on the denial rationale in the redetermination decision, you should know where you will be most vulnerable to attack by the ALJ during the hearing and you **must** be prepared to answer the ALJ's questions directed at those vulnerabilities.

60. What should you do with a vulnerable point in your argument?

Embrace the vulnerability! For example, suppose you are representing a radiation oncologist who is appealing a denial of payment for the robotic stereotactic body radiation therapy (R-SBRT) treatment of a patient with localized prostate cancer. The judge says: "The LCD specifically states R-SBRT cannot be used for the treatment of prostate cancer. Why should I award payment when the doctor knew he was prohibited from using R-SBRT for this patient?"

If you weren't sweating before the hearing, you would probably be sweating when the judge asks that question. But think how effective it would be to respond to the judge with the following answer:

> *Your Honor, we know the LCD policy on the use of R-SBRT for prostate cancer was based on two textbooks and one article published ten years before the patient was treated. We know this is true because the LCD lists those two textbooks and that one article as the source documents used to write the LCD section on "Indications for the use of R-SBRT."*
>
> *We also know the current versions of the same two textbooks, published before this patient was treated, as well as a large number of articles published in peer-reviewed radiation oncology journals before this patient was treated, all support the use of R-SBRT for localized prostate cancer. In addition, ASTRO, the American Society for Radiation Oncology, approved the use of R-SBRT for localized prostate cancer before this patient was treated. The newer version of the textbook sections, the newer articles, and the standard of care published by ASTRO are all included as attachments in the letter brief sent to the QIC.*
>
> *In clinical terms, Your Honor, the use of R-SBRT allowed the radiation oncologist to treat the patient's cancer with much greater accuracy than was possible with the older, LCD-approved intensity modulated radiation therapy (IMRT). And the R-SBRT allowed the radiation oncologist to administer his radiation in five sessions as opposed to the 45 radiation therapy sessions required with the older IMRT. The R-SBRT also allowed the radiation oncologist to treat the patient with half the total dose of radiation that would have been used with IMRT. And finally, Your Honor, R-SBRT is nothing more than an updated and improved version of IMRT.*

No longer sweating? I didn't think so.

61. Will the stated denial reasons always tell you what you have to prove to the ALJ?

Yes. And once you know why payment was denied, you have to counter each denial reason.

62. What are the common denial reasons and what do you have to prove for each?

Here are common reasons for denials and what you have to prove for each:

If the contractor denies payment, stating the service was **not medically reasonable and necessary,** you will have to prove the service *was* medically reasonable and necessary.

If the contractor denies payment stating the service was **experimental/investigational,** you will have to prove the service was *not* experimental/investigational.

If the contractor denies the E&M code stating the **E&M service was included in the procedure code and that procedure code was paid by the contractor,** you will have to prove the E&M code should be paid as a separate service. You will also have to prove you met the E&M code requirements on the date of service at issue.

If the contractor **down-codes** the submitted E&M code, you will have to prove the higher complexity E&M code should be paid based on the complexity of the patient's problem and based on the contents of your progress note on the date of service at issue.

If the contractor's LCD allowed the denied service but the contractor denied payment stating **some requirements were not met** (e.g., the reporting forms required for diabetic shoes were not all submitted, there was an inadequate time interval between the same services, there was no indication of symptoms requiring the provided service, there was no indication of complicating medical factors justifying the provided service), you will have to prove how and why the requirements *were* met, or why the service was medically reasonable and necessary and should, therefore, be paid.

If the overall surgical service qualifies for payment but the contractor states payment was denied for the surgical code at issue because you **unbundled** the primary surgical code in order to bill the code at issue, you will have to prove why the denied surgical service qualifies for payment as a separate and distinct surgical service.

Basically, whatever the MAC asserts as the reason for denial, you will have to prove the opposite is true or that an exception should be made to the denial reason.

63. When required information is missing, how do you argue denied E&M codes?

Here is what I would recommend. First, offer a capsulized version of each patient's problem. Then, quote the CPT clinical example that is similar in complexity to each denied E&M code. Once you convince the judge that the seriousness of each patient's problem is similar to a clinical example in Appendix C of the CPT Manual, the only other thing you must do is prove you met the record-keeping requirements for the use of each code.

If one or more record-keeping requirements are missing in the applicable progress note, you may consider using a modification of the following argument when you are making your presentation to the judge:

Your Honor, in Appendix C of the 2018 CPT Manual, an example for E&M code ________ states: "______________." With very similar complexity, first, last [name of patient] had [describe the patient's problem].

In addition, the section at the very beginning of the CPT Manual on the use of E&M codes states the complexity and seriousness of the patient's problem determines the selection of the correct E&M code. Here, based on the complexity and seriousness of [first, last's] problem and based on the equivalent CPT example, we know the correct E&M code for the claim at issue is __________.

It is true that some of the information in the history/physical examination on the date of service is missing in the _________ E&M code progress note. However, the missing information should not drive the court's decision regarding payment because the missing information was not material to the management of the patient's problem. The clinically significant history and examination findings, needed to manage the patient's care, were included in the submitted progress note.

In summary, the denied __________ code should be paid because the complexity of the patient's problem calls for the E&M code used, because the clinically necessary information by history was obtained, and because the clinically necessary examination was performed.

64. Is an LCD policy binding on an ALJ?

No, an LCD policy is not binding on an ALJ. As stated in 405.1062: "ALJs are not bound by LCDs, but **will** give substantial deference to these policies if they are applicable to a particular case." (Emphasis added.)

65. What is the practical effect of the "substantial deference" rule?

The word "will" does not mean "may" or "can" or "should." The word "will" means the ALJ "must" state in the ALJ's written decision why the LCD policy was not followed (see 405.1062). And the ALJs know the Council (the Medicare Appeals Council) will reverse an ALJ decision on appeal if the ALJ awards payment but does not adequately explain how "substantial deference" was paid to the LCD policy in the ALJ's written decision.

66. Does "substantial deference" affect your burden of proof?

Of course it does. The standard of proof in a Medicare ALJ hearing is by a "preponderance of the evidence" (see 45 CFR Section 150.443). This means, in order for the ALJ to rule in your favor, she just has to find your evidence is 51% more persuasive than Medicare's 49%.

However, the ALJ is not going to rule in your favor when you prove you are right by a mere preponderance of the evidence (51% to 49%). You will have to prove to the ALJ, at least by the standard of "clear and convincing evidence" (75% to 25%), if not by the standard of "beyond a reasonable doubt" (95% to 5%), that you are right and Medicare is wrong.

So, depending on the bone versus cartilage content of the ALJ's spine, your argument has to be either very convincing or incredibly convincing in order to win the ALJ decision when the applicable LCD policy says "no."

67. What are the differences between "substantive" denials and "procedural" denials?

Procedural denials occur when you make a procedural/technical mistake (e.g., you make a clerical error on a claim form or you submit a claim form or an appeal too late).

By contrast, in a substantive denial, even if you fill everything out correctly on the claim form and you get everything submitted on time, Medicare thinks the service doesn't qualify for payment. Why? Because there is a Medicare policy or rule that prohibits payment of the claim. With a substantive denial, Medicare is saying the service you billed should never be paid under the clinical facts surrounding your claim.

68. When are you most likely to win a procedural denial and a substantive denial?

When you are appealing a procedural denial, you are likely to win at the redetermination or reconsideration level of appeal.

When you are appealing a substantive denial, you are unlikely to win before the ALJ hearing.

69. If you sent your patient care documents to the QIC, can you send a letter brief to the ALJ?

Yes. You will tell the judge your letter explains the patient care documents already submitted to the QIC but does not present any new evidence. You will not be able to send the ALJ any articles, textbook sections, or standard of care statements because they would all be "new evidence," but you can send a letter explaining the patient care documents.

70. Will you be notified when your contractor sends the ALJ a position paper?

Probably not. Your MAC may submit a "position paper" to the ALJ regarding the service at issue. And although the contractor is required to send you a copy of any position paper the contractor submits to the ALJ (see 405.1012), in my experience, the contractors **never** send a copy of their position paper to the provider/supplier. When you submit your request for an ALJ hearing, **be sure to ask the ALJ in writing to send you a copy of any position paper submitted by the contractor**, and a week before the hearing, call the ALJ's assistant and ask if a position paper has been submitted by the MAC.

71. The contractor sends a position paper to the ALJ but not to you. What should you do?

At the beginning of the hearing, you should raise the issue of the contractor's failure to send you a copy of the position paper and you should politely ask the ALJ to give no consideration to the contractor's position paper. Under 405.1010, the ALJ must comply with your request and must exclude the position paper.

72. Uh-oh . . . what if you cannot find support for the service you provided?

If you cannot find journal support for the denied service, you may want to rethink the appeal and, more importantly, you may want to rethink the denied service. Maybe you were wrong and should be doing something different.

ABOUT THE DOCUMENTS FOR THE LETTER BRIEF

73. You can always submit a Medicare document. What is a "Medicare document"?

"Medicare documents" are documents written by or relied upon by Medicare and include the following:

a. Medicare Internet-Only Manual sections (e.g., Medicare Program Integrity Manual 100-08 sections)
b. Sections from the CPT (Common Procedural Terminology) Manual (otherwise known as the HCPCS I Manual) written by the AMA (American Medical Association)
c. Sections from the HCPCS II Manual (Healthcare Common Procedure Coding System Level II Codes) written by CMS

d. LCDs (the LCD published by your contractor and the LCDs published by other contractors on the service at issue)
e. Articles published by CMS

74. What are "non-Medicare documents" and when should they be submitted?

"Non-Medicare documents" are documents that were **not** written by or relied upon by Medicare but are the documents needed to persuade the ALJ to award payment. The non-Medicare documents **should always be submitted** as attachments to your letter brief when you request the reconsideration appeal.

"Non-Medicare documents" include the following:

a. All medical records specific to the patient whose denied claim is being appealed
b. Articles published in peer-reviewed journals
c. Textbook sections
d. Summary articles published by non-CMS authorities

75. What are the Medicare Internet-Only Manuals?

The old paper-based Medicare Manual, published by CMS, contained all of the rules and regulations for Medicare. The Medicare Manual has been converted into "Medicare Internet-Only Manuals (IOMs)."

76. Which of the Medicare Internet-Only Manuals explain the rules regarding LCDs?

It is the Medicare Program Integrity Manual (MPIM) that explains how LCDs are written, what LCDs should contain, and what LCDs must not contain.

77. Can you use the Medicare Program Integrity Manual (MPIM) on LCDs to your advantage?

Medicare has gifted you with the following words on LCDs in Section 13.1.3 of Chapter 13 of the MPIM: "Contractors develop LCDs by considering **medical literature**, the **advice of local medical societies and medical consultants**, public comments, and **comments from the provider community.**"

78. What is the strongest evidence for LCD policies and how will you use this?

Chapter 13, Section 13.7.1 of the MPIM states: "Published authoritative evidence derived from definitive randomized clinical trials or other definitive studies is **the strongest evidence** for LCD policies."

If you have articles based on "definitive randomized clinical trials or other definitive studies" from the journals that apply to your specialty or business, you should cite those articles in the letter brief and write something like this:

The article titled "____________" and published in ____________ on [date of publication] states: "__________." Although the LCD policy that was the basis for the denial was correct when the articles cited in the LCD were published, the standard of care for the treatment of (the patient's problem) has evolved. Based on published, definitive studies as of [the date of service at issue], the denied service was medically reasonable and necessary and should be paid.

79. What is the second strongest evidence for LCD policies?

Section 13.7.1 states: The **second strongest evidence** is "general acceptance by the medical community (standard of practice), as supported by sound medical evidence based on scientific data or research studies published in peer-reviewed medical journals."

If this is your supporting evidence you will write something like this:

> *The denied service __________ was the standard of practice in the medical community as of [date of service], as evidenced in the attached article titled "__________" and published in the peer-reviewed journal __________ on [date of publication].*

80. What is the third strongest evidence for LCD policies?

Section 13.7.1 states: "The consensus of expert medical opinion (i.e., recognized authorities in the field); or medical opinion derived from consultations with medical associations or other health care experts." This is the **third strongest evidence** for LCD policies.

As to the **advice of local medical societies and medical consultants and comments from the provider community**, you will reference the written policy statements of the recognized societies that support your treatment for the patient at issue.

If this is your supporting evidence, you will write something like this:

> *The American College of __________ / the American Society of __________ published a policy statement on [date policy statement was published] regarding the treatment of __________. A summary of the policy statement would read as follows: "__________." A complete copy of the policy statement is attached.*

Call your Medicare Carrier Advisory Committee (CAC) representative. It is likely your CAC representative has this "medical opinion" information you are looking for.

81. What is the most common substantive reason used by Medicare to deny payment?

The most common substantive denial code states: "The services you provided were not medically reasonable and necessary."

82. What does the phrase "not medically reasonable and necessary" mean?

This is a Medicare "term of art" that does *not* mean what you think it means. The phrase actually means the service in question is not allowed because there is at least one CMS, Medicare, or contractor rule that prohibits payment for the service.

A medical service may be perfectly reasonable and necessary in the ordinary use of the phrase but will still not be paid. For example, even though a patient desperately needed diabetic shoes, you did not meet the CPT and/or ICD coding requirements on the claim forms and/or you did not meet the LCD documentation requirements. As a result, the service was "not medically reasonable and necessary."

And even if you did meet the CPT and ICD coding requirements, and even if you were initially paid for the diabetic shoes, you may still receive a demand for repayment of overpayment for the diabetic shoes based on a single missing document required for payment.

In other words, if you decide to appeal a demand for repayment of overpayment for a pair of diabetic shoes, guess what the contractor is going to say when you submit copies of your patient care documents that fail to meet the LCD document requirements for diabetic shoes? The contractor is going to uphold the demand for repayment of overpayment because the service was "not medically reasonable and necessary."

83. Where does the phrase "medically reasonable and necessary" come from?

The phrase "medically reasonable and necessary" comes from Section 1862(a)(1)(A) of the Social Security Act (the Act):

> Sec. 1862. [42 U.S.C. 1395y] (a) Notwithstanding any other provision of this title, **no payment may be made** under part A or part B **for** any expenses incurred for **items or services**—
>
> (1)(A) **which**, except for items and services described in a succeeding subparagraph, **are not reasonable and necessary for the diagnosis or treatment of illness** or injury or to improve the functioning of a malformed body member. (Emphasis added.)

84. Is there a list of requirements for "medically reasonable and necessary"?

Yes. The elements of the phrase "medically reasonable and necessary" are detailed in the MPIM, Chapter 13, "Local Coverage Determinations," Section 13.5.1—Reasonable and Necessary Provisions in LCDs.

Make a copy of MPIM Section 13.5.1 and keep it in front of you every time you write a prehearing brief.

You must address each element of 13.5.1 in the prehearing brief you will submit to the QIC and you must include each element of 13.5.1 in the oral argument you will present to the ALJ. Section 13.5.1 of the MPIM reads as follows:

> § 13.5.1: A service may be covered by a contractor if it is reasonable and necessary under 1862(a)(1)(A) of the Act. Contractors shall consider a service to be reasonable and necessary if the contractor determines that the service is:
>
> **Safe and effective;**
>
> **Not experimental or investigational** (exception: routine costs of qualifying clinical trial services with dates of service on or after September 19, 2000, which meet the requirements of the Clinical Trials NCD are considered reasonable and necessary); and
>
> **Appropriate**, including the duration and frequency that is considered appropriate for the service, in terms of whether it is:
>
> - Furnished in accordance with accepted standards of medical practice for the diagnosis or treatment of the patient's condition or to improve the function of a malformed body member;
> - Furnished in a setting appropriate to the patient's medical needs and condition;
> - Ordered and furnished by qualified personnel;
> - One that meets, but does not exceed, the patient's medical need; and
> - At least as beneficial as an existing and available medically appropriate alternative.

85. What "documents" should you have in front of you before you start writing?

a. The progress note for the date of service
b. Any other progress note, procedure report, imaging report, or correspondence that directly supports the billed service

c. A hard copy of the digital photograph of the patient's problem, taken on or near the date of service, with the patient's initials, the date of service, and the patient's Medicare number on a piece of paper as the background for the image. This will be the most convincing piece of evidence you can provide for the judge
d. The initial claim form submitted to Medicare
e. The Remittance Advice denying payment
f. The redetermination appeal request form
g. The redetermination denial letter

86. If you know a service will be denied, what statement should you incorporate in the progress note?

In addition to using clinical photos as described above, here is an overview of what you should consider. If you know a claim **will be** denied as you are providing the service, and you know **why** the claim will be denied, then you know **what** you have to document in the progress note dictated on the day of the service. Here are some examples of "lead-ins" you can use when you are dictating the progress note:

- Although the time interval between today's (CPT code) service, and the same (CPT code) service provided on __________ does not meet the LCD time interval requirement, the service provided today was medically reasonable and necessary (MR&N) because __________.
- The symptoms requiring the provided service included __________.
- The findings on examination and specifically, "__________," provided the medical necessity for the CPT code __________.
- The complicating medical factors justifying the provided service included __________.
- The (CPT code number) surgical service was separate and distinct from the (CPT code) primary surgical procedure for the following reasons: __________.
- The (description of) service was MR&N (medically reasonable and necessary) because _______.
- The (description of) service was not experimental/investigational because __________.
- The (CPT code) E&M code was not part of the (CPT code #) procedure code and is separately payable because __________.
- The (CPT code) E&M code for today's encounter is appropriate because __________.

It takes almost no time to incorporate these phrases into your dictation, and although these phrases and the additional information may not prevent the contractor's denial of payment, it is likely the QIC will pay attention, and it is almost certain the ALJ will take notice.

Tell your transcriptionist to put these explanatory statements **in bold** in your progress notes.

ORGANIZING AND FORMATTING THE LETTER BRIEF

87. What should you send with the CMS-20033 reconsideration appeal request form?

Here is everything you should send in the same envelope with the CMS-20033 reconsideration appeal request [405.966]:

1. A less-than-three-page letter that explains what was wrong with the patient, exactly what you did, why that service was necessary, how you know that was the correct thing to do, and why the denial reasons are wrong—**all in plain English.**

2. If the patient has a problem that can be captured in a photograph, send a printed copy of the digital photograph with the patient's name, Medicare number, and the date the photograph was taken, clearly showing in the picture. **In addition to a copy of the progress note for the date of service in question, the photograph will be the most important evidence you will submit to the QIC and, therefore, to the ALJ.**
3. A copy of all applicable **patient records** (the progress note, procedure report, imaging report, and/or lab findings for the service date at issue, other progress notes, such as initial H&P, and/or letters from referring or co-treating doctors).
4. Peer-reviewed journal articles supporting the service/supply you provided.
5. Textbook section(s) supporting the service/supply you provided.
6. Standard-of-care statements by specialty organizations that are recognized as authorities for your specialty/service/supply and that support the service/supply you provided.

88. How should you organize the letter brief?

Use the same writing outline every time. Having an outline will take the sting out of writing the letter brief and by having a skeleton outline you can always rely on, you will avoid being confused about what goes where.

The first page will have the demographic information about you and will reference the spreadsheet you will submit as Attachment #1 to the letter brief. In successive columns from left to right, that spreadsheet will list the beneficiary's name, Medicare HICN (Health Insurance Claim Number), the MAC appeal number, the date of service, and the procedure code(s) at issue for the date of service.

The remainder of the first page, along with the second and third pages, will contain the answers to the following: what was wrong with the patient, why the problem needed treatment, what you did for the patient, why you know your treatment was correct, and why each denial reason offered by the contractor in the redetermination denial letter was wrong.

89. Where do you find the address for the QIC you are sending your letter brief to?

The address of the QIC where you will send your letter brief can be found at the end of the notice of redetermination letter.

90. How should you format the letter portion of the letter brief?

The letter portion of your letter brief should be less than three pages and should be double-spaced with a font size of 12. You can attach as many supporting documents (e.g., patient care documents, LCDs, journal articles, textbook sections) to the letter as you want to, but the letter should be three pages or less.

91. How should you organize the first page of the letter brief?

Here are some practical suggestions for organizing the first page of the letter brief:

1. Write the letter to the QIC on your office/business **letterhead**.
2. Put the **date** of the letter in the center of the page, under your office address, phone, and fax information.
3. Put in the title of the document in bold caps.
4. Enter the name of the MAC that denied the claim(s) along with notice that the redetermination appeal numbers are included on a spreadsheet as Attachment #1.

5. Attachment #1: In alphabetical order by last name of the patient, the spreadsheet will contain: the beneficiary's name and Medicare HICN number, the MAC appeal number, the date of service, and the procedure code(s) at issue for that date of service—for **each** claim.
6. Along the left-hand margin, put in the **mailing address of the** QIC exactly as it is written in the redetermination decisions.

92. How many claims can you appeal in a single letter brief?

The number of claims is not the issue. It's how you organize your response to the denials or demands for repayment of overpayment that becomes *the* issue for the reader of your letter brief (the ALJ).

93. How should you organize hundreds of codes in a single letter brief?

Let's say you are preparing for an ALJ hearing regarding a repayment-of-overpayment demand that includes claims for 200 patients. And let's assume there are a total of 350 codes for the 200 patients that Medicare says were "overpaid," for a total of $40,000. But when you make a list of the 350 codes, it turns out that there are only 8 separate E&M codes, procedure codes, and/or supply codes in the whole group of 350 codes.

Figure out the amount of money at stake for each of the eight codes. It is very likely two or three of the codes will account for the majority of the $40,000. You should address those two or three codes **first** in the letter brief.

For each code, you will have a general section that defines the code and describes what is required for payment of the code.

Do **not** detail how each patient met those requirements—one patient at a time—in the letter. Do that in a separate attachment for each patient. You do not want to lose the judge's attention by distracting her with these details in the letter itself. The judge will look at the attachments after she reads the letter.

Also, do not give in to the temptation to write first about the single patient with 1 code that appears only once in the 350 codes, just because you want to, for whatever reason.

When the judge reads your letter brief, her attention will be strongest at the beginning of the brief and weakest at the end. Do not waste the opportunity to convince the judge early on, when she is paying the most attention, about the largest portion of the money at issue.

94. How does the number of codes being appealed affect the number of pages in a letter brief?

As a general rule, you get three pages for each denied code. But the general rule depends on the similarity of clinical facts for each group of patients. Let's take the previous example where a matricectomy procedure is performed at both the tibial and fibular borders of the same nail, but only one matricectomy procedure is allowed for payment by the contractor. If there are ten of these patients being appealed at the same hearing, the clinical summary for all ten patients would require one short paragraph:

> *The Medicare identifying information for all of the patients in this appeal is included in the table in Attachment #1 following this letter.*
>
> *All ten patients presented with painfully ingrown tibial and fibular borders of a single nail. In each case, separate surgical procedures were performed at the tibial border and at the fibular border of the same nail, but only one surgical matricectomy procedure code (11750) was allowed for*

each toe. In each case, the second matricectomy procedure code (11750-51) should be allowed for the second, separate surgical procedure performed on the same toe but at a separate surgical site.

The clinical photographs for these patients are found in the patient Attachments following this letter.

Then you will argue for payment of the second surgical procedure based on the presentation in #48 above.

In other claim sets, the clinical facts will vary enough from patient to patient so that even though you are billing for the same procedure code, you will have to give the judge a detailed explanation of the procedure performed on each patient—in each patient attachment to the letter brief. However, less is more. You want to focus your brief on the facts that justify payment of the denied codes and you want to avoid endless facts that will not result in payment.

95. What kind of "demographic" table do you need, and where should it be placed?

Attachment #1 in your letter brief will **always** be a table that will include the following information:

Name of Provider/ Supplier	Name of Patient	Medicare Number	Date of Service	Code(s) at Issue	Redetermination Appeal No.
David Mullens, DPM (first, last, degree, or name and type of business)	Boyd, Ann (last, first)	1A23-B45-CD67	06/11/2018	99213-25, 64455-59 (include all modifiers used on the claim)	The appeal number assigned to the claim by the contractor
David Mullens, DPM (first, last, degree)	Jones, Frank (last, first)	2B34-C56-DE78	06/12/2018		The appeal number assigned to the claim by the contractor
David Mullens, DPM (first, last, degree)	Smith, Steven (last, first)	3C45-D67-EF89	06/13/2018		The appeal number assigned to the claim by the contractor

This "demographic" table will always be the first attached page ("Attachment #1") after the last page of your letter.

96. Do you have to send copies of cited "Medicare" documents as attachments?

No. The judge (the staff attorney who works for the judge) will have quick access to all of the "Medicare" documents cited in your letter.

97. Do you have to send copies of the "non-Medicare documents" as attachments to the letter brief (to the QIC)?

Absolutely, **yes**! The non-Medicare documents, including the patient records, are the crucial evidence in your appeal. Unless you provide this evidence as attachments to your letter brief, you stand no chance of winning.

You can cite the LCDs, Medicare articles, Medicare Manual sections, and the CPT/HCPCS II definitions in the letter, but you will **always** send actual copies of the patient's photos, medical records, articles, textbook sections, and professional organization policies you refer to in your letter as attachments to the letter.

98. How do you organize the documents that share a single attachment number?

The easiest way to answer this is to give an example. If the medical records for Mr. John Smith (HICN: XXX-XX-1234 A) are Attachment #7, and the medical records include an initial H&P progress note, follow-up progress notes, an MRI report, an operative report, and a pathology report, here is how you can organize these documents in the table of contents:

Attachment #7 pages 1–4 of 39: the initial H&P progress note for J.S. (HICN:1234 A)
Attachment #7 pages 5–31 of 39: the follow-up progress notes for J.S. (HICN:1234 A)
Attachment #7 pages 32–35 of 39: the MRI report for J.S. (HICN:1234 A)
Attachment #7 pages 36–37 of 39: the operative report for J.S. (HICN:1234 A)
Attachment #7 pages 38–39 of 39: the pathology report for J.S. (HICN:1234 A)

If there are multiple documents that share a common attachment number (e.g., medical records of a patient), put the document with the earliest date on top and the document with the latest (most recent) date on the bottom.

99. How do you identify the attachment number and page numbers of the attachments?

Order a custom self-inking rubber stamp (e.g., from Amazon.com) that, when pressed to the bottom right-hand corner of each attachment page, reads:

Attachment # __________
Page(s) __________ *of* __________

After writing the number of the attachment, you will handwrite the page number(s) out of the total number of pages in the attachment. If Attachment #7 has 39 pages, and you are stamping the first page of the MRI report pages, you would handwrite 7 after **Attachment #** and you would write **Pages 32–35 of 39** on the second line of the stamped words:

Attachment # 7
Page(s) 32–35 of 39

100. How can you send a diagram and a simple explanation of the patient's problem?

Almost all common medical problems are captured in the Krames pamphlets for patients. Be sure to send the QIC a copy of the Krames pamphlet that demonstrates the patient's problem along with a hard copy of the digital photograph of the patient's problem.

Explain how the diagram in the Krames pamphlet relates to the patient whose claim you are appealing.

101. Can you send your digital photographs of the patient to the QIC in an email?

No. You have to make hard copies of the digital photographs and send them to the QIC when you request the reconsideration appeal. The QIC will forward those photographs to the ALJ after the QIC denies payment and you request the ALJ hearing.

Digital photographs taken on the date of the service at issue, with all of the authenticating information in the background of the picture are best (see #40–42 above).

The longer the time interval between date of the service at issue and the later date of the digital photograph, the less weight the ALJ will give the photograph.

102. What determines the number of attachments you will send with the letter brief?

There are a lot of documents you will *consider* sending to the QIC in anticipation of the ALJ appeal. What you actually send will depend on the complexity and nature of the appeal. For example, let's assume you are fighting a demand for repayment of fees paid for diabetic shoes. In addition to the CMS-20033 reconsideration appeal request form, you would send a photograph of the patient's foot taken when the decision was made to provide the diabetic shoes, a photograph of the patient's feet and the diabetic shoes on the day the shoes were dispensed, the rest of the letter brief that includes the applicable progress note(s), and copies of the LCD-required documentation forms you were able to complete for the patient.

But if you are fighting for payment for a service that is **not allowed in the applicable LCD**, you would send almost all of the following to the QIC:

- A completed CMS-20033 reconsideration appeal request form
- A short (1–3 page) letter that includes a summary of the patient's medical facts, what was done, why it was necessary, the authorities supporting the service, and why and how the related LCD section that prohibits payment has been **misapplied** by the contractor (not why the LCD policy is wrong)
- A demographic table (see #95)
- A table of contents (so the ALJ can find what she is looking for quickly)
- The progress notes, letters from referring or co-treating doctors, procedure reports, imaging reports, and/or lab findings
- Peer-reviewed journal articles supporting the service you provided
- Textbook section(s) supporting the service you provided
- Policy statements by authoritative organizations representing your specialty or business that support the service you provided
- A copy of the CMS-20027 redetermination appeal request form sent to the contractor
- A copy of the redetermination denial letter

103. What should be the order of the documents you attach to your letter brief?

Use the following order for the attachments:

- 1: demographic table
- 2: table of contents
- 3: pertinent parts of Medicare documents (LCDs, Medicare articles, etc.) but **only if those Medicare documents contain "smoking gun" evidence that should persuade the ALJ to decide in your favor.** For example, the page(s) of the version of the LCD that applies to the denied service or supply specifically allowed the service or supply. Otherwise, you will just refer to the Medicare documents in the body of the letter because the ALJs have immediate access to

LCDs. Routinely sending copies of LCDs will require extra work by the ALJ's staff and will destroy forests more quickly without any apparent benefit for anyone
- 4, 5, etc.: copies of the patient care documents for each patient, including photos, progress notes, reports, and initial claim and all claim-related documents sent and received
- Next: journal articles
- Next: textbook sections
- Next: policy statements by authoritative organizations

104. How should you arrange the "patient care documents" attached to the letter brief?

In the attachment for each patient, the first patient care document should be the **photo(s)** of the patient. The next patient care documents should be all of the progress notes and reports for that patient, in chronological order, with the earliest dated progress note on top.

All of the claim-related documents, also in chronological order (with the earliest dated claim on top), should come last. Claim-related documents include the redetermination appeal request and the redetermination denial letter along with any extension, dismissal, or reopening documents associated with the claim.

A lot of people put the claim-related documents on the top of the pile. I think that is a mistake because it is the photograph of the patient that you want the judge to see first when the judge looks at each patient's set of documents. The second thing you want the judge to see are the progress notes that support what the judge sees in the photograph. The claim-related documents are almost an afterthought because the file forwarded to the ALJ from the QIC should already have these. But you should still send copies of the claim-related documents because you don't want to find yourself in the middle of the ALJ hearing only to find the judge does not have one or more of these documents in front of her.

105. How should you arrange "journal articles" attached to the letter brief?

If you are using journal articles to persuade the judge, make sure the articles have been published in peer-reviewed journals. The peer-reviewed journal article most supportive of the contested service should be the first article cited. However, not all journals are created equally. A moderately supportive article in the *New England Journal of Medicine* will be given more weight than a strongly supportive article published in an obscure journal.

Anecdotal reports and articles published by the manufacturer of the equipment or service at issue will be given very little weight, if any weight at all, by the ALJ.

Be very careful about using articles published **after** the contested date of service. The ALJ will be sensitive to the date of service and the date of any article you use to support payment for the denied claim. However, if the later published article cites studies that were published **before** the contested date of service, and those cited studies support the service for which payment was denied, then the later published articles are fine. If this is the case, spell it out for the judge as in:

> *Your Honor, this article was published* ***after*** *the service at issue was provided. However, the article was based on studies published* ***before*** *the service at issue was provided and those studies are listed at the end of the article.*

106. How should you arrange "textbook sections" attached to the letter brief?

Sections from textbooks that are considered authoritative for a specialty or business are very persuasive evidence for ALJs. Make sure you include a photocopy of the title page of the book and the date of publication as well as the photocopy of the relevant textbook section.

107. How should you arrange standard-of-care statements attached to the letter brief?

If you have "smoking gun" evidence that should, on its own, make the ALJ decide in your favor, don't bury that evidence in the back of the letter brief. Put that evidence right up front in the letter brief and put it **in bold.** If the authoritative evidence is overwhelmingly in your favor, and you can write the letter brief in one page—by all means do it. The ALJ will love you for not wasting her time.

In other words, if you have a policy statement of a professional organization that is recognized as authoritative for your specialty or business, and the policy statement **unmistakably** supports your denied service or supply, use it immediately in the letter brief.

You always want to put your strongest evidence at the beginning of the brief because you have a better chance the judge will read it. And, when you are making your presentation to the judge during the hearing, you always want to start with your strongest evidence while you have the judge's attention.

108. What should you do if the LCD did not allow the service?

You will argue the service was medically reasonable and necessary based on the facts. And you will list those facts. In addition, you will have to prove to the ALJ, at least by the standard of "clear and convincing evidence" (75% to 25%) if not by the standard of "beyond a reasonable doubt" (95% to 5%), that the provided service was "**safer than,**" "**more effective than,**" and "**less expensive than**" the allowed service in the LCD.

Use common sense. If the contested service was obviously safer than and more effective than the LCD-indicated service, you are going to win. If the contested service was not as safe as or not as effective as the LCD-allowed service, you will not win.

The attachments you will consider sending when an LCD prohibits the service at issue are listed in #102 above and #119 below.

109. How should you number the pages in your letter brief?

This non-tech trick will save you a lot of aggravation. When you have the entire packet ready to go (the less than three-page brief, the patient care documents, the articles, the textbook sections, etc.), number all of the pages in the lower right-hand corner very lightly with a pencil.

The number 1 will be at the lower right-hand corner of the first page of your letter and all of the pages after that will be numbered in order. This will save you countless headaches when pages of documents are dropped and/or the judge cannot find the document during the hearing that you are referring to. Write the numbers in light pencil because you will almost always have to erase and redo them.

110. Must you prove you sent a copy of the request for the ALJ appeal to each patient?

Yes. Section 405.1014(b)(2) requires you to send a copy of the request for the ALJ appeal to each of the patients whose claims are being appealed.

111. Must you prove each patient received a copy of your request for an ALJ appeal?

No. You only have to prove the copies were sent. You do not have to prove they were received. This makes a huge difference as to the type of mail you will use.

112. Do you have to send a copy of the letter brief to each of the patients?

No. If you are not sending any additional "evidence" with your request for an ALJ appeal, the answer is no. See section 405.1014.

The letter brief was sent with your request for a reconsideration appeal and the CFR sections on reconsideration appeals are silent on this topic.

113. What is the least expensive way to prove you sent a copy of the ALJ appeal request to each patient?

Go to your local post office and get a bunch of "certificate of mailing" forms (Form 3817). You will need to fill out a separate certificate of mailing form for each letter (containing a copy of the ALJ appeal request form) you send to each patient.

Each certificate of mailing form will cost $1.45. You will send each letter as first-class mail with a 55¢ stamp on the envelope. The total cost for this "proof of mailing" is $2. Do not waste money by using "proof of delivery" mail. You don't need to prove each patient received a copy of the ALJ appeal request form. You only need to prove you **sent** each patient a copy of the ALJ appeal request form.

You will take the completed certificate of mailing forms with you when you go to the post office to mail the copies of the ALJ appeal request to the patients.

114. How do you avoid HIPAA violations when using the OMHA-100A form?

When you are requesting an ALJ hearing for only **one beneficiary**, you will just use the OMHA-100 form.

When you are requesting an ALJ hearing for **multiple beneficiaries**, you will use the OMHA-100 form **plus** the OMHA-100A form.

In order to avoid HIPAA violations, you will make enough copies of the completed OMHA-100 form and the completed OMHA-100A form to send one set of both copies to each beneficiary. On each OMHA-100A form, you will redact (black out) the information on all of the patients other than the information on the one patient you are sending that set of copies to.

115. How should you fill out Section 7 on the OMHA-100 form?

Section 7 on the OMHA-100 form asks you to state why you disagree with the reconsideration being appealed.

You will enter: *"Please see the letter brief submitted to the QIC for the reconsideration appeal."*

However, if the QIC added new denial reasons in the reconsideration appeal denial letter, you will also enter: *"In addition, please see the attached letter brief that addresses the new denial reasons offered by the QIC."*

ABOUT WRITING THE "HEART" OF THE LETTER BRIEF

116. What is the best way to describe the problem, what you did, and why it was correct?

Write the shortest possible version of the patient's problem, describe what you did for the patient in lay terms, and include an explanation of why the service should be paid. For example:

> *Mr. J.S., an established patient in the practice, is a 65-year-old type 2 diabetic who returned to the office on January 2, 2017, with a foul-smelling (infected) ulcer on the ball of his left foot of several weeks' duration. Although J.S. did not have a fever, the left foot was swollen and X-rays demonstrated a probable bone infection of the second metatarsal head, directly under the ulcer.*
>
> *In addition to billing for 97602 surgical debridement of the ulcer (cutting away the dead and infected tissue), a 99215 E&M code was billed for the comprehensive history, the comprehensive examination, and the high complexity medical decision-making required for his*

problem. The Medicare contractor denied payment of the 99215 code, stating the E&M service was included in the 97602 wound debridement code.

However, ***the amount of E&M required for Mr. J.S. far exceeded the E&M included in the 97602 code.*** *A copy of the progress note for the January 2, 2017, date of service is included in Attachment #3. The progress note meets all of the CPT requirements for the 99215 code.*

The E&M provided for J.S. is similar to the E&M in the 99215 example for podiatric surgery in the 2017 CPT Manual "Appendix C—Clinical Examples" section.

I am respectfully requesting payment for the 99215 E&M service provided for J.S. on January 2, 2017.

117. What should you write when you did not meet some MAC requirements for a service?

You will have to convince the ALJ that the medical necessity of the service should outweigh the technical reasons for denial. Here is one example of wording you could use in your response:

The [describe the service] was medically reasonable and necessary at the time it was provided for the following reasons.

On [date of service at issue], the findings by history included ________, and the findings by examination included ________. Without the denied service, the patient ________. As a result, it was medically reasonable and necessary to provide the denied service to [first, last] on [date of service]. In addition, the decision to provide this treatment, based on the findings on the date of service, is supported by the attached peer-reviewed journal article(s) and by the attached standard-of-care policy published by ________, the professional organization that oversees the specialty/business of ________.

118. What should you write when the service is prohibited in the contractor's LCD?

Convincing an ALJ to pay for a service when the service is specifically prohibited in the contractor's LCD is **the toughest ALJ appeal.** When you are in this fight, you want to be able to prove at least by clear and convincing evidence (the 75% burden of proof standard) that the denied service was medically reasonable and necessary.

The strongest statement you could make to the ALJ would be:

Your Honor, the [name of the denied service] is ***safer than, more effective than,*** *and* ***less expensive than*** *the LCD-approved [name of the LCD-approved service] for the treatment of [description of the patient's medical problem].*

Realistically, you will be writing some combination of the following statements:

The denied service [describe the service] was medically reasonable and necessary for the following reasons:

The service provided [describe the service] is as safe as/safer than the "indicated" service [describe the "indicated" service] in the LCD and this statement is supported by ________.

The service provided [describe the service] is as effective as/more effective than the "indicated" service [describe the "indicated" service] in the LCD, and this statement is supported by ________.

The service provided [describe the service] is less expensive than the "indicated" service [describe the "indicated" service] in the LCD, and this statement is supported by ________.

Although the service provided for the patient's problem is prohibited in the applicable LCD, based on all of the above, payment should be awarded for the [CPT/HCPCS ________] code service provided for Medicare beneficiary (initials) on [date of encounter].

The closer you are to "safer, more effective, and less expensive," the more likely you are to win.

Assuming the "indicated" service in the LCD and the denied service are equally effective in the treatment of the patient's problem, if the denied service is not as safe as the "indicated" service in the LCD, you are going to lose. If the denied service can be proved safer than the "indicated" service in the LCD, you are going to win. And even though cost is not supposed to be considered by the ALJ, if the denied service is thousands of dollars cheaper than the "indicated" service and everything else is "equal," you absolutely want to raise the issue of cost.

119. What can you do when your contractor says "no" but another contractor says "yes"?

This is why you have to look at the LCDs published by the other contractors regarding denied services. If you don't read the other LCDs, you won't know if another LCD allows the same service your Medicare contractor does not allow.

What is the most common reason two Medicare contractors have conflicting LCD policies regarding the same service? In my experience, the most likely reason was that one contractor was relying on older medical literature and the other contractor was relying on newer medical literature. You must check on the cited literature at the back of the LCD to determine how your contractor arrived at its coverage policy.

If you determine the service at issue has been denied because your contractor is relying on outdated literature, it is easy to write the appeal for the ALJ. Here is an example of what you can say:

The medical literature cited in the [name of contractor] LCD (L__________) regarding the denied service is out of date. Current medical literature, recognized as authoritative by the contractor, supports payment of the denied service. The current medical literature includes all of the following: __________.

In addition, although the LCD, L__________, prohibits the denied service, the LCD, L__________, published by [name of other contractor] allows the denied service under the same clinical circumstances. The difference between the two LCD policies is that my contractor's LCD, L__________, is based on older literature, while LCD L__________ is based on current literature.

120. What should you do if an applicable, older LCD says "no" but the current LCD says "yes"?

Look at the documents the current version of the LCD relies on. The literature relied upon by the authors of the LCD is listed toward the end of the LCD. It is very possible the articles relied upon by the authors of the newer version of the same LCD were published at or before the time the contested service was provided. If so, your argument would be:

The articles and textbooks relied upon by the authors of the newest version of the LCD, L__________, were published before the (billing code) service was provided for [first, last] (the Medicare beneficiary). The newest version of the LCD correctly allows the denied service for the Medicare beneficiary's problem [description of diagnosis/name of disease].

The older version of the LCD, although in effect at the time the service was provided, has been misapplied. The literature relied upon by the authors of the newest version of the LCD demonstrates the medical standard for the contested service had changed by the time the denied services were provided.

121. What can you do when a claim is denied as "not medically reasonable and necessary"?

First, establish the evaluation and management portion of the patient's problem before you argue in favor of payment for the procedure performed or the supply/item dispensed. Here is how you could respond:

A photograph of the patient's problem, with the patient's initials, the patient's Medicare number, and the date of the photograph all clearly evident in the background is included as Attachment # ___. The photograph demonstrates _______.

The patient is a ___-year-old male/female with [description of problem], who was seen in the office [or other location] on [date of encounter] complaining of/for follow-up of [complaint or problem being followed up].

The patient's history revealed the following: _______.

The patient's examination revealed the following: _______.

The diagnosis was _______.

Treatment included _______.

The complexity of medical decision-making was [straightforward/of low complexity/ of moderate complexity/of high complexity] based on the [minimal/limited/multiple/ extensive] number of diagnoses or management options; based on the [minimal/limited/ moderate/extensive] amount and/or complexity of data to be reviewed; and based on the [minimal/low/moderate/high] risk of complications and/or morbidity or mortality. See the patient records in Attachment #___.

Here are the contractor's reasons for denial and why each reason is wrong: _______.

The [name of contractor] LCD that applies to the contested service is L_______. L_______ states: "________."

An article from a peer-reviewed journal, with a diagram (or photograph) of a patient with an (almost) identical problem/deformity is included as Attachment #___. The article states_______.

The treatment guidelines for this problem, as published in the textbooks _______, _______, and _______, are enclosed as textbook sections in Attachment #___. The textbook(s) state(s) _______.

The treatment guidelines for this problem, as published by the [name of specialty organization], are enclosed as Attachment #___. The treatment guidelines state _______.

Based on all of the above, I am respectfully requesting payment for the medically necessary and reasonable service provided to [first, last] on [date].

122. What must you prove when a claim is denied as "experimental/investigational"?

You have to prove to the judge that the service was not "experimental" or "investigational." But this is not as easy as it seems because Medicare has **no** definition of "experimental/investigational."

123. Will you be surprised when a claim is denied as "experimental or investigational"?

Almost never. You know, or should know after the first denial for the same service, that the service you are providing is considered to be experimental or investigational by your Medicare contractor.

124. What can you do when a critical term such as "experimental or investigational" is not defined by Medicare?

When faced with terms that are not defined by Medicare, look to other sources for definitions.

If you cannot find a definition for a term on the http://Medicare.gov website, look at for-profit company websites.

If you cannot find the definition on for-profit company websites, you can always quote an authoritative source such as the *Merriam-Webster* dictionary.

The easiest thing to do, however, is to put the phrase "definition of ________" into the Internet search bar and let it do the work for you. You are looking for the definition that works best for you and is written by an unquestionably authoritative source.

125. Can you use the Anthem BC BS definition of "investigational"?

Yes. The Anthem BC BS, ADMIN.00005 document on "Investigational Criteria" states:

> "Investigational" means that the procedure, treatment, supply, device, equipment, facility or drug (all services) does not meet the WellPoint Technology Evaluation Criteria because it does not meet **one or more** of the following criteria:
> have final approval from the appropriate government regulatory body; **or**
> have the credible scientific evidence published in peer-reviewed medical literature generally recognized by the relevant medical community which permits reasonable conclusions concerning the effect of the procedure, treatment, supply, device, equipment, facility or drug (all services) on health outcomes; **or**
> be proven materially to improve the net health outcome; **or**
> be as beneficial as any established alternative; **or**
> show improvement outside the investigational settings.

126. How would you use Anthem's definition of "investigational"?

"Investigational" is a big step up from "experimental," and Medicare is almost always denying payment because the service was considered "investigational" rather than "experimental."

In your letter brief, you will tell the ALJ:

> *Even though Medicare fails to define the phrase "experimental or investigational," Anthem BC BS has provided a detailed definition for the term "investigational." Here is Anthem's definition and here is why the service I provided for [name of patient] was not experimental or investigational: ________.*

First, you will provide the entire BC BS definition for "investigational" (see above).

Then, you will write something like the following:

The [describe the service] provided for [name of patient] was not "experimental or investigational."

The [describe the service] has final approval from [name of appropriate government regulatory body]. A copy of that approval is attached to this letter as Attachment #___.

The [describe the service] is supported by credible scientific evidence published in peer-reviewed medical literature recognized by the [name of the relevant medical community]. These studies permit reasonable conclusions concerning the effect of [describe the service] on health outcomes. Several of these peer-reviewed journal articles are attached to this letter as Attachments # ___–___.

The [describe the service] has been proven to materially improve the net health outcome of the patients who received this service. Examples of studies proving this point are attached to the letter as Attachments #___–___.

The [describe the service] is as beneficial as any established alternative. A comparison of the [describe the service] to the established alternative service approved in the LCD is available in peer-reviewed journal articles attached to this letter as Attachments #___–___.

The [describe the service] shows patient improvement outside investigational settings. These results are evident in the peer-reviewed journal articles attached to this letter as Attachments #___–___.

The service at issue [describe the service], is as safe as/safer than, is more effective than/as effective as, and is less expensive than/no more expensive than the LCD-approved service [describe the LCD-approved service].

For all of these objective reasons, the denied service is not "experimental/investigative" and should be paid.

127. What do you tell the ALJ when the "vendor" assured you Medicare would pay?

Please do not bother arguing that the vendor who sold you a piece of diagnostic or treatment equipment (or convinced you to provide an expensive service) assured you that the service meets all of the requirements for Medicare payment. Vendors are not always completely truthful.

When you are considering the purchase of a new, and usually expensive, piece of equipment, or you are considering providing a service associated with a big fee, have the vendor send you written proof that the equipment/service meets all of your Medicare contractor's requirements for payment—**before** you buy the equipment/before you provide the service.

Make the vendor send you redacted (blacked out) copies of the Remittance Advice notices, previously known as Explanation of Medicare Benefits (EOMBs), from your Medicare contractor demonstrating payment for the equipment you are thinking about buying. Make sure you check with your contractor as to the combination of ICD and CPT codes that will qualify you for payment—**before** you buy the equipment or provide the service.

Vendors engage in bait-and-switch techniques in order to sell their product. And just because someone gets paid for using a piece of equipment or providing a service by using a wrong ICD and/or CPT code, that doesn't mean the RAC will fail to discover this scheme *after* you have paid for the equipment; *after* you have used and billed for the services related to the equipment or after you have provided the big fee service; and *after* you have been erroneously paid by the contractor.

128. What if the vendor actually signed a piece of paper assuring Medicare payment?

Do not bother asking the vendor to sign a piece of paper stating the equipment/service meets all of Medicare's requirements for payment. The vendor knows you are not going to waste the time and money needed to go after them. And even if you do, and the vendor then goes belly-up, who are you going to collect from once you have a judgment?

Name a single provider or supplier who has successfully gone after a vendor after Medicare has made the provider or supplier repay the money billed for the services provided with the vendor's equipment.

Be smart **before** you buy expensive equipment/before you provide big fee services rather than trying to be smart after you have been taken to the cleaners/after you have been forced to repay a very large demand for repayment of overpayment.

129. An example of a vendor's magic show: the selling of platelet-rich plasma (PRP) for the repair of ruptured tendons around the ankle.

In 2013, I had to research the topic of platelet-rich plasma for a client, and there were literally thousands of published anecdotal reports on the use of PRP. But there wasn't one double-blind study published in a peer-reviewed journal supporting effectiveness. How could this be? Easy. Something that sounds good and has a big fee associated with it makes critical judgment go away. And as more and more people come to believe in the "emperor's new clothes," the less critical everyone is about reality.

Some of you will respond with: How can you do a double-blind study with something like PRP when the patient is expecting you to use it? The answer is easy. Two or more university hospitals can tell all of their ruptured Achilles tendon patients requiring surgery and/or all of their ruptured posterior tibial tendon patients requiring surgery that they are going to use or not use PRP at the time of the repair. Although the surgeon would know which patients received the PRP, the patient and the research coordinator recording the postoperative findings would not know.

I am **not** saying PRP does not work. I am saying I was amazed to find thousands of anecdotal reports and not one controlled study when I researched this.

130. How should you decide whether to cite and include a document?

When you are asking yourself whether to quote/cite a document in the letter and whether to include a copy of that document as an attachment to the letter, ask yourself this two-part question: **Will the judge read and understand this document?** If the answer is yes, ask yourself the next question: **Will this document sway the judge in favor of payment?** If the answer is yes to both questions, cite it and include it.

No matter how attractive a document may be, if the judge will not read it, if the judge will not understand it, or if the document will not sway the judge in favor of payment, don't cite it and don't send it.

131. Should you rely on common sense when you are writing the letter brief?

Yes. Suppose you are appearing before an ALJ during a video teleconference hearing regarding nonpayment of diabetic shoes and you have been smart enough to have the patient attend the hearing. For a moment, pretend you are the ALJ. The one and only question you would have as the judge would be: Should I award payment?

The best, quickest, and surest way to convince the judge is to have the patient take off their shoes and show the judge the missing toe(s), partial amputation, plantar diabetic ulcer, and so on.

A common sense presentation of the contractor's indications for diabetic shoes in the letter brief with the on-camera presentation of the patient's foot during the hearing will result in a ten-second knockout. The hearing is over and you won. The rest of your conversation with the judge is just for the purpose of completing the record.

132. What are the contractor's strongest arguments against payment?

Pretend you are an attorney representing the contractor. Now, tear your arguments apart. Where are your weaknesses? No case is perfect. Find your weaknesses before the judge finds them.

When you find a weakness in your argument, embrace it. Think about how you can best address that weakness in your letter brief and/or how you will answer the judge's questions about that weakness during the hearing.

You should assume if you are able to find the weakness, the judge will find it as well.

133. Where do you include the contractor's arguments in your letter brief?

It depends. If the contractor's denial is based on a single factual assertion and you can prove that assertion is wrong, you will put the contractor's denial reason and your proof the contractor is wrong right at the beginning of the letter brief. For example, if the contractor denied payment stating the applicable LCD prohibits the billed service, and the applicable version of the LCD actually allows the billed service, you would put all of this at the very beginning of the letter brief.

On the other hand, if the contractor's argument is not wrong but the contractor's argument should not determine the outcome of the hearing, you will put the contractor's argument and your counterargument at the end of the letter brief. For example, if the contractor states the denied service is allowed but was provided too frequently, you will present all of the clinical information supporting the need for the service when the service was provided and will address the contractor's denial reasons after you have made it clear the denied service was medically reasonable and necessary when it was provided based on the clinical facts.

134. What do you do with a weakness in the contractor's argument against payment?

If you discover an **important** weakness in the contractor's argument, address it in the first part of the letter. Leave out the adjectives. Just tell the judge why the contractor's argument is wrong.

135. What do you do with a weakness in your argument for payment?

If you discover an **important** weakness in your request for payment, you can be certain that point will be brought up by the judge during the hearing and you must address that weakness in your letter.

136. What do you do with a questionable weakness in an argument?

If you discover a **questionable** weakness in the contractor's argument or in your request for payment but that weakness will **not** determine the outcome of the ALJ hearing, leave it out of the letter or address it in a footnote.

137. You didn't send a letter brief to the QIC. Can you send a letter brief to the ALJ?

If you sent all of the patient care documents to the QIC, you can write and send a letter brief to the ALJ based on the patient care documents. Your first sentence in the letter brief will read: "*Your*

Honor, this letter organizes and explains the evidence already submitted to the QIC. However, this letter contains ***no new evidence.***"

But remember, if you did not send the articles, textbook sections, and standard of care statements to the QIC, you cannot send these items to the ALJ. You can only send the ALJ a letter explaining the previously submitted patient care documents.

138. If you send a letter brief to the ALJ, do you have to send copies to the patients?

Yes. See 405.1014. By sending the letter brief to the QIC, you won't have to send copies to all the patients whose claims are at issue as you will if you wait to send the letter brief, for the first time, to the ALJ.

139. Will the ALJ accept your letter brief under these facts?

Why not? And if the ALJ hearing is about something as visual as the diabetic problems that justify therapeutic shoes and you were smart enough to include hard copies of the digital images taken during treatment when you sent your evidence to the QIC, you stand a very good chance of winning payment. Even if you did not submit any digital images to the QIC, if the patient will appear at the hearing, you can have the patient show the judge the deformities that required the use of therapeutic shoes.

AFTER YOU WRITE THE LETTER BRIEF . . .

140. Does your letter say what you want it to say and will the ALJ understand it?

This is important enough to repeat. When you finish the letter, a layperson should be able to read your letter brief and understand the nature of the patient's problem, what you did and why you did it, why your treatment was the best choice for the patient, and why the contractor's denial reasons are wrong.

Do not get fancy. Stay with plain English. Have someone with no medical education read your letter and then have that person tell you what the letter says. If that person gets it, then the ALJ will get it. If that person does not understand what you have written, it is likely the ALJ will not understand what you have written either.

141. What should you do if you can't find support for the denied service?

If you cannot find journal support for denied service, you may want to rethink the appeal, and more importantly, you may want to rethink the denied service. Maybe you were wrong and should be doing something different.

142. Did you present your strongest evidence first?

The judge's interest will fade very, very quickly. Get your strongest piece of evidence in front of the judge at the very beginning of the letter. If you are not sure what your strongest piece of evidence is, here are my recommendations:

If you have a photograph that captures the patient's problem, use it first in the letter and use it first during the ALJ hearing.

If you don't have a photograph but you do have a clear-cut statement by a recognized authority that what you did was entirely correct, use that first.

If you don't have a photograph or a statement by a recognized authority, but you do have a peer-reviewed journal article supporting the service at issue—use that first. Whatever you do, do not waste the beginning of the letter and/or the beginning of the hearing with information about unimportant issues or worse, non-issues.

Get to the point immediately. The judge is not interested in a display of knowledge regarding a topic in medicine. The judge just wants to know if you deserve to be paid for the service you provided.

143. Other than the QIC, who else do you have to send the letter brief to?

No one. The QIC will forward your letter brief to the ALJ's office. While you must send copies of the ALJ appeal request form to each of the patients whose claims are the subject of the appeal (see 405.1014), you are **not** required to send them copies of the letter brief sent to the QIC.

144. How much emotion should you include in your letter brief?

None. Look for the adjectives in your letter brief and get rid of them.

The ALJ will be turned off by emotion in your letter brief and will be really turned off by emotion in your oral argument during the hearing. Think about this: Do you find yourself positively engaged when a Medicare beneficiary starts whining to you about the treatment they received at the hands of other providers or about how unfair Medicare is?

The ALJ will stop paying attention to what you have written and what you are saying when you start whining in your letter and/or when you start whining as you speak during the hearing. A display of emotion will result in the exact opposite effect you are trying to achieve.

145. What should you do if the QIC raises new arguments in the reconsideration decision?

If the QIC supports the contractor's denial and offers additional reasons why your claim should not be paid, do you get to refute the additional new denial reasons offered by the QIC? Absolutely, **yes**. You will send a separate letter brief to the ALJ that lists all of the QIC's new reasons for denial and explains why all of those reasons are wrong.

Under 405.1028, a provider/supplier always has good cause to send the ALJ a letter explaining why the new denial reasons offered by the QIC are wrong.

If the QIC raises new arguments in their denial letter, you will write and submit a second, short letter brief to the ALJ. The table you will use as Attachment #1 to the second letter brief will look like this:

Name of patient	Medicare number	Beneficiary address, city, state, zip	Date of service	Code(s) at issue	QIC appeal number	Date copy of ALJ request sent to beneficiary
Smith, Robert (last, first)	444555666A	22 Campbell Rd., Palo Alto, CA 94303	06/11/2019	99213-25, 64455-59 (include all modifiers used on the claim)	The appeal number assigned to the claim by the QIC	12/19/2019

You will limit your second brief to the new arguments raised by the QIC. Make it easy for the judge. List the new denial reasons and explain why each new reason is wrong.

146. What if you forgot to include an important piece of evidence in the letter sent to the QIC?

Relax. If everything in your letter brief makes sense and the evidence you failed to send is even loosely referenced in the letter brief, chances are the ALJ will allow that late-submitted piece of evidence to be admitted for the ALJ appeal.

147. Does any of this apply to you if your medical group does all your billing and appeals?

Knowing what you are doing with billing—and knowing how to fight effectively when payment for your services is denied—is a professional survival skill that you have to master and keep current. And for those of you who work in large groups and think someone else is taking care of all your billing concerns, that just isn't realistic.

If you are not regularly checking on what is and what is not being billed, what is being denied, and what is being done about the denials, you are losing money, possibly a lot of money. This is like turning your checkbook over to someone else and hoping they will take care of all your financial needs. Unless that other person is your spouse, it doesn't happen.

148. If you don't want to write letter briefs and do ALJ hearings, what should you do?

I am supposed to write something like this: If you are on top of your billing but you just don't want to write letter briefs and you don't want to defend yourself at ALJ hearings, call someone like me, a health care attorney, who will be happy to write the letter brief and will be happy to represent you at the ALJ hearing all on a contingency fee basis. At the end of the day, receiving 60% of the allowed Medicare fee as the provider/supplier is a lot better than receiving 0% of the allowed Medicare fee.

What I wanted to write was this: "Call me! Call me! I will represent you on a contingency fee basis, I am very experienced, I am hardworking, I am easy to work with, and I get results."

20

Administrative Law Judge (ALJ) Appeals

20a

Submitting the Request for an ALJ Appeal
42 CFR §§ 405.1000–405.1054

OUTLINE

1. What happened?
2. How much time do you have to submit an ALJ appeal request?
3. How does the ALJ office calculate the date you received the reconsideration denial?
4. The denial letter is dated September 5. The denial envelope is postmarked September 12. How do you calculate the due date for the ALJ appeal?
5. How much money has to be at issue to qualify for an ALJ appeal, and how is this determined?
6. Does CMS have a new form to request an ALJ hearing?
7. How do you fill in the OMHA-100 form?
8. Is there a box on the OMHA-100 form to request a video teleconference (VTC) hearing?
9. When should you request a VTC hearing instead of a phone hearing?
10. How do you request a VTC hearing?
11. What if the ALJ asks for a "good cause" letter to qualify for a VTC hearing?
12. How does the ALJ determine which VTC center will be used for the hearing?
13. Why is it a bad idea to let the judge determine which VTC center will be used for the hearing?
14. How can you make sure the video teleconference center is close to your location?
15. What should you do if the QIC denies payment and adds new denial reasons?
16. What if you want to submit new evidence when you request an ALJ hearing?

17. What is "new" evidence?
18. What is not "new" evidence?
19. What will you have to do to get the ALJ to accept "new" evidence?
20. Do all the ALJs enforce the "no new evidence" rule in the same manner?
21. What if you submitted some patient care documents to the QIC and you want to submit additional patient care documents for the ALJ hearing?
22. Can you submit a newer version of a text relied upon by the contractor in the LCD?
23. Can you submit articles and book sections that are newer than those present in the LCD?
24. Can you use the Medicare Program Integrity Manual to bolster your argument when you want to submit "new" evidence to the ALJ?
25. If you cannot make a "good cause" argument, what can you tell the judge if "new" evidence was mentioned, but not included, in the documents sent to the QIC?
26. If you cannot make a "good cause" argument, what can you tell the judge if your "new" evidence for denied E&M codes is related to documents relied upon by the QIC?
27. What is your most important evidence when you request a reconsideration appeal?
28. What if you don't have the time to write a prehearing letter brief to the QIC?

1. What happened?

The Medicare contractor denied the initial claim for payment.
The Medicare contractor denied the subsequent redetermination appeal.
The QIC denied the reconsideration appeal.

Now you will submit a request for an ALJ appeal.

2. How much time do you have to submit an ALJ appeal request?

Your ALJ appeal request must reach the ALJ office specified in the reconsideration denial letter within **60 calendar days** of the date you received the reconsideration denial. See 405.1002.

3. How does the ALJ office calculate the date you received the reconsideration denial?

The date you received the reconsideration denial will be presumed to be five calendar days after the date on the reconsideration denial letter unless there is evidence to the contrary. See 405.1002(a)(3).

Your "evidence to the contrary" will be the postmarked date on the envelope containing the reconsideration denial. You will argue, if necessary, that the date you received the reconsideration decision was five days *after the postmarked date* on the envelope containing the reconsideration denial letter rather than five days after the date on the reconsideration denial letter.

4. The denial letter is dated September 5. The denial envelope is postmarked September 12. How do you calculate the due date for the ALJ appeal?

If you were smart enough to keep the denial envelope, you get 65 days after September 12 to get the request for an ALJ appeal to the ALJ office. Unless you keep the denial envelope containing the QIC denial letter, the ALJ office will use September 5 as the starting date for the calculation.

Scan the denial envelopes along with the denial letters into the appeal file for each patient and keep the denial envelopes stapled to the denial letters. The date on the reconsideration denial envelope will allow you to **set the calendar in your favor** by giving you 60 plus 5 (65) days **after** the postmarked date on the denial envelope.

5. How much money has to be at issue to qualify for an ALJ appeal, and how is this determined?

For 2019, the amount in controversy (AIC) was $160. The AIC for 2020 is $170.

The amount in controversy does **not** mean the fee you charged for the service that was denied. The AIC is the Medicare-allowed amount for the service at issue, minus any deductible and minus any co-pay. **The AIC is the amount Medicare will actually pay you if you win the ALJ decision.**

For our example, and let's make this easy, assume the patient has already paid the yearly deductible. If you charge $500 for a service that is denied, and Medicare only allows $80 for that service (when Medicare pays for the service), and the patient has a 20% co-pay, the amount in controversy for that denied service is $80 minus the $16 co-pay = $64.

Here is the same example:

You charge $500 for a service.
The Medicare contractor denies payment for the service.
However, the Medicare-allowed amount for that service, when paid, is $80.
The Medicare payment for the claim was $0.
If Medicare paid the claim, Medicare would pay $64 and the patient would owe a $16 copayment (20% of the allowed amount).
$80 minus $16 = $64. The amount in controversy for this claim is $64.

This service, for which you billed $500, would not satisfy the 2020 AIC requirement for an ALJ appeal ($170 minimum AIC).

6. Does CMS have a new form to request an ALJ hearing?

Yes. As of January 2017, CMS has a new (OMHA-100) form to request an ALJ hearing and CMS has an additional (OMHA-100A) form to use if you are requesting a hearing for multiple beneficiaries.

7. How do you fill in the OMHA-100 form?

Print a copy of the OMHA-100 form and keep it in front of you as you read the following suggestions on how to fill out each section on the form.

Section 1: Which Medicare Part are you appealing?

Check which Medicare Part you are appealing: Part A, Part B, Part C, or Part D.

Section 2: Which party are you?

Check the box next to "provider or supplier."

Section 3: What is your (the appealing party's) information?

Fill in all your contact information.

Section 4: What is the representative's information?

If you are represented by an attorney, the attorney will fill in Section 4, along with the rest of this form.

Section 5: What is being appealed?

Fill in Section 5 if you are appealing a single denied claim.

If you are appealing denials for multiple beneficiaries, use the **OMHA-100A** form instead of filling in Section 5.

If you are appealing denials for multiple beneficiaries, you will write "See the attached OMHA-100A form" in Section 5.

Section 6: For appeals of prescription drugs only.

This section is only for appeals of prescription drugs on Part D.

Section 7: Why do you disagree with the reconsideration or dismissal being appealed?

One of the following will apply:

1. When the denial reasons offered by the contractor in the redetermination decision and the denial reasons offered by the QIC in the reconsideration decision are identical, you will write the following in Section 7 of the OMHA-100 form: *"Please see the letter brief submitted to the QIC when the reconsideration appeal was requested."*
2. When the reconsideration denial letter contains *new* denial reasons that were not offered by the contractor in the redetermination denial letter, you must send the ALJ a second letter brief that addresses the QIC's new denial reasons.

   Your right to respond to the QIC's new denial reasons is stated in 405.1028(b) and you will write the following in Section 7 of the OMHA-100 form: *"Please see the letter brief submitted to the QIC when the reconsideration appeal was requested, and please see the additional attached letter brief I am submitting in response to the new denial reasons offered by the QIC in the reconsideration denial letter."*
3. If the QIC dismissed your appeal, you can ask the ALJ to reverse the dismissal but you must get the request to the ALJ within 65 days of the QIC dismissal. See 405.1004. In Section 7 of the OMHA-100 form, you will write the following: *"Please see the attached letter brief asking the ALJ to reverse the QIC's dismissal of my claim."*

Section 8: Are you submitting evidence with this request, or do you plan to submit evidence?

1. When the denial reasons offered by the contractor in the redetermination decision and the denial reasons offered by the QIC in the reconsideration decision are identical—AND YOU SUBMITTED A LETTER BRIEF TO THE QIC—you will check the "I am **not** planning to submit evidence at this time" box. You will also check the "**Yes**" box next to the question "Was the evidence already submitted for the matter that you are appealing?"
2. When the reconsideration denial letter contains new reasons for the denial of payment that were not offered by the contractor in the redetermination denial letter, you will check the "I am submitting evidence with this request" box. You will also check the "**No**" box next to the question: "Was the evidence already submitted for the matter that you are appealing?" Don't worry, the ALJ must accept your letter that refutes the new denial reasons offered by the QIC. See 405.1028.

3. When you are using the ALJ appeal to request a reversal of the QIC's dismissal of your claim, you will check the "I am submitting evidence with this request" box. You will also check the "**No**" box next to the question "Was the evidence already submitted for the matter that you are appealing?"
4. If you are submitting your letter brief with all the patient care documents *for the first time*, when you request the ALJ hearing you will have to submit a "good cause" statement explaining why you are submitting your evidence late (see 405.1028). Now you should worry because unless you have a "good cause" reason for the late submission, the ALJ may read your letter brief, but it is likely the ALJ will not consider your letter brief in making a payment decision.

Section 9: Is there other information about your appeal that we should know? Are you aggregating claims to meet the amount in controversy (AIC) requirement?

If you are aggregating (combining) claims in order to meet the $170 AIC requirement and the total amount of the claims you are appealing is **less than $200**, why are you doing all of this work? This makes no sense.

On the other hand, if you are aggregating similar/identical claims in order to meet the $170 AIC requirement and the total amount of the claims you are appealing is **more than $500**, you are absolutely doing the right thing.

Are you waiving the oral hearing before an ALJ and requesting a decision based on the record?

No. Never do this. You should always have an oral hearing because you will be presented with opportunities during the hearing to make your case stronger and clearer for the ALJ.

Does the request involve claims that were part of a statistical sample?

If yes, please explain the status of any appeals for claims in the sample that are not included in this request.

If you are dealing with a "statistical sample," that single fact implies many claims are at issue and also implies Medicare will be applying the results of the ALJ hearing to many (perhaps hundreds or thousands) other claims you have billed. Get an attorney. You are way over your head here and the stakes are too high to be "winging" it.

Section 10: Certification of copies sent to other parties.

When you appeal a denial of payment to an ALJ, you must prove you sent a copy of the OMHA-100 appeal form to each Medicare beneficiary with a claim at issue. **You do not have to prove the beneficiary *received* the copy; you only have to prove you *sent* the copy.** See 405.1014.

Use the U.S. Postal Service form 3817, "Certificate of Mailing," to send the copies of your ALJ appeal request form to the Medicare beneficiaries. You will include a copy of the stamped certificate of mailing form for each beneficiary in your letter brief sent to the QIC.

8. Is there a box on the OMHA-100 form to request a video teleconference (VTC) hearing?

No. CMS created the OMHA-100 form for you to fill out and submit a request for an ALJ appeal but the OMHA-100 form does **not** have a box to request a video teleconference (VTC) hearing. Why not? CMS does not want to pay for VTC hearings, so CMS did not put any information about VTC hearings on the OMHA-100 form.

9. When should you request a VTC hearing instead of a phone hearing?

You should **always** request a VTC hearing. You want to see the judge in real time so you can tell if you have the judge's attention and whether you need to stop presenting your argument in order to help the judge find the document or photograph you are talking about. If the judge is searching for a document or a photograph while you are speaking, she isn't going to get anything you are saying.

In addition, any time a patient's problem is easily appreciated and understood just by looking at the affected body part, you can walk the ALJ through the photos of the patient that you cleverly submitted to the QIC for the reconsideration appeal. A picture is still worth a thousand articles!

10. How do you request a VTC hearing?

See 405.1000(b). Because the OMHA-100 form does **not** have a checkoff box to request a VTC hearing, I am recommending you do **three** things:

1. Section 9 of the OMHA-100 form asks: "Are you waiving the oral hearing before an ALJ and requesting a decision based on the record?" You will check the "**No**" box.
2. You will staple a letter to the completed OMHA-100 form specifically requesting a video teleconference (VTC) hearing. The letter will say something like this:

   Your Honor, I am requesting a video teleconference hearing in order to explain the photographs previously submitted in the letter brief to the QIC. In addition, I will ask the patient(s) to appear at the hearing so the Court can ask the patient(s) questions.

3. You will follow up by calling the ALJ's secretary a week later and confirming approval of your request for the video teleconference hearing.

11. What if the ALJ asks for a "good cause" letter to qualify for a VTC hearing?

You are entitled to a video teleconference hearing without having to justify your request. See 405.1020.

However, instead of getting angry when the ALJ asks for an explanation of why you want a VTC hearing, use this moment as an opportunity to frame the patient's problem for the judge. Send a short letter to the judge that describes the patient's medical problem in a few short sentences. Then, tell the judge the patient's medical problem is best understood by viewing the images sent to the QIC and having those images explained, and that a VTC hearing is the best way to accomplish this.

12. How does the ALJ determine which VTC center will be used for the hearing?

The ALJ's office will find a "nearby" approved video teleconference center and will make the arrangements for use of the facility.

13. Why is it a bad idea to let the judge determine which VTC center will be used for the hearing?

The judge doesn't care if you have to travel twenty miles to a VTC center, but you do.

14. How can you make sure the video teleconference center is close to your location?

Put "[name of your city] video teleconferencing centers" into your Internet search bar and several locations will come up. Call the video teleconference centers closest to you to determine which center(s) are approved for Medicare hearings. Then, fax the judge's secretary with a request to have the video teleconference hearing at the center you want to use.

Provide the secretary with all of the contact information for the conference center in the body of the fax and ask the secretary to send you written confirmation regarding use of that conference center for the hearing.

15. What should you do if the QIC denies payment and adds new denial reasons?

This is important enough to repeat: If new issues are raised by the QIC, you must submit a separate letter brief to the ALJ that explains why the QIC's **new reasons for denial** of payment are wrong. An ALJ is required to find "good cause" for this "new evidence." See 405.1028(b).

16. What if you want to submit new evidence when you request an ALJ hearing?

You will have a very tough time getting the ALJ to consider any new evidence when the ALJ decides your claim. Unless the QIC offered new and different denial reasons, all of your evidence must be submitted when you request the QIC appeal.

17. What is "new" evidence?

All of the following would qualify as "new" evidence if they are being submitted for the first time when you submit the request for an ALJ appeal: copies of all applicable **patient records** (progress notes, procedure reports, imaging reports, and/or lab reports); hard copies of photos of the patient; letters from referring or co-treating doctors); published statements by specialty organizations supporting the service you provided; peer-reviewed journal articles supporting the service you provided; and textbook section(s) supporting the service you provided.

18. What is not "new" evidence?

Any document written by or relied upon by Medicare/CMS is not new evidence. For example, the applicable LCD articles and other documents cited in the LCD, the CPT Manual, the HCPCS II Manual, the Medicare Manual, and the Code of Federal Regulations are not new evidence. Portions of these documents can be submitted at any time during an appeal.

19. What will you have to do to get the ALJ to accept "new" evidence?

If you want to submit "new" evidence to the ALJ—evidence that was not sent along with the reconsideration appeal request—you will have to send a "**good cause**" statement explaining why the ALJ should accept the new evidence. And any "new" evidence will have to meet the "good cause" requirements (405.942[b][2] and [b][3]) in order to get the ALJ to consider the newly submitted evidence. Section 405.966, "Evidence to be submitted with the reconsideration request," states:

> When filing a request for reconsideration, you should present evidence and allegations of fact or law related to the issue in dispute and explain why you disagree with the initial determination and the redetermination. Any **missing documentation** identified in the notice of redetermination must be submitted with your request for reconsideration. Absent **good cause**, failure to submit all evidence, including any documentation requested in the notice of redetermination, **PRECLUDES (disqualifies)** subsequent consideration of that evidence (by the ALJ). (Emphasis added.)

The "good cause" requirements for the admission of "new" evidence for the ALJ hearing are not defined by Medicare. The ALJs get to make this subjective decision.

20. Do all the ALJs enforce the "no new evidence" rule in the same manner?

No. Sometimes an ALJ will allow new evidence based on a weak explanation, and other times an ALJ will not allow new evidence unless the doctor can provide a strong 405.966 "good cause" argument. Here is the bottom line: You do not want to put yourself in the position of hoping an ALJ will admit your new evidence. Submit all the evidence you are relying on when you request the reconsideration appeal.

21. What if you submitted some patient care documents to the QIC and you want to submit additional patient care documents for the ALJ hearing?

If you have already submitted some patient care documents to the QIC, but there are other patient care documents—such as other progress notes or consultation reports—that you want the ALJ to consider, I would write something like this to the ALJ:

> *Your Honor, these late-submitted patient care documents provide greater detail for the patient care documents already submitted to the QIC, but the additional documents do not raise any new issues.*

22. Can you submit a newer version of a text relied upon by the contractor in the LCD?

If the contractor's LCD policy relies on an older version of a textbook to deny payment for the service you provided but the newer version of the same textbook supports the service you provided, you will write something like this to the ALJ:

> *Your Honor, the contractor's LCD relies on the textbook, [title of text] by [name of author], to establish the accepted medical standard of care regarding the [name or description of service] provided for [first, last name of patient]. However, the more recent version of the same textbook, published <u>before</u> the service date in question, supports the treatment provided for [first, last name of patient]. Because this textbook is cited by the contractor in the LCD, a newer version of the same textbook published before the date of service at issue should not be excluded as "new evidence."*

23. Can you submit articles and book sections that are newer than those present in the LCD?

If the contractor's LCD policy relies on old textbooks and articles to deny payment for the service you provided but newer textbooks and articles *published before the date of service at issue* support the service you provided, you will write something like this to the ALJ:

> *Your Honor, the contractor's LCD relies on textbooks and articles that were current at the time the first version of the LCD, L_______, was published in [year of publication]. However, authoritative textbooks and articles that were published before the date of service at issue [month and year of service] support the denied service as medically reasonable and necessary. See Attachments ____–____.*

24. Can you use the Medicare Program Integrity Manual to bolster your argument when you want to submit "new" evidence to the ALJ?

Your Honor, Section 13.5.1 of the Medicare Program Integrity Manual deals with medically "Reasonable and Necessary Provisions in LCD" and may be paraphrased in part as follows: "Contractors shall consider a service to be reasonable and necessary if the service is furnished in accordance with accepted standards of medical practice for the diagnosis or treatment of the patient's condition."

The accepted standards of medical practice for [first, last name of Medicare beneficiary] on [date of the service at issue] included [description of treatment], as supported in the textbook(s)/article(s) enclosed as Attachment(s) ____– ____. Because the contractor is presumed to know the accepted standard of medical practice regarding the service at issue, these textbook sections/articles should not be viewed as "new evidence."

25. If you cannot make a "good cause" argument, what can you tell the judge if "new" evidence was mentioned, but not included, in the documents sent to the QIC?

When a professional organization representing your specialty or business has a published policy statement on the treatment of the patient's condition and you previously submitted that policy statement to the QIC, if that policy statement cites articles you now want to submit to the judge, here is what I would write to the judge:

*Your Honor, these additional documents are incorporated by reference in the evidence previously **submitted to** the QIC. The [name of professional organization] policy statement previously submitted specifically references the enclosed articles.*

26. If you cannot make a "good cause" argument, what can you tell the judge if your "new" evidence for denied E&M codes is related to documents relied upon by the QIC?

Your Honor, the QIC relies upon the CPT Manual for billing standards and the CPT Manual includes a list of clinical examples for the use of each E&M code. Included in that list are the E&M codes at issue in this dispute. The documents now being submitted explain in greater detail how and why the CPT E&M clinical examples are equivalent to the E&M codes at issue.

27. What is your most important evidence when you request a reconsideration appeal?

The patient care records, including photographs of the patient, and literature supporting the services provided are the most important pieces of evidence you will want the ALJ to consider. That evidence must be submitted when you request the reconsideration appeal.

28. What if you don't have the time to write a prehearing letter brief to the QIC?

Do not give in to the temptation to go to hearing without submitting a prehearing letter brief to the QIC for the ALJ. Lack of preparation and overconfidence are a lethal combination in any court. Without a prehearing letter brief, there is nothing to tie all your patient care documents together. And the judge may not take the time to sort through your documents to try and make sense of them.

If you know you will not write the letter brief, call someone (like me) who will represent you on a contingency fee basis and will not only write the letter brief but will also represent you at the hearing. At the end of the day, if you walk away with 60% of the Medicare-allowed amount, that's a whole lot better than walking away with 0% of the Medicare-allowed amount.

20b

Sending a Proposed Decision with the Request for an ALJ Appeal

OUTLINE

1. Who sends and who receives the proposed decision?
2. Is a proposed decision written in the voice of the provider?
3. When will you send the proposed decision?
4. Should you attach your proposed decision to the ALJ appeal request form?
5. Where will you send the request for an ALJ hearing and the proposed decision?
6. Must you send a copy of the ALJ request and proposed decision to each beneficiary?
7. As a party to your ALJ hearing, does CMS or a contractor get a copy of the proposed decision?
8. If CMS or a medical review contractor is a party at your ALJ hearing, how will you know where to send the copy of the proposed decision?
9. Which mail service should you use to send the copies of the proposed decision to the other parties to the hearing?
10. If CMS or a medical review contractor is a "nonparty participant" at the ALJ hearing, must you send a copy of the proposed decision to that entity?
11. What happens when OMHA receives your request for an ALJ appeal?
12. What support staff does an ALJ have, and who reads your request for the hearing?
13. What is your goal when the ALJ's attorney advisor receives your proposed decision?
14. Why is the ALJ's attorney advisor likely to read your letter brief after reading your proposed decision?
15. The ALJ's attorney advisor reads your proposed decision, your letter brief, and whatever Medicare has submitted. What does the attorney advisor do next?
16. How can you draw the attorney advisor's attention to your proposed decision?
17. What information should you include on the cover sheet sent with a proposed decision?
18. How many documents will you be sending when you request an ALJ hearing?
19. What is the most important part of a proposed decision?
20. What does the ALJ need in order to find in favor of the provider?
21. Why should a proposed decision be submitted with the request for an ALJ appeal?
22. Why do you want the ALJ to read your version of the dispute before the ALJ reads Medicare's version?
23. What does "framing" the argument mean and how is that related to the ALJ reading your version of the dispute before she reads Medicare's version of the dispute?
24. What is an example of framing the dispute?

25. Are you allowed to tell the ALJ what to write in the ALJ's written decision?
26. Will the judge be offended by your submission of a proposed decision?
27. At what point do providers usually seek the help of an attorney?
28. Why do providers wait so long to ask for legal representation?
29. What do most providers submit to the QIC for the reconsideration appeal?
30. If most providers submit a copy of the beneficiary's medical records along with an incomplete explanation why Medicare should pay, who submits the letter brief?
31. If a letter brief is not submitted at or before the reconsideration appeal, what does that do to the importance of the proposed decision?
32. Yes or no: The letter brief and the proposed decision do the same thing.
33. If a letter brief was sent to the QIC, what kind of proposed decision should the health care attorney submit?
34. Why would the health care attorney want to submit a proposed decision to the ALJ if the provider has already submitted an acceptable letter brief to the QIC?
35. What parts of that letter brief will need to be edited and condensed for the proposed decision?
36. What is "substantial deference"?
37. When an ALJ finds in favor of a provider, which portion of the written decision will be most heavily examined by the Council on appeal?
38. Is the ALJ team applying a "preponderance of the evidence" standard as they read your partial proposed decision?
39. Who wouldn't want two bites of the apple?
40. If the story is adequately told in the letter brief, can the proposed decision focus on the analysis?
41. Will the ALJ use your proposed decision, word for word, when writing the decision?
42. If the ALJ is not allowed to use your proposed decision, what's the point in writing it?
43. Who usually writes the proposed decision?
44. Any provider can write a proposed decision but almost no provider will. Why not?
45. When should a health care attorney think twice about representing a provider?
46. What does the CFR say about the contents of a written ALJ decision?
47. In addition to the CFR, who tells the ALJ what the written decisions must contain?
48. What does OMHA expect in a complete ALJ written decision?
49. Should a provider's proposed decision contain all the sections included in a complete ALJ written decision?
50. What does the "Procedural History" include?
51. Do you need to tell the ALJ the procedural history of your appeal?
52. What does the term "issue(s)" refer to?
53. Do you need to tell the ALJ the issues in your appeal?
54. What does the phrase "findings of fact" refer to?
55. When will an ALJ refuse to consider the "findings of fact"?
56. What is the difference between the "findings of fact" in other legal disputes and in an ALJ appeal?
57. How can you make it easy for the ALJ team to cut and paste portions of your "findings of fact" and "analysis" sections?
58. What does "legal framework" refer to?
59. Do you need to write anything about OMHA's Review Authority in a proposed decision?
60. Under the "Legal Framework" heading, do you need to write anything about the "principles of law" in a proposed decision?

61. Most commonly, which "principles of law" apply to the denials resolved by ALJ hearings?
62. As to substantive denials, what can a provider do to defuse an LCD rule or a Medicare policy article rule?
63. In the proposed decision, what are the "conclusions of law"?
64. In the proposed decision, what is the "order"?
65. Why is the analysis the most difficult part of the written decision for the ALJ?
66. Do you always need to include the findings of fact in your partial proposed decision?
67. Should the findings of fact do more than just recite the facts about the medical history and the denied service or supply?
68. How can you structure the findings of fact to convince the ALJ team the denied service was medically reasonable and necessary?
69. Should you use the findings of fact section to write a book on the beneficiary's problem?
70. What should you do about medical issues not related to payment?
71. Should you present findings of fact as a story or as a series of numbered statements?
72. When you present the findings of fact as a short story, do you have to cite the medical record documents attached to the letter brief or the proposed decision?
73. Will the health care attorney representing the provider submit a proposed decision as a complete ALJ written decision?
74. Should the medical service or supply "findings of fact" be weaved together in the same paragraphs or should they be presented separately?
75. Here is a findings of fact statement for a fictional beneficiary, John Smith, regarding diabetic therapeutic shoe services.
76. Should you include a section on OMHA's Review Authority?
77. As an example, what Medicare laws would be included in an appeal regarding diabetic therapeutic shoe services?
78. A letter brief was previously submitted to the QIC. How will you cite the patient care documents and standard-of-care policy statements to prove the denied service was medically reasonable and necessary?
79. For our hypothetical diabetic therapeutic shoe service appeal, what documents were submitted to the QIC?
80. What problems does our provider, Dr. Jones, have to deal with when the ALJ hearing is requested?
81. What would be the outcome of the appeal if Dr. Jones is silent regarding the missing documents?
82. How should Dr. Jones address the missing documents/information issue?
83. Would a provider know "limited discovery" is allowed when the MAC or other medical review contractor elects to be a party at the hearing?
84. Will the request for limited discovery be sent with the proposed decision as a separate document?
85. How will the provider write the analysis section of the proposed decision?
86. How will the ALJ's analysis incorporate the provider's analysis, the results of the limited discovery, and the testimony at the hearing?
87. What did our example provider do wrong?
88. Would a health care attorney working on a contingency fee basis put this kind of effort into a single diabetic therapeutic shoe service claim?
89. Would a provider be willing to pay a health care attorney on an hourly basis for a single diabetic therapeutic shoe service claim?

90. What about the situation where a provider is the target of an overpayment audit and submits medical records for several beneficiaries, but the total amount at issue is less than $5,000? For that amount of money, what's the point?
91. Why should providers fight post-payment audits when the amount of money for the claim is small?
92. How should the requirements for diabetic therapeutic shoe services be changed?
93. If you are an attorney representing a provider, should you have the provider help you with the findings of fact and the analysis?
94. Should a provider consider listing the Medicare requirements for a denied service in the exact order and language used by Medicare in the applicable LCD and/or Medicare article and, after each listed requirement, explain how that requirement was met?
95. Can we summarize the most important points for providers doing their own appeals?

WHAT IS A PROPOSED DECISION?

A "proposed decision" is what a provider would like to receive from the ALJ: A favorable decision ordering payment for a denied service or supply, or a favorable decision that rejects Medicare's demand for repayment of overpayment.

1. Who sends and who receives the proposed decision?

The provider sends the "proposed decision" to the ALJ.

2. Is a proposed decision written in the voice of the provider?

No. A proposed decision is written in the voice of the judge. A proposed decision is what the provider wants the judge to write in her written decision after the hearing.

3. When will you send the proposed decision?

You will send the proposed decision when you request the ALJ hearing.

4. Should you attach your proposed decision to the ALJ appeal request form?

Yes. You will staple the completed OMHA-100 (Request for ALJ Hearing) form to the proposed decision. The OMHA-100 form goes on top of the proposed decision.

5. Where will you send the request for an ALJ hearing and the proposed decision?

The QIC denial letter will tell you where to send the request for an ALJ hearing. Currently, you will send the request for the ALJ hearing/proposed decision to the Office of Medicare Hearings and Appeals (OMHA) at:

OMHA Centralized Docketing
200 Public Square, Suite 1260
Cleveland, OH 44114-2316

6. Must you send a copy of the ALJ request and proposed decision to each beneficiary?

Yes.

7. As a party to your ALJ hearing, does CMS or a contractor get a copy of the proposed decision?

Anything you send to the ALJ must be sent to all other **parties** to the appeal. That includes all the beneficiaries whose claims are at issue.

8. If CMS or a medical review contractor is a party at your ALJ hearing, how will you know where to send the copy of the proposed decision?

You will receive notice from CMS or its medical review contractor of its decision to participate as a party in your ALJ hearing. That notice will include the address where you will send a copy of the proposed decision.

9. Which mail service should you use to send the copies of the proposed decision to the other parties to the hearing?

Send each copy with a proof of mailing certificate.

10. If CMS or a medical review contractor is a "nonparty participant" at the ALJ hearing, must you send a copy of the proposed decision to that entity?

No. You are only required to send copies of your proposed decision to the other parties to the hearing.

11. What happens when OMHA receives your request for an ALJ appeal?

The OMHA docketing department gets your ALJ appeal request and assigns it to an ALJ. Although OMHA may try to assign your case to an ALJ in your regional ALJ office, if no ALJ is available in your regional ALJ office, OMHA will assign your case to the next available ALJ at any of the regional ALJ offices.

Your claim file and your request for the ALJ appeal is then sent to the ALJ assigned to your appeal.

12. What support staff does an ALJ have, and who reads your request for the hearing?

Each ALJ has a "team" that usually consists of the ALJ, two attorney advisors, and two legal assistants.

Your request for an ALJ hearing is usually given to one of two attorney advisors working for the ALJ. The attorney advisor who reads your "request for an ALJ appeal" will likely be the attorney who writes the ALJ's written decision after the hearing.

13. What is your goal when the ALJ's attorney advisor receives your proposed decision?

You first want the attorney advisor to read your proposed decision. You then want the attorney advisor to read the letter brief you previously sent to the QIC. And you want the attorney advisor to read your documents **before** the attorney advisor reads whatever Medicare has submitted to the ALJ.

14. Why is the ALJ's attorney advisor likely to read your letter brief after reading your proposed decision?

The attorney advisor will have to look at the patient care documents attached to the letter brief/request for the reconsideration appeal in order to find the patient care documents you mention in the proposed decision. In addition, your brief medical history and legal analysis in the proposed decision will grab the attorney advisor's interest in your letter brief.

15. The ALJ's attorney advisor reads your proposed decision, your letter brief, and whatever Medicare has submitted. What does the attorney advisor do next?

The attorney advisor will then prepare a "substantive review" for the ALJ. And you want that substantive review to recommend a finding in your favor based on your down-to-earth, common-sense presentation validated by known medical authorities.

In the substantive review, you want the attorney advisor to conclude the arguments in your favor are much, much stronger than the arguments offered against you by Medicare.

16. How can you draw the attorney advisor's attention to your proposed decision?

Bob Soltis, a retired ALJ, wrote *How to Handle Your Medicare Hearing.* In his book, Bob recommends printing the proposed decision on **bright pink paper** and to place a cover sheet, also printed on bright pink paper, on top of your "Request for an ALJ Hearing." These are not good recommendations. These are *great* recommendations.

17. What information should you include on the cover sheet sent with a proposed decision?

Your cover sheet should include the following statements in large bold print:

Attention: Attorney Advisor
or Legal Assistant:
[Name of Provider]
Requests a Fully Favorable
On the Record Decision.
A Proposed Decision Is Attached.
OMHA Central Ops: Please leave this sheet on top of the Hearing Request.

Use **bright colored paper** (e.g., bright pink) for both the cover sheet and the proposed decision to get the attention of the OMHA docketing clerk and to get the attention of the ALJ attorney advisor. These two pink documents will stand out in the stack of white documents that make up the rest of the claim file.

18. How many documents will you be sending when you request an ALJ hearing?

You will send three documents. The document on top will be the cover sheet printed on bright pink paper. The next document will be the completed OMHA-100 (Request for ALJ Hearing) form. The third document will be the proposed decision, also printed on bright pink paper.

19. What is the most important part of a proposed decision?

The most important part of a proposed decision is the legal analysis in which the Medicare laws (the Medicare rules, regulations, and statutes that apply to the disputed service/supply) are applied to the findings of fact (the beneficiary's medical history and the facts regarding the denied service or supply).

20. What does the ALJ need in order to find in favor of the provider?

The ALJ needs answers to the following questions (see Chapter 19e, "The Letter Brief") in order to award in favor of the provider:

a. **In lay terms, what kind of problem does the patient have?** The ALJ must have a basic understanding of the patient's problem in order to rule in your favor.
b. **Why did the problem require treatment?** Do not take this question for granted. You must convince the judge the patient's problem needed to be treated.
c. **What service/supply did you provide for the patient's problem?** Keep it simple and state exactly why the denied service/supply was the best and most logical choice for the patient.
d. **How do you know that treatment was the correct thing to do?** What medical authorities support what you did? Provide copies of those authorities as attachments to the letter brief.
e. **Why is each denial reason offered by the contractor in the redetermination denial letter wrong?** No matter how silly the contractor's reasons may be, you have to address and pull apart each denial reason.

If the ALJ concludes the provider's service/supply was medically reasonable and necessary, the ALJ will likely decide in your favor. The ALJ team will provide the rest of the information required in the written decision.

WHY SHOULD A PROVIDER SUBMIT A PROPOSED DECISION?

21. Why should a proposed decision be submitted with the request for an ALJ appeal?

- You should submit a proposed decision because you want the ALJ to read your version of the dispute **before** the ALJ reads Medicare's version of the dispute.
- You should submit a proposed decision because you want to **frame the dispute** for the ALJ.
- You should submit a proposed decision because you want **to help the ALJ with** the most critical part of the written decision—**the analysis (breakdown)**.

22. Why do you want the ALJ to read your version of the dispute before the ALJ reads Medicare's version?

Having the judge read your version of the dispute first will have a big influence on the outcome of the appeal. Why? In any dispute, the party that speaks first makes the biggest impression on a neutral third party listening to the dispute. It's just the way our minds work.

23. What does "framing" the argument mean and how is that related to the ALJ reading your version of the dispute before she reads Medicare's version of the dispute?

If your proposed decision, and hopefully the photographs submitted to the QIC, capture the attention of the ALJ team, they will take the time to read the letter brief you submitted to the QIC **before** they read the contractor's and the QIC's denial reasons.

If your written documents make sense and your photographs support your arguments, the ALJ team will be thinking: "Why would the contractor and the QIC deny this service/supply that was obviously medically reasonable and necessary?"

Going first allows you to frame the argument by telling the story the way you want the ALJ to view the dispute. Going first allows you to create a favorable bias for your version of the dispute before the ALJ team reads the other side's version.

24. What is an example of framing the dispute?

If, for example, the dispute concerns payment for diabetic therapeutic shoe services, you first want to prove to the ALJ there is no question the beneficiary is diabetic, no question the beneficiary has a qualifying condition for the diabetic therapeutic shoe service, and no question the diabetic therapeutic shoe services were provided as billed.

You then want to let the ALJ know the denial of payment was based only on the absence of one or two "reporting" documents required by the contractor. By framing the dispute in this manner, you are making a powerful form-over-substance argument. That is, if the missing documents were required to prove the beneficiary is diabetic, the beneficiary has a qualifying condition for the diabetic therapeutic shoe service, and the diabetic therapeutic shoe services were provided as billed—why should payment be denied when all three requirements have unquestionably been met?

Medicare's denial reasons based on the one or two incomplete or absent record-keeping forms now seem foolish and the ALJ team will have that mind-set as they begin reading Medicare's arguments.

25. Are you allowed to tell the ALJ what to write in the ALJ's written decision?

Sort of. You are not actually "telling" the judge what to write. But if the judge finds in your favor, she can use any portion of your proposed decision as part of her written decision.

However, the judge is not allowed to completely adopt your entire proposed decision.

26. Will the judge be offended by your submission of a proposed decision?

Absolutely not. The ALJ team will be thankful for your summarized, documented view of the dispute.

27. At what point do providers usually seek the help of an attorney?

Most providers ask for legal representation **after** they get the reconsideration denial from the QIC.

28. Why do providers wait so long to ask for legal representation?

The providers want to see if they can win the appeal without having to pay an attorney. It's what lawyers would do if they were the providers.

29. What do most providers submit to the QIC for the reconsideration appeal?

Most providers submit a copy of the beneficiary's medical records without adequately explaining why the provider should be paid.

30. If most providers submit a copy of the beneficiary's medical records along with an incomplete explanation why Medicare should pay, who submits the letter brief?

Most commonly, a letter brief is **not** submitted at or before the reconsideration appeal.

31. If a letter brief is not submitted at or before the reconsideration appeal, what does that do to the importance of the proposed decision?

Without a previously submitted letter brief serving as a road map for the ALJ team, the proposed decision becomes **the critical document** in the appeals process.

And without a previously submitted letter brief, the proposed decision is the provider's only **unopposed opportunity** to persuade the ALJ team that the denied service or supply was medically reasonable and necessary and that legal analysis supports payment of the service or supply.

IF A LETTER BRIEF WAS SENT TO THE QIC, WHY SHOULD A PROPOSED DECISION BE SENT TO THE ALJ?

32. Yes or no: The letter brief and the proposed decision do the same thing.

Yes and no. When the letter brief and the proposed decision are both well written, the letter brief tells the longer version of the beneficiary's story while the proposed decision focuses on applying the law to the facts—the analysis. And it is the analysis that will determine the ALJ's decision.

33. If a letter brief was sent to the QIC, what kind of proposed decision should the health care attorney submit?

It depends on the quality of the letter brief.

If the letter brief is of poor quality, the health care attorney will have to write the proposed decision as if no letter brief has been written.

If the letter brief is acceptable, the health care attorney should edit and condense the relevant portions of the letter brief for the proposed decision.

34. Why would the health care attorney want to submit a proposed decision to the ALJ if the provider has already submitted an acceptable letter brief to the QIC?

The letter brief is written in the voice of the provider.

By contrast, the proposed decision is written in the voice of the judge.

For an ALJ who decides in your favor, the most difficult part of the written decision is the analysis: How the ALJ gave "substantial deference" to the nonbinding Medicare rule(s) relied upon by the contractor and the QIC, and why the judge decided not to follow those nonbinding rule(s) (see 405.1062). It is almost certain the provider's attorney will do a better job applying the law to the facts in the proposed decision than did the provider in the letter brief to the QIC.

35. What parts of that letter brief will need to be edited and condensed for the proposed decision?

The medical findings of fact (the beneficiary's medical history related to the denied service/supply) and the findings of fact related to the service/supply (the critical facts regarding the denied service or supply) will need to be edited and condensed. Then the Medicare law (rules, regulations, and statutes) will have to be applied to the findings of fact for the analysis.

36. What is "substantial deference"?

Medicare has not defined "substantial deference." But the ALJ is expected to give "substantial deference" to any Medicare rule that applies to the service at issue.

37. When an ALJ finds in favor of a provider, which portion of the written decision will be most heavily examined by the Council on appeal?

When a provider receives a favorable ALJ decision and that ALJ decision is appealed, it is the "analysis" section of the ALJ's written decision that the Council looks at closest in deciding whether to sustain or overrule the ALJ's decision.

You should use the "proposed decision" to give the ALJ the clearest explanation of why the Medicare law relied upon by the contractor and the QIC should not be followed in your appeal.

38. Is the ALJ team applying a "preponderance of the evidence" standard as they read your partial proposed decision?

Absolutely not. You must provide the ALJ with a "compelling, extenuating, or unusual circumstance" in order to overcome Medicare's denial reasons.

39. Who wouldn't want two bites of the apple?

A wonderfully written letter brief followed by a concise analysis in the proposed decision is the best of all possible worlds. Make it easy for the ALJ team to decide in your favor.

40. If the story is adequately told in the letter brief, can the proposed decision focus on the analysis?

Yes. As much as possible, you want the analysis to be the focus of the proposed decision.

41. Will the ALJ use your proposed decision, word for word, when writing the decision?

No. The ALJs are not allowed to adopt a provider's proposed decision and publish it as the ALJ's decision.

Even if the ALJ agrees with your position, and even if she adopts some portions of your proposed decision, once she approves the final edited version of the written ALJ decision, it is likely that final version will bear little resemblance to your proposed decision.

42. If the ALJ is not allowed to use your proposed decision, what's the point in writing it?

You are not sending your proposed decision in order to ghostwrite the written decision. The point of submitting the proposed decision is to get your case-specific medical facts, your case-specific service or supply facts, and your legal analysis in front of the ALJ's attorney advisor as the first thing that attorney advisor reads about your case.

THE PROPOSED DECISION

43. Who usually writes the proposed decision?

Most commonly, it is the health care attorney representing the provider who will write the proposed decision.

44. Any provider can write a proposed decision but almost no provider will. Why not?

If a provider has already submitted a letter brief, it is unrealistic to think that the provider will also write a proposed decision. It just doesn't happen.

And if you can't motivate the provider to write a short letter explaining the medical records submitted to the QIC, it is unrealistic to think that the provider is going to write a proposed decision.

45. When should a health care attorney think twice about representing a provider?

If the provider has received the reconsideration decision and the provider did **not** submit copies of the beneficiary's medical records, the health care attorney should think twice about accepting the request for representation. If the attorney is working on an hourly basis and it is impossible to get the beneficiary's medical records entered into evidence for the hearing, the provider/client is going to be very unhappy about a big legal bill with no chance of winning. If the attorney is working on a contingency fee basis and it is impossible to get the beneficiary's medical records entered into evidence for the hearing, the attorney will spend a lot of unpaid time getting nothing accomplished.

If there is no good cause argument that can be made regarding the late submission of the medical records, the health care attorney should probably turn down the request for representation.

Instead, the health care attorney should use the opportunity to let the provider know the next time the provider only has to submit copies of the beneficiary's medical records at or before the reconsideration appeal request in order for the attorney to zealously represent the provider in an ALJ appeal.

WHAT MUST A WRITTEN ALJ DECISION CONTAIN?

46. What does the CFR say about the contents of a written ALJ decision?

See 405.1046, which requires the ALJ to include:

> The findings of fact, the conclusions of law, and the reasons for the decision in the written decision. The written decision must be based on evidence offered at the hearing or otherwise admitted into the record and must include any independent findings and conclusions of the ALJ. The decision must be written in a manner calculated to be understood by a beneficiary and must include the specific reasons for the determination, including, to the extent appropriate, a summary of any clinical or scientific evidence used in making the determination; and for any new evidence that was submitted for the first time at the OMHA level and subjected to a good cause determination pursuant to § 405.1028, a discussion of the new evidence and the good cause determination that was made.

47. In addition to the CFR, who tells the ALJ what the written decisions must contain?

The Office of Medicare Hearings and Appeals (OMHA) tells the ALJs how to write the ALJ decisions and what information the decisions must contain.

48. What does OMHA expect in a complete ALJ written decision?

As outlined on the Office of Medicare Hearings and Appeals form, OMHA-152, all ALJ written decisions include the following:

1. Procedural History
2. Issue(s)
3. Findings of Fact
4. Legal Framework
    a. OMHA Review Authority
        i. Jurisdiction
        ii. Scope of Review
        iii. Standard of Review

   b. Principles of Law
      i. Statutes
      ii. Regulations
      iii. Policy
5. Analysis
6. Conclusions of Law
7. Order

49. Should a provider's proposed decision contain all the sections included in a complete ALJ written decision?

No. See the following questions and answers. When we use the phrase "provider's proposed decision," we are referring to a **partial proposed decision** that will only include sections helpful to the ALJ team.

50. What does the "Procedural History" include?

The "Procedural History" refers to the history of the denied claim.

When was the service at issue provided?
When was the initial claim received by the contractor?
When was the initial claim denied?
What were the contractor's stated denial reasons?
When was the redetermination appeal received by the contractor?
When was the redetermination appeal denied?
What were the contractor's stated denial reasons?
When was the reconsideration appeal received by the QIC?
When was the reconsideration appeal denied?
What were the QIC's stated denial reasons?
When was the ALJ appeal received at OMHA?

51. Do you need to tell the ALJ the procedural history of your appeal?

No. The ALJ and her attorney advisor have the procedural history and there is no need for you to repeat it.

52. What does the term "issue(s)" refer to?

"Issue(s)" refers to the contractor's initial denial reasons, the redetermination denial reasons, and the reconsideration denial reasons—and whether the service at issue should be paid despite those denial reasons.

But the essential issue is always the same: whether the provider should be paid for the denied service or supply.

53. Do you need to tell the ALJ the issues in your appeal?

No. The ALJ and her attorney advisors know the ultimate issue is always whether the provider should be paid for the denied code(s).

54. What does the phrase "findings of fact" refer to?

The findings of fact include the beneficiary's medical history (medical findings of fact) and the facts related to the denied service or supply.

The **medical findings of fact** include the answers to all the following questions:

What medical problem(s) did the beneficiary have that required the denied service or supply?
Why did the problem require treatment?
What other medical problems, if any, did the beneficiary have that complicated his/her care? If a comorbidity (another medical condition) makes the problem at issue more difficult to treat or places the beneficiary at greater risk, include it in the medical findings of fact.

The **findings of fact related to the denied service or supply** include the answers to all the following questions:

What exact denied service or supply was provided to the beneficiary?
What medical authorities support the denied service or supply as the correct choice in similar clinical circumstances?
Why was that service or supply selected by the provider over other choices?
Why was that service or supply selected by the provider over the "indicated" (contractor-allowed) service or supply published in the LCD?

55. When will an ALJ refuse to consider the "findings of fact"?

The beneficiary's medical records are the "evidence" that supports the medical findings of fact.

When a provider fails to submit the beneficiary's medical records at or before the reconsideration appeal, the ALJ is **not allowed** to consider those medical records during the ALJ appeal unless the provider has a "good cause" reason for the late submission.

The "findings of fact related to the denied service or supply" are the published explanations of the denied service or supply along with the published medical authorities that support the use of the denied service or supply in the beneficiary's clinical circumstances. These documents are the "evidence" that explain and support the denied service or supply.

As is the case with the beneficiary's medical records, when a provider fails to submit the "findings of fact related to the denied service or supply" at or before the reconsideration appeal, the ALJ is **not allowed** to consider those documents during the ALJ appeal unless the provider has a "good cause" reason for the late submission.

And any late-submitted evidence allowed by the ALJ requires an explanation in the written decision as to how the petitioner met the good cause requirements in 42 CFR Sections 1018 and 1028. If you are trying to submit the beneficiary's medical records and/or the "findings of fact related to the denied service or supply" for the first time at the time of the ALJ hearing, it is unlikely you will succeed.

56. What is the difference between the "findings of fact" in other legal disputes and in an ALJ appeal?

In most legal disputes, the "findings of fact" are challenged by the parties. For example, one party says, "The defendant was speeding." The other party says, "The defendant was not speeding."

However, in Medicare ALJ appeals, the "findings of fact" are not usually disputed. Instead, Medicare ALJ appeals usually revolve around "how" the Medicare rules and regulations are applied to the "findings of fact" and not whether there are opposing versions of the "findings of fact."

57. How can you make it easy for the ALJ team to cut and paste portions of your "findings of fact" and "analysis" sections?

Write the proposed decision in Microsoft Word. Burn a copy of the proposed decision onto a CD. Send the CD with the printed proposed decision. This will make it simple for the attorney advisor to cut and paste your "findings of fact" and "analysis" sections into the ALJ's written decision.

58. What does "legal framework" refer to?

The "legal framework" refers to the Medicare rules, regulations, and statutes that apply to the service at issue.

59. Do you need to write anything about OMHA's Review Authority in a proposed decision?

No. The ALJ's attorney advisor already has a menu of paragraphs in her computer regarding OMHA's Review Authority. That menu includes the paragraphs on jurisdiction, scope of review, and standard of review that will be incorporated in the body of the written ALJ decision.

The provider does not need to write anything about jurisdiction, scope of review, and standard of review in the proposed decision.

60. Under the "Legal Framework" heading, do you need to write anything about the "principles of law" in a proposed decision?

Yes. Although the ALJ's attorney advisor has immediate access to the statutes, regulations, and policies that apply to the service or supply at issue, these are the Medicare "laws" that must be applied to the service or supply in the analysis. And you can cut and paste the applicable statutes, regulations, and policies in a matter of seconds.

From every point of view, it makes sense to include the "black letter law" sections, the word-for-word statutes, regulations, and policies that apply to the dispute in the proposed decision before you begin the analysis.

61. Most commonly, which "principles of law" apply to the denials resolved by ALJ hearings?

Medicare denials can be divided into procedural and substantive denials.

Most commonly, the "principles of law" that apply to **procedural denials** come from the 42 CFR sections regarding appeals and are the CFR sections that deal with the late submission of an appeal request or the late submission of copies of the patient care records needed for a favorable ALJ decision. Procedural denials are very difficult to overcome because Medicare's "good cause" requirements in 405.1028 are almost impossible to meet.

The "principles of law" that apply to **substantive denials**, on the other hand, are usually an LCD rule or a Medicare policy article rule that prohibits payment for the provided service or supply. Substantive denials are not difficult to overcome when the service or supply was medically reasonable and necessary.

62. As to substantive denials, what can a provider do to defuse an LCD rule or a Medicare policy article rule?

There are at least two avenues available to the provider.

In the best-case scenario, the Medicare "rule" was **out of date** when the service was provided. And on the date the service or supply was provided, the standard of care clearly supported the denied service or supply.

When the Medicare "rule" was **not out of date**, the provider will have to prove the denied service was the **best choice** for the beneficiary under the clinical facts at the time the service was provided. The provider will have to prove, by considerably more than a preponderance of the evidence, that the denied service was safer than, more effective than, and hopefully, less expensive than the service required by Medicare under identical clinical circumstances.

Unfortunately, the ALJ team is aware of the heightened possibility of appeal when the ALJ finds in favor of a provider based on "best choice." Therefore, a "best choice" defense must be based on obviously safer than/more effective than grounds.

Not uncommonly, when a Medicare "rule" is out of date, the provider can and should use both the "out of date" and the "best choice" arguments.

63. In the proposed decision, what are the "conclusions of law"?

Based on the analysis, the conclusion of law is the judge's decision whether the service or supply at issue should be paid, should be denied, or whether the case must be remanded for additional findings.

The ALJ will reach one of the following "conclusions of law":

1. The Medicare rules applied to the medical facts support payment of the previously denied service.
2. The Medicare rules applied to the medical facts do not support payment of the previously denied service.
3. The ALJ appeal is dismissed. See 405.1052.
4. The ALJ appeal is remanded to the QIC, 405.1056, because:
   a. An official copy of the redetermination or reconsideration is missing in the case file;
   b. No redetermination of the claim was made; or
   c. The QIC's dismissal of a request for reconsideration was in error.

64. In the proposed decision, what is the "order"?

The "order" refers to the judge's order at the end of the written decision.

The ALJ will issue one of the following "orders":

1. The contractor is ordered to pay the previously denied service.
2. The contractor's demand for repayment of overpayment is denied.
3. The previous denial of payment is upheld.
4. The contractor's demand for repayment of overpayment is upheld.
5. The ALJ appeal is dismissed.
6. The ALJ appeal is remanded to the QIC:
   a. For the missing official copy of the redetermination or reconsideration;
   b. To re-adjudicate the request for reconsideration because no redetermination of the claim was made;
   c. To provide a reconsideration decision on the claim that was erroneously (mistakenly) dismissed by the QIC.

65. Why is the analysis the most difficult part of the written decision for the ALJ?

This bears repeating. For an ALJ who decides in favor of the provider, the most difficult part of the written decision is the analysis: How did the ALJ give "substantial deference" to the nonbinding Medicare rule(s) relied upon by the contractor and the QIC, and why did the judge award payment instead of following the nonbinding rule(s)?

When an ALJ decision is appealed by the Medicare contractor or by the Medicare Advantage plan, see 405.1048, the "analysis" is exactly where the Medicare Appeals Council will look in deciding whether to sustain or overrule the ALJ's decision. As a result, the provider should use the "proposed decision" to give the ALJ the clearest explanation of why the applicable Medicare rule(s) should not be followed in the appeal.

WHAT WILL THE PARTIAL PROPOSED DECISION SENT TO THE ALJ BY THE PROVIDER INCLUDE?

66. Do you always need to include the findings of fact in your partial proposed decision?

Yes.

67. Should the findings of fact do more than just recite the facts about the medical history and the denied service or supply?

Yes. The findings of fact section should be written to convince the ALJ team the denied service was medically reasonable and necessary. Write the findings of fact section so anyone can understand the beneficiary's problem and why the provided service or supply was medically reasonable and necessary.

68. How can you structure the findings of fact to convince the ALJ team the denied service was medically reasonable and necessary?

Incorporate the findings of fact within the story of the beneficiary's care. Where do you start a story? At the beginning!

Bring the reader into the exam room where and when the provider made the decision to provide the denied service or supply. Every good movie draws the audience into the story and you want to do the same. Tell the reader what the beneficiary told the provider during the history portion of the exam and always refer to the beneficiary by his or her name. Never use the word "beneficiary."

69. Should you use the findings of fact section to write a book on the beneficiary's problem?

No. You just want to write enough so the reader will understand the nature of the problem and why the specific treatment/supply choice was made.

70. What should you do about medical issues not related to payment?

Do not bore the ALJ with medical facts that are not relevant (related) to your appeal. For example, if the issue is whether you should be paid for diabetic therapeutic shoe services, do not waste paragraphs in your "findings of fact" section telling the ALJ about the beneficiary's colon cancer surgery.

71. Should you present findings of fact as a story or as a series of numbered statements?

Which do you think is easier to read, several paragraphs that tell a story from beginning to end, or a page of numbered statements with an attachment number and page number at the end of each statement? I think the answer is "several paragraphs."

Your findings of fact should easily fit on one side of one page with double-spaced printing and a font size of at least 12. Remember, you want the ALJ team to understand the major reasons why you should prevail and you want to keep the reader's attention from start to finish. Presenting the beneficiary's relevant medical history as a short story is the best way to accomplish these goals.

72. When you present the findings of fact as a short story, do you have to cite the medical record documents attached to the letter brief or the proposed decision?

No. Before you write the findings of fact, you will write something like the following: *"The medical record documents supporting the findings of fact were submitted to the QIC (and were included as attachments to the letter brief/to the request for a reconsideration appeal form)."*

73. Will the health care attorney representing the provider submit a proposed decision as a complete ALJ written decision?

Again, no.

STRUCTURE THE "FINDINGS OF FACT" SECTION OF THE PROPOSED DECISION

74. Should the medical service or supply "findings of fact" be weaved together in the same paragraphs or should they be presented separately?

It depends on the complexity of the denied service or supply. For example, if diabetic therapeutic shoe services are the subject of the appeal, there is no need to separate the service from the medical findings because the topics are simple and easily understood.

On the other hand, if the service is complex and requires real effort to explain clearly, I think you should consider separating the findings of fact regarding the denied service from the medical findings of fact. An example would be the denied use of robotic stereotactic body radiation therapy (R-SBRT) when the type of radiation therapy approved in the LCD for the beneficiary's cancer is intensity modulated radiation therapy (IMRT). You will first have to explain both R-SBRT and IMRT, and the differences between these two forms of radiation therapy before you explain why R-SBRT was a better choice than IMRT for the beneficiary.

In addition, the attorney advisor has to "get it" the first time she reads your proposed decision. Why? Because that attorney advisor has hundreds of claims stacked by her desk and she isn't going to take time she doesn't have to research poorly explained concepts in your proposed decision. Your explanation must be so clear that a high school senior can understand what you have written the very first time she reads it.

75. Here is a findings of fact statement for a fictional beneficiary, John Smith, regarding diabetic therapeutic shoe services.

We will purposely make this example difficult for a very good reason. If you can prove a service was medically reasonable and necessary, you can win the ALJ decision even if the provider has not complied with all the LCD or policy article rules. You just have to be persistent and thorough.

Here are the **bad facts** our hypothetical provider must deal with in the appeal:

1. The beneficiary is a noncompliant, type 2 diabetic male with a plantar ulcer.
2. When seen for diabetes management every four or five months, the beneficiary's internist does **not** examine the beneficiary's feet.

3. When the beneficiary told a friend about the "sore" on the bottom of his foot, the friend recommended the beneficiary see the provider for his foot problem.
4. When the beneficiary saw the provider for the first time in October 2017, the beneficiary's internist was unaware of the plantar ulcer.
5. The beneficiary's internist and the provider do not get along.
6. At the initial office visit, the provider had the beneficiary sign a "release" form allowing the provider to share the beneficiary's medical information with other treating doctors and with Medicare.
7. When the provider sent the beneficiary's internist a "Statement of Certifying Physician for Therapeutic Shoes" form and a separate note asking the internist to complete and sign the form and to return it in the addressed and stamped envelope, the provider got no response. The provider has a copy of the mailed request in the beneficiary's chart.
8. The provider also asked the beneficiary to speak with his internist and to ask the internist to complete and return the "Statement of Certifying Physician for Therapeutic Shoes" form. The provider's request was noted in the beneficiary's chart. But no "certifying physician" form was received from the internist.
9. When the provider sent another note and a pre-addressed and stamped return envelope to the internist asking for a copy of the internist's progress note from the last visit before the beneficiary's first visit with the provider, the provider got no response. The provider has a copy of the mailed request in the beneficiary's chart.
10. The provider's diabetic therapeutic shoe service claims were paid by the contractor but the Durable Medical Equipment (DME) RAC performed a post-payment audit and asked for copies of the medical records and the shoe service reporting forms from the provider. The provider's beneficiary care records (progress notes) were fine but the provider's required diabetic therapeutic shoe service reporting forms were lacking.
11. The RAC told the MAC to demand the repayment of overpayment because some of the required reporting forms were missing.
12. The provider sent copies of the patient care notes (progress notes) and copies of the requests sent to the patient's internist to the QIC for a reconsideration appeal. But the provider did not submit a letter brief to the QIC when the progress notes were submitted.
13. The provider asked the beneficiary to participate in the video teleconference ALJ hearing so the beneficiary could tell the judge about the treatment of his diabetes by the certifying physician and so the beneficiary could show the judge the foot that required treatment. The beneficiary refused.
14. The DME RAC sent a notice to the ALJ and to the provider of its intent to be a **party** at the ALJ hearing. And the Medicare Administrative Contractor sent a notice to the ALJ and to the provider of its intent to be a **nonparty** participant at the ALJ hearing.

Here is the "findings of fact" submitted by the provider in the proposed decision for this ALJ appeal.

The beneficiary care documents (progress notes) proving the following findings of fact were submitted to the QIC for the reconsideration appeal.

Mr. John Smith is a 68-year-old, type 2 diabetic who was first seen by the provider, Dr. Roberta Jones, on October 10, 2017, for treatment of an ulcer on the bottom of his right foot of approximately one month's duration. Photos of Mr. Smith's feet were taken at the time of the initial office visit and copies of the photos were submitted to the QIC.

Mr. Smith states he has been seeing his internist, Dr. Tom White, for care of his diabetes for more than five years and that Dr. White sees him every four to five months for management of his diabetes. However, Mr. Smith states Dr. White does not have Mr. Smith remove his shoes for a foot examination when seen for management of the diabetes, and states Dr. White was unaware of the ulcer when Mr. Smith was seen by Dr. Jones in October of 2017.

Mr. Smith states he has developed diabetic neuropathy in both lower extremities over the past three years. The diabetic neuropathy was first diagnosed by Dr. White and was confirmed by a local neurologist, Dr. Carol Thomas, in 2016.

In addition to his diabetic neuropathy, Mr. Smith has a right bunion deformity. The right big toe underrides the adjacent right second toe, producing a right hammertoe second deformity. As a result of the combined bunion and hammertoe deformities, the beneficiary's right second metatarsal head is pushed down, toward the sole of the foot, as the beneficiary stands and walks.

The lack of sensation in the beneficiary's foot due to the diabetic neuropathy combined with the downward pressure of the right second toe joint against the skin on the bottom of the foot resulted in ulceration of the skin under the right second toe joint. When first seen by Dr. Jones, the ulcer at the bottom of the right second toe joint was measured as 2 cm long, 1 cm wide, and 0.5 cm deep. Fortunately, the ulcer was not infected.

Dr. Jones fabricated custom shoe insoles (orthotics) from foam impressions of Mr. Smith's feet taken on October 10, 2017. Dr. Jones has also seen Mr. Smith for weekly debridement of the hard, calloused edges of the ulcer. Otherwise, the calloused margins of the ulcer would act like a hard, foreign body, further eroding and enlarging the margins of the ulcer.

On October 20, 2017, the custom shoe insoles (orthotics) were dispensed along with appropriately sized extra-depth shoes and examination revealed a good fit of both the orthotics and the shoes. Photos of Mr. Smith's feet, orthotics, and shoes were taken on October 20, 2017, and were submitted to the QIC. As of December 12, 2017, the ulcer was significantly smaller.

HOW WILL THE LEGAL FRAMEWORK SECTION OF THE PROPOSED DECISION BE WRITTEN?

76. Should you include a section on OMHA's Review Authority?

No. As stated above, the attorney advisor has a pull-down menu of paragraphs the ALJ wants to use for her written decisions.

77. As an example, what Medicare laws would be included in an appeal regarding diabetic therapeutic shoe services?

For diabetic therapeutic shoe services, the Principles of Law section would include sections of the LCD L33369 and sections from A52501 Medicare Policy Article. Some ALJs would include complete copies of both documents within the body of the written ALJ decision. We will simply summarize the L33369 and A52501 requirements as follows:

1. The beneficiary has diabetes mellitus.
2. The certifying physician has documented in the beneficiary's medical record one or more of the following conditions:

   a. Previous amputation of part or all of either foot; or
   b. History of previous ulceration of either foot; or
   c. History of pre-ulcerative calluses of either foot; or
   d. Peripheral neuropathy with callus formation on either foot; or
   e. Foot deformity of either foot; or
   f. Poor circulation in either foot; and
3. The Certifying Physician has certified that indications (1) and (2) are met and that he/she is treating the beneficiary under a comprehensive plan of care of his/her diabetes and that the beneficiary needs diabetic shoes.
   a. The Certifying Physician must have an in-person visit with the beneficiary during which diabetes management is addressed within six months prior to delivery of the shoes/inserts and must
   b. Sign the certification statement on or after the date of the in-person visit and within three months prior to the delivery of the therapeutic shoes/inserts.
4. Prior to selecting the specific items that will be provided, the supplier must conduct and document an in-person evaluation of the beneficiary.
5. At the time of an in-person delivery to the beneficiary of the items selected, the supplier must conduct an objective assessment of the fit of the shoe and inserts and document the results.

HOW SHOULD THE PROVIDER STRUCTURE THE ANALYSIS SECTION OF THE PROPOSED DECISION?

78. A letter brief was previously submitted to the QIC. How will you cite the patient care documents and standard-of-care policy statements to prove the denied service was medically reasonable and necessary?

If a letter brief was submitted to the QIC, you will write something like the following:

> *The patient care documents and the standard-of-care policy documents that were included as attachments to the letter brief previously submitted to the QIC will be cited in the following analysis. We will cite to the* ***same attachment numbers*** *used when these documents were submitted to the QIC. We will* ***not*** *attach identical copies of the same patient care documents and the same standard-of-care policy documents to this proposed decision.*

79. For our hypothetical diabetic therapeutic shoe service appeal, what documents were submitted to the QIC?

For our diabetic therapeutic shoe service example, we will use the hypothetical presented above in the findings of fact. We will assume the only documents submitted to the QIC, along with the reconsideration appeal request form, were copies of the patient's progress notes, clinical photographs of the patient's feet, and copies of the unanswered requests mailed by the provider to the internist for a "Statement of Certifying Physician for Therapeutic Shoes" form and for a copy of the internist's progress note from the last visit before the beneficiary's first visit with the provider.

80. What problems does our provider, Dr. Jones, have to deal with when the ALJ hearing is requested?

Dr. Jones has to deal with the absent "Statement of Certifying Physician for Therapeutic Shoes" document and the absent progress note(s) from the internist documenting the beneficiary has been under a comprehensive plan of care for his diabetes.

81. What would be the outcome of the appeal if Dr. Jones is silent regarding the missing documents?

If Dr. Jones does not address the missing documents when the hearing is requested and cannot answer the judge's questions during the hearing regarding the missing information, Dr. Jones will lose the ALJ appeal.

82. How should Dr. Jones address the missing documents/information issue?

Dr. Jones should convert the missing documents problem into an opportunity. Because the DME RAC has given notice of its intent to participate in the hearing as a party, Dr. Jones is allowed limited discovery under 405.1037.

When Dr. Jones receives notice of the DME RAC's intent to participate as a "party," Dr. Jones should send the ALJ a separate request that reads something like the following:

> *Dear Judge [last name],*
>
> *In good faith, I mailed Dr. White requests for the two missing documents required in the A52501 Medicare Policy Article: the "Statement of Certifying Physician for Therapeutic Shoes" form and the progress note from Dr. White's last visit with Mr. Smith prior to my first appointment with Mr. Smith. Copies of those mailed requests were submitted to the QIC. In bad faith, and apparently due to long-standing personal grievance, Dr. White failed to respond to either request.*
>
> *Because the DME RAC has based the demand for repayment of overpayment on these two missing documents, and because the DME RAC elected to be a party to the hearing, I am respectfully requesting limited discovery as allowed under 42 CFR § 405.1037. Specifically, I am requesting copies of the Medicare claim forms submitted by Dr. White for his office visits with Mr. Smith between January 1, 2016, and October 10, 2017. Those claim forms will include an ICD-10 code for type 2 diabetes and will support a finding by the Court that Mr. Smith is diabetic and was seen every four to five months between January 2016 and October 2017 for management of his diabetes.*
>
> *Sincerely,*
> *Roberta Jones, DPM*
> *Cc: DME RAC*
> *Cc: Mr. John Smith*

83. Would a provider know "limited discovery" is allowed when the MAC or other medical review contractor elects to be a party at the hearing?

Absolutely not. This is why providers need health care attorneys for ALJ appeals.

84. Will the request for limited discovery be sent with the proposed decision as a separate document?

No. The request for limited discovery cannot be sent until the DME RAC chooses to be a party to the hearing. And that won't happen until after the DME RAC is made aware of the appeal.

85. How will the provider write the analysis section of the proposed decision?

The provider's "analysis" for the proposed decision will read as follows. Remember, the analysis is different from the findings of fact above:

> *The documents submitted to the QIC by Dr. Jones included copies of two mail requests sent by Dr. Jones to Dr. White for a completed "Statement of Certifying Physician for Therapeutic Shoes" form and for a copy of Dr. White's progress notes from the most recent visit before Mr. Smith's first visit with Dr. Jones. Dr. White did not respond to either request.*
>
> *The progress notes submitted by Dr. Jones state Mr. John Smith was a "68-year-old, type 2 diabetic with previously diagnosed peripheral neuropathy" when first seen by Dr. Jones on October 10, 2017, for treatment of "an ulcer on the bottom of his right foot of approximately one month's duration." The authenticated clinical photographs submitted by Dr. Jones to the QIC reveal an ulcer on the bottom of Mr. Smith's right foot under the second ("metatarsal phalangeal") toe joint.*
>
> *The patient history obtained by Dr. Jones on October 10, 2017, reveals the diagnosis of diabetic peripheral neuropathy was made by Dr. White in 2016. The "diabetic peripheral neuropathy" diagnosis was then confirmed by Dr. Carol Thomas, a board-certified neurologist. A copy of Dr. Thomas's neurology consultation report was submitted to the QIC by Dr. Jones. In addition, at the initial office visit, Mr. Smith stated that while he is seen by Dr. White every four or five months for management of his diabetes, that Dr. White does not have Mr. Smith remove his shoes and socks for a foot exam when seen for his diabetes management visits.*
>
> *On October 10, 2017, Dr. Jones measured the ulcer on the bottom of the right second toe joint as "2 cm long, 1 cm wide, and 0.5 cm deep." Custom shoe insoles were fabricated and on October 20, 2017, the custom shoe insoles were dispensed along with appropriately sized extra-depth shoes. A November 20, 2017, photo demonstrated the ulcer was smaller in all dimensions.*
>
> *Based on Dr. Jones's patient care records, based on the neurological examination by Dr. Thomas in 2016, and based on the clinical photos taken at the initial office visit and on the day the shoes and orthotics were dispensed, the court concludes the beneficiary was a type 2 diabetic with diabetic neuropathy and a diabetic ulcer under the right second toe joint, and was being followed every four to five months by Dr. White for management of his diabetes when he was first seen by Dr. Jones on October 10, 2017.*
>
> *The record-keeping requirements in the Medicare article A52501 and in the LCD L33369 were written to make sure a beneficiary receiving diabetic therapeutic shoe services is diabetic, is being followed for management of the diabetes, has a qualifying condition for diabetic therapeutic shoe services, and that the diabetic therapeutic shoe services were provided as billed.*

In this case, two of the record-keeping forms were incomplete, resulting in the RAC demand for repayment of overpayment. However, the provider made best efforts to obtain the missing forms from the internist and it is the opinion of the Court that the intent of the Medicare rules regarding diabetic therapeutic shoe services have all been met. I am therefore finding in favor of the provider.

86. How will the ALJ's analysis incorporate the provider's analysis, the results of the limited discovery, and the testimony obtained from the hearing?

At the request of the DME RAC, the MAC sent Dr. Jones a demand for repayment of overpayment for the diabetic therapeutic shoe services provided for the beneficiary. The basis for the repayment demand was the absence of a "Statement of Certifying Physician for Therapeutic Shoes" form and the absence of a progress note from the certifying physician (Dr. White), demonstrating the beneficiary had been seen for diabetic management within six months prior to delivery of the diabetic therapeutic shoe service.

The documents submitted to the QIC by Dr. Jones included copies of two unanswered mail requests sent by Dr. Jones to Dr. White for a completed "Statement of Certifying Physician for Therapeutic Shoes" form and for a copy of Dr. White's progress notes from the most recent visit before Mr. Smith's first visit with Dr. Jones.

Upon receiving notice of the hearing, the DME RAC elected to be a party. Dr. Jones then submitted a request for limited discovery, asking for copies of the Medicare claim forms submitted by Dr. White for office visits with the beneficiary between January 1, 2016, and October 10, 2017. Dr. Jones stated the claim forms were relevant to prove the certifying physician's regular management of the beneficiary's diabetes at and before the time of the diabetic therapeutic shoe services.

Because the DME RAC elected to be a party to the hearing, because the documents requested by Dr. Jones were relevant to the hearing, and because the records show Dr. Jones made best efforts to obtain the missing documents from the certifying physician, Dr. Jones's request for limited discovery under 42 CFR §405.1037 was granted. Copies of those claim forms, provided by the Medicare Administrative Contractor, show the beneficiary was seen by Dr. White every four to five months between January 1, 2016, and October 10, 2017, for management of his diabetes. And every claim form submitted by Dr. White included the ICD-10 code E11.40 for type 2 diabetes with diabetic neuropathy.

The patient history obtained by Dr. Jones on October 10, 2017, also revealed the diagnosis of diabetic peripheral neuropathy was made by Dr. White in 2016. The "diabetic peripheral neuropathy" diagnosis was then confirmed by Dr. Carol Thomas, a board-certified neurologist. A copy of Dr. Thomas's neurology consultation report was submitted to the QIC by Dr. Jones.

Dr. Jones's October 10, 2017, progress note states Mr. John Smith was a "68-year-old, type 2 diabetic with previously diagnosed peripheral neuropathy" when he was first seen for treatment of the "ulcer on the bottom of his right foot of approximately one month's duration." The authenticated clinical photographs from the same date, submitted by Dr. Jones to the QIC, reveal an ulcer on the bottom of Mr. Smith's right foot under the second ("metatarsal phalangeal") toe joint.

During the video teleconference ALJ hearing, Dr. Jones referred to the beneficiary's X-rays and clinical photographs submitted to the QIC and explained as follows:

> *The beneficiary has a bunion deformity of the right foot. The right big toe underrides the adjacent right second toe—so the right second toe is forced to override the big toe. The resulting abnormal shape of the second toe, from a side view, is called a "hammertoe" deformity.*
>
> *As a result of the combined bunion and hammertoe deformities, the beneficiary's right second (metatarsal phalangeal) toe joint bony prominence is pushed down, toward the sole of the foot, as the beneficiary stands and walks.*
>
> *The lack of sensation in the beneficiary's foot due to the diabetic neuropathy combined with the downward pressure of the right second toe joint against the skin on the bottom of the foot resulted in ulceration of the skin under the second toe joint.*

On October 10, 2017, Dr. Jones measured the ulcer on the bottom of the right second toe joint as "2 cm long, 1 cm wide, and 0.5 cm deep." Custom shoe insoles were fabricated and on October 20, 2017, the custom shoe insoles were dispensed along with appropriately sized extra-depth shoes. A November 20, 2017, photo demonstrated the ulcer was smaller in all dimensions.

During the hearing, the DME RAC representative did not refute any of the statements made by Dr. Jones regarding her findings and/or treatment of the beneficiary.

Based on Dr. Jones's patient care records and photographs, based on the neurological examination by Dr. Thomas in 2016, and based on the claim forms submitted to Medicare by Dr. White for the beneficiary's office visits between January 1, 2016, and October 10, 2017, the court concludes the beneficiary was a type 2 diabetic with diabetic neuropathy and a diabetic ulcer under the right second toe joint, and was being followed every four to five months by Dr. White for management of his diabetes when he was first seen by Dr. Jones on October 10, 2017.

The record-keeping requirements in the Medicare article A52501 and in the LCD L33369 were written to make sure a beneficiary receiving diabetic therapeutic shoe services is diabetic, is being followed for management of the diabetes, has a qualifying condition for diabetic therapeutic shoe services, and that the diabetic therapeutic shoe services were provided as billed.

In this case, two of the record-keeping forms were incomplete, resulting in the RAC demand for a repayment of overpayment. However, the intent of the Medicare rules regarding diabetic therapeutic shoe services have all been met and the diabetic therapeutic shoe services, as billed, were provided. I am therefore finding in favor of the provider.

87. What did our example provider do wrong?

So many things!

When a service (e.g., diabetic therapeutic shoe services) or supply is listed as an "issue" on the A/B RAC or DME RAC website, you must have a detailed plan in place for that service or supply based on the assumption you will be targeted for a post-payment audit regarding that service or supply.

In the case of diabetic therapeutic shoe services, **NEVER EVER** provide these services until you have a completely filled out, signed, and dated Certifying Physician Statement in your hands. And always have the patient sign a release that allows you to get copies of the reports from the patient's other diabetes-related doctors (e.g., endocrinologists, neurologists, and vascular surgeons). Have your office call for copies of those reports the first day you see the patient.

88. Would a health care attorney working on a contingency fee basis put this kind of effort into a single diabetic therapeutic shoe service claim?
No!

89. Would a provider be willing to pay a health care attorney on an hourly basis for a single diabetic therapeutic shoe service claim?
No!

90. What about the situation where a provider is the target of an overpayment audit and submits medical records for several beneficiaries, but the total amount at issue is less than $5,000? For that amount of money, what's the point?
Most licensed medical providers have a rider on their medical malpractice policy that entitles them to at least $10,000 in attorneys' fees for representation in administrative actions. As the target of a DME RAC, repayment of overpayment audit, the provider would qualify for that representation.

91. Why should providers fight post-payment audits when the amount of money for the claim is small?
As an example, unless and until the providers fight and win hundreds if not thousands of ALJ hearings regarding diabetic therapeutic shoe services, Medicare will have zero motivation to change the requirements for diabetic therapeutic shoe services. And see the quote from the Medicare Program Integrity Manual on page 21 regarding overpayment audits.

92. How should the requirements for diabetic therapeutic shoe services be changed?
The provider should not have to produce documents from a third party, the "certifying physician," in order to be paid for the diabetic therapeutic shoe services.

93. If you are an attorney representing a provider, should you have the provider help you with the findings of fact and the analysis?
Yes. If you are an attorney representing a provider, the "findings of fact" and the "analysis" are two areas in which the provider should be involved. No matter how much you think you know about the beneficiary's medical problem, and no matter how much you think you know about the denied service, the provider knows more.

You may have to ask the provider to tell you the "story" several times, but it will be well worth it because you will learn things you will include in the letter brief, in the proposed decision, and in your direct examination of the provider and/or expert during the hearing you would otherwise miss.

WHEN THE PROVIDER REPRESENTS HERSELF AND WRITES THE PARTIAL PROPOSED DECISION . . .

94. Should a provider consider listing the Medicare requirements for a denied service in the exact order and language used by Medicare in the applicable LCD and/or Medicare article and, after each listed requirement, explain how that requirement was met?
Yes. You always want to make it easy for the ALJ to decide in your favor. And this formula approach makes it flat out simple for the provider to write the analysis and for the ALJ team to use the provider's analysis.

95. Can we summarize the most important points for providers doing their own appeals?

Yes.

- Use short, simple sentences.
- Make the beneficiary's medical findings of fact as brief as possible and use lay terms instead of medical terms whenever you can.
- Do not include the beneficiary's serious medical problems that are unrelated to the problem at issue.
- Make the findings of fact related to the denied service or supply as short and simple as possible but include the authorities that support the use of that service or supply under identical clinical circumstances.
- For the analysis, cite and include the actual Medicare LCD or Article rule that applies. Then reprint that rule, sentence by sentence, and start each new sentence of the rule on the following line.
- Go back and write in *italics* after each sentence of the rule how the requirements of that sentence were met, or why the requirements of that sentence should be overlooked in this case.
- If photographs of the beneficiary's problem were submitted to the QIC, direct the reader's attention to those photographs in the medical findings of fact.
- If even a one-page letter brief was submitted to the QIC, direct the reader's attention to that letter brief at the very beginning of the proposed decision.
- When the applicable LCD *supports* the denied treatment, your proposed decision should describe the beneficiary's problem in lay terms, your treatment of the beneficiary's problem, why you did what you did, and directly refer to the LCD sections that support your denied treatment.
- When the applicable LCD *prohibits* the denied treatment but the articles and textbooks cited in the LCD are old, and peer-reviewed articles and textbooks published before you provided the denied service support your treatment, tell the reader:

  The LCD policy was correct when originally published.

  However, the peer-reviewed journals and the versions of the LCD-cited textbooks published **before** the denied service was provided all support the denied treatment.

- You will distinguish the up-to-date publications—available before you provided the denied treatment—from the out-of-date publications relied upon by the contractor in the LCD and/or article.
- When the applicable LCD *prohibits* the denied treatment and the articles and textbooks cited in the LCD are *up-to-date* but there were **extenuating circumstances** that made your choice the better choice of treatment for the beneficiary on the date at issue, spend your time explaining the medicine and your choice of treatment in detail.
- By the time the ALJ's attorney advisor finishes reading your proposed decision, the attorney advisor has to "get it." Unless the attorney advisor understands what was wrong with the beneficiary, what you did and why you did it, and concludes your denied treatment was medically reasonable and necessary, you will not "get" a favorable decision.

20c

Extending the Time Limit for an ALJ Appeal

OUTLINE

1. Why do you have to get the ALJ appeal request in on time?
2. What should you do if you are up against the deadline to request an ALJ appeal?
3. If you are already a few weeks late, can you still submit a request for an extension of the time limit to submit the request for an ALJ appeal?
4. Why is it likely your request for an extension won't succeed?
5. If your request for an extension is granted, what then?
6. What is the bottom line regarding requests for ALJ appeals?

1. Why do you have to get the ALJ appeal request in on time?

You either get the ALJ appeal request in on time or your appeal is over unless you can prove to the ALJ that your appeal request is late because of reasons beyond your control. Maybe that will happen once or twice in your entire practice/business lifetime.

2. What should you do if you are up against the deadline to request an ALJ appeal?

If you are right up against the time limit for submitting the request for an ALJ appeal, fill out the OMHA-100 form and submit it by registered overnight mail to the ALJ office designated in the reconsideration denial letter.

3. If you are already a few weeks late, can you still submit a request for an extension of the time limit to submit the request for an ALJ appeal?

Yes. If you have already missed the time deadline to submit a request for an ALJ appeal but are only a few weeks late, under 405.1014(e)(1) you can request an extension for good cause. See 405.942(b)(2) and 405.942(b)(3).

A request for an extension of time must be in writing, must give the reasons why the request for a hearing was not filed within the stated time period, and must be filed with the entity specified in the notice of reconsideration.

4. Why is it likely your request for an extension won't succeed?

Unless you can prove you failed to file the request for an ALJ appeal for **reasons beyond your control**, the appeal is over.

5. If your request for an extension is granted, what then?

In the unlikely event the ALJ grants an extension of time for submission of the appeal, you are back in the game and will be allowed to file your request for an ALJ appeal.

6. What is the bottom line regarding requests for ALJ appeals?

Realistically, you have to get the ALJ appeal in **on time** or it's over.

20d

Fighting the Dismissal of an ALJ Appeal

OUTLINE

1. What happened?
2. Why was the ALJ appeal dismissed?
3. Why is it unlikely you will get an extension to file a request for an ALJ hearing?
4. What happens when the ALJ rejects your good cause excuse for a late-submitted appeal?

1. What happened?

Your ALJ appeal has been dismissed by the ALJ (405.1052).

2. Why was the ALJ appeal dismissed?

Your ALJ appeal was dismissed because:

- You failed to submit the ALJ hearing request **on time** (405.1052), and
- The ALJ has not found good cause for extending the time deadline as provided in 405.1014(c).

3. Why is it unlikely you will get an extension to file a request for an ALJ hearing?

You can find the requirements for a "good cause" extension of the deadline to file a request for an ALJ hearing in (405.942[b]). It should sound familiar when I tell you "circumstances beyond your control" are the only acceptable reasons for a late-submitted ALJ appeal.

4. What happens when the ALJ rejects your good cause excuse for a late-submitted appeal?

If the ALJ does not accept your good cause excuse for a late-submitted ALJ appeal request (see 405.1054), your appeal is over. And the dismissal of a request for an ALJ appeal is binding unless it is reversed by the Council under 405.1108(b).

20e

Reopening an ALJ Appeal

OUTLINE

1. How long do you have to ask the ALJ to reopen the ALJ hearing decision?
2. What is required to convince an ALJ to reopen the ALJ's decision?
3. What are the 405.986 good cause requirements to reopen?
4. What would be an example of "good cause"?
5. How frequently do ALJs reopen decisions?

1. How long do you have to ask the ALJ to reopen the ALJ hearing decision?

You are allowed to ask the ALJ to reopen the ALJ hearing decision within 180 calendar days from the date of the review decision for good cause in accordance with 405.980.

2. What is required to convince an ALJ to reopen the ALJ's decision?

You will have to prove "good cause" in accordance with 405.986 in order to get the ALJ to reopen the decision.

3. What are the 405.986 good cause requirements to reopen?

There is "good cause" to reopen the ALJ decision when:

- There is new and material evidence that was not available or known at the time of the decision and that
- May result in a different conclusion; or
- The evidence that was considered in making the decision clearly shows on its face that an obvious error was made at the time of the decision.

4. What would be an example of "good cause"?

An example of "good cause" would be an ALJ decision based on an earlier or later version of the applicable LCD that did not allow the service in question, while the LCD that was actually in effect at the time of the service did allow the service in question.

5. How frequently do ALJs reopen decisions?

I have yet to see an ALJ reopen a decision. But I have been successful in getting the Council to reopen an ALJ's decision and decide in my client's favor when the LCD example above applied.

20f

Presenting Your Case to the ALJ

OUTLINE

1. How should you "perform" as you present your case to the ALJ?
2. How much time has the ALJ set aside for your hearing?
3. If the hearing is by video teleconference (VTC), what should you wear?
4. How should you address the judge?
5. Do you need an outline for the hearing?
6. What will you do with the hearing outline?
7. How will the hearing proceed?
8. What happens after the judge identifies everyone in the room?
9. What should you do if the judge states your letter brief was compelling on the issues?
10. What should you do if the judge states the letter brief was compelling but gives no guidance as to what she wants to hear?
11. How can you decide what to present and what to discard *during* the hearing?
12. The judge asks if the beneficiaries will be responsible for the 20% co-pay. How should you respond?
13. If the judge does not bring up the 20% co-pay issue, should you?
14. Will the judge ask if you want to make an opening statement?
15. What should you do if the judge plows right into the hearing without asking if you want to make an opening statement?
16. What should your opening statement consist of?
17. If you sent a letter brief to the QIC and/or a proposed decision to the ALJ, how should you respond if the judge asks if you want to make an opening statement?
18. How should you proceed when the judge gives you permission to present your arguments?
19. Why should you go to the photographs immediately?
20. How should you finish the presentation of the photographs?
21. If no photos were submitted, how should you proceed?
22. How can you determine what your strongest piece of evidence is?
23. How do you get your presentation into near-perfect form?
24. How should you speak to the judge as you make the presentation?
25. What happens if the judge interrupts your presentation?
26. Is it okay to rephrase the judge's question before you answer her question?
27. But what if the judge's question reveals she is missing an important point?

28. What if you naturally speak quickly?
29. When is it okay to interrupt the judge when she is speaking?
30. What determines the outcome of the hearing, and how long will it take the judge to decide?
31. What will the judge ask you?
32. Is it okay to read your answers to the judge?
33. What is the difference between a perfect answer read to the judge and a conversational answer that is slightly incomplete?
34. How much emotion should you include in your oral presentation to the judge?
35. What do you do if the judge asks you a question you cannot answer?
36. What happens when an ALJ catches a provider in a lie?
37. What if you forget to tell the judge something important?
38. Do you need an assistant with access to a fax machine in the room with you?
39. What "standard of proof" applies to an ALJ hearing?
40. Is it okay to tell the judge which Medicare rules apply to your hearing?
41. Do you need an attorney for the hearing?
42. Instead of an attorney, how about a friend who is an "expert"?
43. You do not have an attorney. You do have an expert. What must you do before the hearing?
44. What should you do with your expert before the hearing?
45. Why is it a bad idea to ask your expert any new question during the hearing?
46. What if an issue has been discussed but is not yet checked off on your list of issues?
47. Should you ever begin your presentation to the judge with arguments not related to the QIC denial reasons?
48. Does a display of emotion help convince the judge your argument is the more correct of the two opposing arguments?
49. Can you attack the Medicare rule in your appeal for payment?
50. But what if the Medicare rule is wrong and that is the basis of your appeal?
51. Can you tell whether you have won or lost an ALJ hearing based on the judge's conduct during the hearing?

1. How should you "perform" as you present your case to the ALJ?

Be prepared, be humble, and be brief.

2. How much time has the ALJ set aside for your hearing?

The ALJ wants your hearing to last **no more than 30 minutes**, and the closer you can get to 15 minutes, the better. While your case is all important to you, your hearing is one of several the judge must get through during the day.

3. If the hearing is by video teleconference (VTC), what should you wear?

Dress as though you are going to Superior Court. This means a sport coat and tie for men and suitable corresponding clothes for women. The ALJs are all attorneys and whether they say so or not, they will be offended if you appear before them in a sweatshirt.

4. How should you address the judge?

You will always address the judge as "Your Honor."

5. Do you need an outline for the hearing?

Yes. When you start writing the outline for your hearing, it will consist of short paragraphs for each topic/part of the hearing. As you rehearse your presentation in front of a mirror, you will reduce the outline from a paragraph for each topic, to a sentence for each topic, to a phrase or word for each topic.

When the hearing outline is finished and the rehearsals are completed, the entire outline should fit on one side of one page, with each topic in large print—starting with the beginning topic at the top of the page and the ending topic at the bottom of the page.

6. What will you do with the hearing outline?

During the hearing, you will check off each topic as the topic is covered. When the judge interrupts your presentation with a question, you will leave the outline and answer whatever questions the judge has. When the judge allows you to return to your presentation, you will return to the last unchecked topic on your hearing outline and pick up where you left off.

In the heat of battle, it is very easy to lose track of where you are with your presentation. The one-page list of topics will allow you to cover all the important points you want to make during the hearing.

7. How will the hearing proceed?

On camera, the judge will take her seat at the judge's bench and, after identifying herself, will ask you to identify yourself and anyone else in the room with you. The judge will want everyone in the room with you in view of the camera. Please note:

I will use the pronoun "her" to describe the judge rather than writing "him/her" every time I refer to the judge.

I will use the term "provider" to mean the provider and/or the provider's attorney throughout the rest of this section.

I will use the term "service" to mean either a service or supply.

8. What happens after the judge identifies everyone in the room?

The judge will make some introductory remarks for the record, such as the date, the case number, and so on. The judge will then swear in the provider and any witness(es).

9. What should you do if the judge states your letter brief was compelling on the issues?

If the judge tells you, during opening remarks, that she found your letter brief to be compelling/convincing on the issues, **do not torture her** by sticking with your predetermined outline for the hearing. Ask the judge to give you guidance as to what the Court would like to hear, if anything, regarding the issues before the Court. Do not wrestle defeat from the jaws of victory.

10. What should you do if the judge states the letter brief was compelling but gives no guidance as to what she wants to hear?

If the judge says your letter brief or proposed decision was compelling/convincing but then gives you no guidance as to what she would like to hear, stick with your outline but eliminate everything other than the most important facts supporting the denied service and the most important facts that refute the denial reasons.

11. How can you decide what to present and what to discard *during* the hearing?

You can't. So, use a yellow highlighter **before the hearing** to mark the topics on your outline that will be presented at hearing if the judge tells you your letter brief was incredibly persuasive but then gives you no guidance as to what she would like to hear.

12. The judge asks if the beneficiaries will be responsible for the 20% co-pay. How should you respond?

At the beginning of the hearing, the judge will ask the provider about the 20% co-pay each beneficiary will have to pay in the event of a favorable decision. The judge will have to protect the beneficiaries to a greater extent if you are going to bill the co-pays because the beneficiaries are (usually) not present at the hearing. The judge will be more relaxed if you tell her you will not bill the co-pays. But whichever way you go with this, you should decide on your answer before the hearing starts.

As a general rule, I think you should always tell the judge you are going to bill the 20% co-pay in the event of a favorable decision. There is no reason to give up 20% of the already reduced, Medicare-allowed amount on every denied claim you appeal. And I don't think an ALJ decision ever hinges on your decision regarding the 20% co-pay.

13. If the judge does not bring up the 20% co-pay issue, should you?

No.

14. Will the judge ask if you want to make an opening statement?

Maybe, maybe not.

15. What should you do if the judge plows right into the hearing without asking if you want to make an opening statement?

It depends on the judge's opening remarks.

The best argument **against** an opening statement is that the ALJ read your case file the previous night and shouldn't be bored with having to listen to what she already knows. If the judge says something like: "*Okay, I know this case is about [whatever the case is about] and I know the service was denied because [the reason the service/supply was denied],*" there is no reason to make an opening statement.

The best argument **in favor** of an opening statement is that the ALJs are swamped with cases so you should think about using a one-minute opening statement to summarize what the dispute is about and what you are going to prove during the hearing. If the judge says anything like: "*Okay, what is this case about?*" then you absolutely want to make an opening statement. And without saying you are going to make an opening statement, you will make an opening statement.

16. What should your opening statement consist of?

If you decide to make an opening statement, keep it under a minute and in plain English tell the ALJ the short version of what service was provided, why it was denied, and what you are going to present at the hearing in support of the service.

The purpose of the opening statement is to bring the judge up to speed so you can present your case without the judge looking like she is completely lost.

17. If you sent a letter brief to the QIC and/or a proposed decision to the ALJ, how should you respond if the judge asks if you want to make an opening statement?

Your Honor, if the court received a copy of the letter brief (sent to the QIC for the reconsideration appeal) and/or the proposed decision, then I [the plaintiff—you] would like to present my arguments in favor of payment without making an opening statement.

Do not ask the judge if she has read your letter brief or your proposed decision. That would be insulting. You have to assume, if the judge says she has received a copy of the letter brief, that she has read it. If the judge has read the letter brief and/or proposed decision, an opening statement would be a waste of the judge's time.

18. How should you proceed when the judge gives you permission to present your arguments?

If you previously submitted photographs of the patient's problem, I would recommend going to the photographs immediately. Tell the judge the page number of the first photograph in the letter brief you want the judge to look at and wait until she has the photograph in front of her. Then, walk the judge through the photographs, describing the nature of the patient's problem, the patient's symptoms, the relationship of the patient's problem to any systemic disease, exactly what you did for the patient on the date of service at issue, why you did it, and how you know it was the correct thing to do.

19. Why should you go to the photographs immediately?

The judge will pay complete attention as you explain what the photographs reveal. As long as your explanation is simple, straightforward, and obvious, this is your best chance at winning a favorable decision.

20. How should you finish the presentation of the photographs?

You will finish your argument by referencing the articles and authorities that support your statements about the clinical findings revealed by the photographs. Hopefully, copies of those articles and authorities were included with your letter brief. But remember, you are telling the judge a story as you use the photographs.

21. If no photos were submitted, how should you proceed?

Go to your strongest piece of evidence first. As examples:

If the denial was based on a missing required document but the obvious purpose of that document was met, show how the purpose of the document was met.

If the LCD "indication" requirement was out of date when the denied service was provided, show how the recognized authorities supported the denied service.

If medical circumstances supported the denied service over Medicare's choice of service, put the judge in the treatment room and explain why the denied service was a safer, and/or more effective (and hopefully, less expensive) choice for the beneficiary.

22. How can you determine what your strongest piece of evidence is?

Put yourself in the position of the judge. What is the one question that must be answered to the judge's satisfaction to get a favorable decision? The evidence that provides that answer is your strongest evidence.

23. How do you get your presentation into near-perfect form?

Practice the presentation at home in front of a mirror. Outline everything you want to say in the order you want to say it. Reduce the outline from whole sentences to phrases to words as you practice. This will enable you to say what you have to say in a conversational tone. Practice the presentation four or five times and keep it under two minutes.

24. How should you speak to the judge as you make the presentation?

Be yourself. Talk to the judge as though you are talking to a smart patient. Use plain English and watch the judge's response as she listens to you and looks at the pictures. If the judge is frowning, stop and ask the judge if she has a question about what you are saying or about what she is looking at.

25. What happens if the judge interrupts your presentation?

It is likely the judge will interrupt you to ask one or more questions before you are finished with your two-minute presentation. Place a check mark on your outline in front of you so you can pick up where you left off after you answer the judge's question.

26. Is it okay to rephrase the judge's question before you answer her question?

No! It is not okay. Answer the question the judge is asking.

And think about the judge's question before you answer. But do not answer the question you think she should be asking. Always answer the actual question she is asking.

27. But what if the judge's question reveals she is missing an important point?

After you answer the judge's question and she allows you to return to your presentation, that would be the time to rephrase the judge's earlier question so you can say what you want to say on the subject.

28. What if you naturally speak quickly?

Not good. Speak slowly. Watch any news show and concentrate on the speed of the person delivering the news. They always speak slowly and deliberately and that is how you should speak during the hearing.

29. When is it okay to interrupt the judge when she is speaking?

Never. The judge can and will interrupt you, but you are NEVER EVER to interrupt the judge when she is speaking. When the judge is speaking, you are silent. Period.

30. What determines the outcome of the hearing, and how long will it take the judge to decide?

In most cases, your letter brief/proposed decision and the first two minutes of the hearing will determine the outcome of the appeal.

You may be upset to read this, but the outcome of most jury trials is determined by the time the opposing attorneys have finished their opening statements—before a shred of evidence has been presented. If your letter brief/proposed decision presents a convincing argument supported by appropriate medical sources, and your two-minute, common-sense presentation rings true to the judge, chances are you will win.

31. What will the judge ask you?

Assume the judge has read your brief before the hearing. And the judge will read it if the letter part of the brief is no longer than three pages. Then pretend you are the judge and make a list of the questions you would ask a provider/supplier appearing before you regarding the same denial. This isn't tricky. The judge wants to know if your service was "medically reasonable and necessary," whether your service was "experimental or investigative," and why she should find in your favor if the service was prohibited in the LCD. Therefore, you want to prepare for the hearing by writing out short answers to the following questions:

- Why was the service medically reasonable?
- Why was the service medically necessary?
- If the contractor said the service was "experimental or investigative," why do you say it wasn't?
- If the contractor's LCD prohibits the service you provided, why should the judge allow it?

You also want to make a list of every other denial reason offered by the contractor or the QIC, and you want to write out a short response to each of those denial reasons.

32. Is it okay to read your answers to the judge?

Absolutely not. As soon as you start reading, the judge will stop paying attention to what you are saying. The hearing is a conversation between you and the judge. Think about it. If you are debating a topic with someone and they start reading something from a piece of paper, are you still paying attention? Of course not. And the judge is not going to pay attention to whatever you are reading, either.

33. What is the difference between a perfect answer read to the judge and a conversational answer that is slightly incomplete?

A conversational explanation that is slightly incomplete beats a stilted, read-from-a-piece-of-paper explanation every time.

34. How much emotion should you include in your oral presentation to the judge?

None.

35. What do you do if the judge asks you a question you cannot answer?

If the judge asks you a question you cannot answer, tell her you do not know the answer but will respond with a written answer to the question within one day (if the judge wants you to). But do not wing it.

And remember, it's okay not to know the answer to a question.

36. What happens when an ALJ catches a provider in a lie?

When an ALJ catches a provider intentionally misrepresenting a fact, the provider will not only lose the hearing, the provider will forever lose credibility with the judge. And it is likely the judge will share the experience with the other ALJs in her regional office.

No matter how much money is at stake in a case, never, ever lie to an ALJ.

37. What if you forget to tell the judge something important?

You can send the judge a post-hearing letter with the missing information. But don't forget to copy the other parties to the hearing (the beneficiaries and the MAC or other Medicare review contractor) with the missing information letter.

And unless the missing information is so important that you think it will determine the outcome of the hearing, don't send it.

38. Do you need an assistant with access to a fax machine in the room with you?

Have an assistant—who can fax any needed document to the ALJ during the hearing—in the room with you during the hearing. Be sure to tell the judge at the beginning of the hearing that the assistant is in the room with you.

39. What "standard of proof" applies to an ALJ hearing?

Supposedly, you have to prove you should be paid by a "preponderance of the evidence." This means you must prove it is 51% more likely **you** are correct, as opposed to 49% the MAC (or the RAC, CERT, UPIC, or SMRC) and the QIC are correct.

Is it ever that close? No. The judge will want a comfortable margin.

Why? The judge does not want to be overruled by the Council in the event the contractor appeals the ALJ decision.

40. Is it okay to tell the judge which Medicare rules apply to your hearing?

No. Do not tell the ALJ which Medicare rules (laws) apply to your hearing. The judge will stop listening as soon as you start down that path. The only thing the judge wants to hear from you is why the denied treatment was medically reasonable and necessary.

41. Do you need an attorney for the hearing?

If you think you need an expert—because there is so much money at stake, because the issues are complex, because you are too nervous to represent yourself—consider having a health care attorney represent you at the hearing.

42. Instead of an attorney, how about a friend who is an "expert"?

Okay. Don't worry about it. The judge will qualify the expert before the expert testifies and the judge will ask the expert whatever the judge wants to know.

43. You do not have an attorney. You do have an expert. What must you do before the hearing?

You must send the judge and the other parties **a copy of the expert's curriculum vitae** (résumé) before the hearing. Do not show up at hearing with an unannounced expert. Judges don't like that.

44. What should you do with your expert before the hearing?

Write out all the questions you want to ask your expert in front of the ALJ. Then write out all the answers to those questions. And review all the questions and answers with your expert before the hearing.

45. Why is it a bad idea to ask your expert any new question during the hearing?

You may not like the answer. Most health care attorneys will tell you they never ask their expert a question during an ALJ hearing if they don't already know the answer to the question.

46. What if an issue has been discussed but is not yet checked off on your list of issues?

Do not waste the court's time by covering issues that have already been addressed in response to the judge's questions.

47. Should you ever begin your presentation to the judge with arguments not related to the QIC denial reasons?

No. Do not begin the letter brief or your presentation to the judge with arguments not related to the QIC denial reasons. Whether the judge is reading your letter brief or is listening to your oral argument during hearing, she will be focused on the QIC denial reasons. You want to be focused on the same thing the judge is focused on.

48. Does a display of emotion help convince the judge your argument is the more correct of the two opposing arguments?

No. And the ALJ does not want drama. You may be outraged by the conduct of the carrier and the QIC but the ALJ will only be outraged if you start behaving emotionally. The ALJ is simply doing her job and will be very annoyed by an emotionally charged presentation.

49. Can you attack the Medicare rule in your appeal for payment?

No. The law is never at issue. If you are arguing the "law" is wrong, you have already lost the argument and the appeal. Instead, you will be arguing that the Medicare rule has been misinterpreted or misapplied.

50. But what if the Medicare rule is wrong and that is the basis of your appeal?

Here is an example of something you can say when the Medicare rule, usually an LCD rule, is wrong: *"The ALJ should decline to follow the contractor's interpretation of the LCD for the claim at issue. However, the appellant is not asking the ALJ to set aside or review the validity of the LCD for the purpose of this appeal."*

51. Can you tell whether you have won or lost an ALJ hearing based on the judge's conduct during the hearing?

Not usually. I have received favorable decisions from ALJs who were aggressive and surly throughout the hearing and I have received unfavorable decisions from ALJs who were charming and positive throughout the hearing.

20g

Other Things You Need to Know About ALJ Hearings

OUTLINE

1. What can you do when the same judge is assigned to your hearings and that judge always rules against you?
2. Does the ALJ rely on redetermination and reconsideration denial reasons?
3. Does the de novo status of the ALJ hearing affect your preparation for the hearing and your presentation to the ALJ?
4. Is the ALJ hearing really a de novo hearing?
5. What will the proposed decision do?
6. Are the ALJs under pressure to deny payments?
7. Can CMS and/or your MAC participate as a "party" or as a "nonparty" participant in your ALJ hearing?
8. Can CMS *and* one or more of its medical review contractors (MAC, RAC, CERT, UPIC, or SMRC) elect to be "parties" to your ALJ hearing?
9. Can CMS and one or more of its medical review contractors (MAC, RAC, CERT, UPIC, or SMRC) elect to be "nonparty participants" to your ALJ hearing?
10. When should a provider have legal representation at an ALJ hearing?
11. Why is it a bad idea to represent yourself when a medical review contractor is a party to your hearing or is a nonparty participant to your hearing?
12. When CMS and/or the contractor participates as a nonparty participant, what can CMS and/or the contractor do, and what are they not allowed to do?
13. What should you do if the MAC, RAC, CERT, SMRC, or UPIC is a nonparty participant but still tries to cross-examine you or your witness during the hearing?
14. What should you do if CMS, as a nonparty participant, submits articles or textbooks to the ALJ to support the contractor's position?
15. When are you most likely to hear that CMS, as a nonparty participant, has submitted articles or textbooks to the ALJ to support the contractor's position?
16. What does "ex parte" mean?
17. What obligations do you have regarding ex parte communications with the ALJ?
18. Do you have to send a copy of the letter brief to the MAC?
19. What can the MAC, RAC, CERT, SMRC, or UPIC do as a party participant?
20. Does a MAC have to get permission from CMS before the MAC can elect to participate in your ALJ hearing as a party?
21. Does a MAC have to get permission from CMS before the MAC elects to be a nonparty participant in an ALJ hearing?

22. Why would a contractor ever choose to participate as a nonparty participant?
23. What does it mean when two or more Medicare entities are participating in your hearing?
24. Is it likely the medical review contractors will participate in more hearings in the future?
25. What are the issues that drive the decision by CMS and/or the MAC to participate as a party or as a nonparty participant?
26. What is the most important issue when CMS and/or the contractor decide to participate in an ALJ hearing?
27. What must CMS and/or the MAC do if they want to participate as a nonparty or as a party?
28. What should you do when CMS and/or the contractor miss the deadline to give notice of participation?
29. Does CMS or the MAC have to give notice of intent to participate in order to send the ALJ a position paper?
30. When CMS or the MAC "submits" a position paper to the ALJ, is CMS or the MAC required to "send" a copy of the position paper to you?
31. Assuming you receive a position paper five days before the hearing, is that enough time to prepare a response?
32. How can you prevent CMS or the MAC from ambushing you with a position paper sent only to the ALJ?
33. Why am I spending time on position papers sent by CMS or, more likely, the MAC to the ALJ?

As of August 2017, more than **$6.5 billion** in claims were tied up in pending appeals, and appeals were taking an average of over **1,000 days** to process (from the date of the request for an appeal to the date of the judge's published decision).

1. What can you do when the same judge is assigned to your hearings and that judge always rules against you?

In 5 U.S.C. Section 3105, it states (in summary): "Administrative law judges shall be assigned to cases **in rotation.**" Emphasis added. Because health care attorneys representing other providers and suppliers know who the problem judges are, and because those attorneys will complain to the supervising ALJ about that judge, it is the unrepresented provider or supplier who will be assigned that judge.

When you are assigned to the same ALJ over and over again and that judge consistently denies payment, there is something you can do about it. Call the regional ALJ office, find out who the supervising ALJ is, and write a letter to the supervising ALJ asking to have your cases rotated as required under 5 U.S.C. Section 3105. Chances are, you won't see that problem ALJ for a long time.

2. Does the ALJ rely on redetermination and reconsideration denial reasons?

No. ALJ hearings are "de novo" hearings. See 405.1000. A de novo hearing means your case is being tried before the ALJ as if it had not been heard before, and as if no decision had been previously rendered. A de novo hearing means the ALJ weighs all of the evidence in your case and comes to a decision based on her own findings.

3. Does the de novo status of the ALJ hearing affect your preparation for the hearing and your presentation to the ALJ?

Of course it does. You have to make sure the ALJ has all the relevant evidence in front of her at the time of the hearing, and this means you have to include all of the relevant evidence (patient care records, photographs, etc.) in the letter brief to the QIC.

In addition, you have to compact the entire letter brief into a two-minute presentation that takes the form of a story. The letter brief and the two-minute presentation will determine the outcome of the hearing.

4. Is the ALJ hearing really a de novo hearing?

Of course not. The ALJ isn't starting from scratch. Without exaggeration, each ALJ has thousands of backlogged cases because the federal government has not hired the number of ALJs needed to process all the Medicare appeals in a timely manner. As a result, the starting point for the ALJ is the list of denial reasons offered by the contractor and the QIC. Unless you submit a proposed decision along with the request for the ALJ hearing, the contractor and the QIC get to frame the dispute and the ALJ will expect you to prove the contractor's and the QIC's denial reasons are wrong.

5. What will the proposed decision do?

The proposed decision will result in the ALJ team (the ALJ's attorney advisor and the ALJ) reading your side of the dispute before they read Medicare's version of the dispute.

6. Are the ALJs under pressure to deny payments?

Yes. The ALJs are under pressure from the Office of the Inspector General (OIG) to deny the claims that have been denied by the contractors and the QICs. See the OIG article "Improvements Are Needed at the Administrative Law Judge Level of Medicare Appeals" at https://oig.hhs.gov/oei/reports/oei-02-10-00340.pdf. Basically, the OIG is critical of the ALJs for failing to adhere strictly to Medicare rules.

Thankfully, the ALJs are independent of CMS. And the ALJs know CMS and contractor BS when they smell it. The ALJs also know CMS and the contractors have a big advantage by being able to frame the dispute with their denial reasons that are published against the backdrop of Medicare articles and contractor LCDs. The ALJ hearing may be a de novo hearing, but only after CMS and the contractor have already been given a big head start.

7. Can CMS and/or your MAC participate as a "party" or as a "nonparty" participant in your ALJ hearing?

Yes. See 405.1010 and 405.1012.

8. Can CMS *and* one or more of its medical review contractors (MAC, RAC, CERT, UPIC, or SMRC) elect to be "parties" to your ALJ hearing?

No. Medicare is allowed to send only **one party** to your hearing. See 405.1012(d)(1).

9. Can CMS and one or more of its medical review contractors (MAC, RAC, CERT, UPIC, or SMRC) elect to be "nonparty participants" to your ALJ hearing?

Yes. See 405.1012(d)(1).

10. When should a provider have legal representation at an ALJ hearing?

If the Medicare Administrative Contractor is the Medicare "party" to your hearing, you may choose to represent yourself and that's okay.

If one of the other Medical Review Contractors is the Medicare "party" to your hearing, you are crazy to represent yourself. Medicare may be coming after you.

If the MAC is the Medicare "party" to your hearing, and one or more of the other Medical Review Contractors are nonparty participants to your hearing, you are very crazy to represent yourself. Medicare is coming after you.

11. Why is it a bad idea to represent yourself when a medical review contractor is a party to your hearing or is a nonparty participant to your hearing?

When a RAC, CERT, UPIC, or SMRC representative is at your hearing, you should assume they are looking at more than the claims at issue. You should assume they are looking at you—and not in a good way.

The last thing you want to do is become a target for one or more of the medical review contractors.

The first thing you want to do is to win cleanly and convincingly in front of the ALJ. You do not want the Medical Review Contractors thinking they should keep an eye on you in the future.

12. When CMS and/or the contractor participates as a nonparty participant, what can CMS and/or the contractor do, and what are they not allowed to do?

When CMS and or the contractor participate as **nonparty** participants, under 405.1010, CMS and/or the contractor:

- Can file position papers with the ALJ or provide testimony to clarify factual or policy issues in a case, but
- Cannot call witnesses or cross-examine (question) the provider's witness and
- Cannot submit evidence (articles, textbooks, etc.) to the ALJ supporting their position.

13. What should you do if the MAC, RAC, CERT, SMRC, or UPIC is a nonparty participant but still tries to cross-examine you or your witness during the hearing?

You will object to the ALJ. For example, you would say something like the following.

> *Your Honor, the contractor is a nonparty participant in this hearing and does not have the right to cross-examine me (or my witness). Please instruct the contractor to stop this prohibited behavior.*

14. What should you do if CMS, as a nonparty participant, submits articles or textbooks to the ALJ to support the contractor's position?

If CMS or the ALJ gives you notice of the submission of articles or textbooks by CMS to the ALJ before the hearing, you will send the judge a written objection. Here is an example of a written objection:

> *Your Honor, the contractor is a nonparty participant and is not allowed to submit evidence supporting the contractor's position. Please delete the contractor's submitted article from the case file and please instruct the contractor to stop this prohibited behavior.*

15. When are you most likely to hear that CMS, as a nonparty participant, has submitted articles or textbooks to the ALJ to support the contractor's position?

It is likely you will **not** hear about the articles until CMS (the contractor, RAC, CERT, SMRC, or UPIC) starts talking about the articles during the hearing. In that case you should object as follows:

Your Honor, CMS (e.g., the contractor) is a nonparty participant in this hearing. As a nonparty participant, the contractor is prohibited from submitting evidence supporting its position. However, the contractor has not only submitted prohibited evidence, but has also done this "ex parte." I am respectfully asking you to delete the prohibited article from the case file and am requesting the court give no weight to the other documents submitted by the contractor. This request is reasonable because the contractor was aware of its unlawful conduct at the time the contractor submitted the prohibited article.

16. What does "ex parte" mean?

"Ex parte" means the contractor has illegally communicated with the judge without giving you notice. In this case, the ex parte communication is made much worse because the subject of the communication was an illegal document and the contractor knew it was illegal when it was submitted.

17. What obligations do you have regarding ex parte communications with the ALJ?

You have exactly the same obligations CMS and the contractors have. Any communication you have with the ALJ must be shared with the other parties.

18. Do you have to send a copy of the letter brief to the MAC?

No. You do not have to send the contractor a copy of the letter brief that you sent to the QIC because that letter brief will be included in the case file sent to the ALJ, and the contractor has a right to see everything in the case file.

19. What can the MAC, RAC, CERT, SMRC, or UPIC do as a party participant?

In 405.1012, it says that CMS and/or the contractor may participate as **party** participants. As a party participant, CMS and/or the contractor:

1. Can file position papers with the ALJ or provide testimony to clarify factual or policy issues in a case.
2. Can call witnesses or cross-examine the appellant's witnesses.
3. Can submit evidence (articles, textbooks, etc.) to the ALJ supporting their position.

20. Does a MAC have to get permission from CMS before the MAC can elect to participate in your ALJ hearing as a party?

Yes.

21. Does a MAC have to get permission from CMS before the MAC elects to be a nonparty participant in an ALJ hearing?

No.

22. Why would a contractor ever choose to participate as a nonparty participant?

A contractor may decide to allow the RAC to be a party participant while the contractor is a nonparty participant.

23. What does it mean when two or more Medicare entities are participating in your hearing?

As a general rule, if you have two or more Medicare entities participating in your hearing, you are absolutely in their crosshairs.

24. Is it likely the medical review contractors will participate in more hearings in the future?

Yes. As CMS tightens up on payments, the contractors will participate in more ALJ hearings.

25. What are the issues that drive the decision by CMS and/or the MAC to participate as a party or as a nonparty participant?

According to the Medicare Change Request 8501, these are the issues CMS and the contractor look at in deciding whether to participate in an ALJ hearing:

- The policy implications in the case
- The amount of money at issue
- The source of the denial
- Program integrity matters in the case
- The extent to which the case is about a recurring issue

26. What is the most important issue when CMS and/or the contractor decide to participate in an ALJ hearing?

The amount of money is, of course, the most important issue. When a small amount of money is at issue, CMS and the contractor will not show up at a hearing.

27. What must CMS and/or the MAC do if they want to participate as a nonparty or as a party?

If CMS or the contractor decide to participate as party participants or as nonparty participants, they must notify the ALJ and the appellant within ten calendar days of receiving the notice of hearing that they intend to participate in the hearing. But very frequently, CMS and or the contractor fail to notify the ALJ and/or the provider within the required ten calendar days after CMS and/or the contractor receive notice of the hearing.

28. What should you do when CMS and/or the contractor miss the deadline to give notice of participation?

If CMS and/or the contractor decide to participate as 405.1010 nonparty participants or as 405.1012 party participants, but fail to notify the ALJ or you of their intent to participate within ten calendar days of receiving the notice of hearing, here is what you should do.

You will object on the record at the beginning of the hearing to the participation of CMS and/or the contractor. Here is what you should say:

> *Your Honor, I object to the participation of [the name of your MAC and/or the name of the Medical Review Contractor] in this hearing. I am also asking the court to reject any evidence submitted for this hearing by [the name of your MAC and/or the name of the Medical Review Contractor]. I received late notice [or I received no notice] of their participation before the*

hearing. Sections 405.1010 and 405.1012 state CMS and/or the contractor were required to notify me no later than ten calendar days after receiving the notice of hearing that they intended to be a party. They failed to notify me within the required ten days.

If you lose the ALJ hearing decision, you will appeal to the Council, asking the Council to return the case to the ALJ for a second hearing with instructions to the ALJ to deny CMS and/or the contractor the right to take part in the hearing either as a party or as a nonparty participant and for the ALJ to ignore any documents previously submitted to the ALJ by CMS and/or the contractor.

29. Does CMS or the MAC have to give notice of intent to participate in order to send the ALJ a position paper?

Sections 405.1010 and 405.1012 suggest the answer to this question is "no." These CFR sections state CMS or the contractor have to give notice of intent to participate in the hearing as a party, but these CFR sections say nothing about the mere submission of a position paper to the ALJ.

30. When CMS or the MAC "submits" a position paper to the ALJ, is CMS or the MAC required to "send" a copy of the position paper to you?

Technically, yes. But the verbs "submit" and "send" have very different meanings. Sections 405.1010 and 405.1012 both state any position paper written by CMS or a contractor must be "**submitted**" to the ALJ at least five days before the hearing.

Sections 405.1010 and 405.1012 both state any position paper written by CMS or a contractor must be "**sent**" to you at least five days before the hearing. This means any position paper written by CMS or a contractor doesn't even have to reach you before the hearing. It just means CMS or a contractor have to be able to prove they sent you a copy of the position paper at least five days before the hearing.

31. Assuming you receive a position paper five days before the hearing, is that enough time to prepare a response?

Are you kidding? This is hearing by ambush. Let's assume your hearing is on a Monday. If you receive the position paper(s) before the end of business on the Wednesday of the previous week, is that enough time to prepare? Come on. And remember, according to these code sections, CMS and its contractors are not even required to get their position papers to you before the hearing.

32. How can you prevent CMS or the MAC from ambushing you with a position paper sent only to the ALJ?

Two weeks before the hearing, contact the ALJ's assistant. Ask the ALJ's assistant to contact you immediately if CMS or the contractor submits a position paper or any other evidence to the ALJ, and ask the assistant to send you copies of the position paper or other evidence sent to the ALJ by CMS or the contractor. Simultaneously, send the ALJ's assistant an identical written request by email. And in the body of the email, ask the ALJ's assistant to acknowledge receipt of the email by return email the same day.

33. Why am I spending time on position papers sent by CMS or, more likely, the MAC to the ALJ?

I have never once received a copy of a position paper sent to the ALJ by a contractor.

21

Medicare Appeals Council Appeals

42 CFR Sections 405.1100–405.1140

Unless the ALJ has denied payment based on an **obviously incorrect interpretation of the applicable LCD policy** regarding the denied treatment, don't bother appealing to the Council. The Council judges will support any lower-level denial of payment—if there is **any** reasonable basis for the denial. For example, even if you can prove the denied service was safer, more effective, and less expensive for the beneficiary than the LCD-indicated service, you will lose.

On the other hand, if the contractor, the QIC, and the ALJ have all applied the LCD policy in an obviously incorrect manner, then you absolutely should appeal to the Council.

Use Medicare form DAB-101 and follow the instructions very carefully. Have a person good with details review your appeal before you send it. The Council judges will not tolerate any departure from the instructions.

Along with the completed DAB-101 form, send the Council a letter (see 405.1120) that explains exactly how and why the ALJ incorrectly applied the LCD policy regarding the denied service. Again, the error will have to be obvious in order to succeed in a Council appeal.

For example, if the contested service was allowed, according to the LCD in effect at the time the service was provided, but the service was not allowed in a later version of the LCD—and the ALJ mistakenly applied the later LCD policy—the Council judges will find in your favor (assuming all other requirements are met).

Send your Medicare Appeals Council appeal to:

Department of Health and Human Services
Department Appeals Board
Medicare Appeals Council, MS 6127
Cohen Building Room G-644
330 Independence Ave., S.W.
Washington, D.C. 20201

Attach a copy of the ALJ decision to the request for the Council appeal. Be sure to send copies of the Council appeal by proof of delivery to the Medicare beneficiaries whose claims are being appealed.

You may not get a decision from the Council for almost two years.

22

Medicare Audits

OUTLINE

1. Can a provider (provider/supplier) just ignore a Medicare audit?
2. Can a provider always appeal the results of a Medicare audit?
3. How are Medicare audits appealed?
4. At what level of appeal is a provider most likely to win?
5. Who performs Medicare audits?
6. How does Medicare refer to these outside auditing companies?
7. How can you find the names, the contact information, and a description of the services provided by each of the medical review contractors for your area?
8. How many medical review contractors is a provider who engages in some DME services exposed to?
9. How many MACs, RACs, UPICs, CERTs, and SMRCs are there nationwide?
10. What do all the medical review contractors have in common?
11. Where can you find a "complete" list of the reasons why Medicare has decided your medically reviewed claim(s) should not be paid?
12. What does Medicare say about its goal of "lowering the improper payment rate"?
13. What does "CMS strives in every case to pay the right amount to a legitimate provider, for covered, correctly coded and correctly billed services" mean?
14. What is the "CMS strategy for the past"?
15. What are the different types of claim reviews used by the RACs?
16. What kind of simple claim review is used by the RACs?
17. Do a lot of RAC-discovered improper payments come through data mining?
18. How do the RACs perform complex claim review?
19. What percentage of RAC-discovered improper payments come through complex review?
20. Are the RACs allowed to blanket-review any service they want to?
21. Are all the medical review contractors paid in the same manner?
22. What is the "CMS strategy for the present"?
23. What is the "CMS strategy for the future"?
24. What is a MAC?

25. How many different types of MACs are there?
26. Who are the MACs?
27. What "administrative" services are performed by the MACs?
28. What does "the MACs process (pay or deny all submitted) claims" mean?
29. How do the MACs initially process claims?
30. What does the statement "the MACs, on their own, investigate suspected overpayments" mean?
31. What is "complex medical review" of a claim?
32. Can you ignore an ADR letter?
33. What happens if you ignore an ADR request?
34. What does "the MACs demand repayment of overpayments revealed by their own investigations" mean?
35. What does "the MACs demand repayment of overpayments upon request by the RACs, the CERT, and the SMRC" mean?
36. Do the MACs, the RACs, the CERT, and the SMRC all find the same numbers of overpayments?
37. Are demands for repayment of overpayment ever sent to a provider by a RAC, the CERT, or the SMRC?
38. How should a provider view the MACs' "enforcement weapons"?
39. Can a provider appeal the use of all these enforcement weapons?
40. What do the RACs do?
41. How many A/B RACs are there?
42. Does each A/B RAC have its own website?
43. How many DMEPOS (durable medical equipment, prosthetics, orthotics, and supplies) RACs are there?
44. What happens when a RAC identifies an improper payment?
45. What happens when a provider doesn't pay upon notice from the RAC of an overpayment?
46. Are overpayments always collected by the MACs?
47. What does the RAC do when an automated (proprietary software) or semiautomated review reveals an overpayment?
48. What are RAC automated reviews based on?
49. What is the difference between a RAC automated review and a RAC semiautomated review?
50. What is a RAC required to do when an overpayment is discovered as a result of a complex review?
51. What are complex reviews based on?
52. Who has to approve the RACs' widespread review of a topic?
53. What are the topics approved for widespread review by the RACs called?
54. What percentage of appealed RAC "overpayments" are successfully overturned?
55. What medical review methods are used by the RACs?
56. Again, how are the RACs paid?
57. What percentage of your payments do the RACs get to keep?
58. How are the RAC contingency fees determined and what happens to the contingency fee if the "improper payment" is overturned on appeal?
59. How can you find the Medicare Statement of Work for the RACs?
60. What does UPIC stand for?
61. What do the UPIC contractors do?
62. What actions can the UPICs take?
63. What happens when a UPIC suspects fraud?

64. Does the UPIC take any direct action against the providers?
65. Do the UPICs investigate possible fraud in all the Medicare programs?
66. What does CERT stand for?
67. Which Medicare publications should you read regarding the CERT?
68. What is the primary responsibility of the CERT contractors?
69. What is the CERT contractors' secondary responsibility?
70. How many CERT contractors are there?
71. For Medicare appeals, does it matter what each CERT contractor does?
72. How does the CERT determine the national Medicare payment error rate?
73. Which Medicare review contractors (MACs, RACs, CERT, UPICs, SMRC) perform random audits?
74. How does Medicare use the results of the CERT study?
75. Do the CERT contractors ever refer a provider for a fraud investigation?
76. How were the CERT review standards changed in 2009?
77. Before 2009, under the "totality of the circumstances" test, how did the CERT review medical records?
78. As of 2009, under the "more stringent review" (inflexible checklist) test, how is the CERT reviewing medical records?
79. What does the SMRC (supplemental medical review contractor) do?
80. When a claim is submitted, how does a MAC decide whether to pay or deny the claim?
81. What is a non-complex medical review?
82. What non-complex review programs are used by the MACs to process claims?
83. In addition to the CWF software, what other non-complex (automated) software is used by the MACs to determine whether a claim should be paid?
84. What do the NCCI programs include?
85. What is the CCI program?
86. What does the PTP software do?
87. What does the MUE software do?
88. What does the add-on CPT code prepayment claim review software do?

1. Can a provider (provider/supplier) just ignore a Medicare audit?

No. A provider cannot ignore a Medicare audit. Even a seemingly minor audit can have disastrous results on a Medicare practice/business.

2. Can a provider always appeal the results of a Medicare audit?

Yes. Every provider is entitled to appeal the results of any audit.

3. How are Medicare audits appealed?

A Medicare audit is appealed the exact same way a denied claim is appealed: a redetermination appeal, followed by a reconsideration appeal, followed by an ALJ appeal.

4. At what level of appeal is a provider most likely to win?

The ALJ hearing is the only level of appeal where the playing field is level and a provider can win an audit appeal decision.

5. Who performs Medicare audits?

Medicare has hired outside auditing companies to review Medicare payments.

6. How does Medicare refer to these outside auditing companies?

Medicare calls these outside auditing companies "medical review contractors."

7. How can you find the names, the contact information, and a description of the services provided by each of the medical review contractors for your area?

Search "CMS.gov Review Contractor Directory—Interactive Map," select your state on the first page, and click!

8. How many medical review contractors is a provider who engages in some DME services exposed to?

A/B MAC: Part A/Part B Medicare Administrative Contractor
A/B RAC: Part A/Part B Recovery Audit Contractor
CERT Contractor: Comprehensive Error Rate Testing Contractor
DME MAC: Durable Medical Equipment MAC
DME RAC: Durable Medical Equipment RAC
UPIC: Uniform Program Integrity Contractor
SMRC: Supplemental Medical Review Contractor

9. How many MACs, RACs, UPICs, CERTs, and SMRCs are there nationwide?

A/B MACs: 12
A/B RACs: 4
DMEPOS (durable medical equipment, prosthetics, orthotics, and supplies) MACs: 4
DMEPOS RAC: 1
CERT: 1
UPICs: 7
SMRC: 1

10. What do all the medical review contractors have in common?

All of the medical review contractors are for-profit companies.

11. Where can you find a "complete" list of the reasons why Medicare has decided your medically reviewed claim(s) should not be paid?

Go to the "Review Reason Codes and Statements" at www.Medicare.gov for an explanation why your medically reviewed claim was denied. But please note, the medical review contractors (MACs, RACs, CERTs, SMRCs, and UPICs) have previously "developed and maintained (their own) lists of denial reason codes and statements." Medicare is now editing these "review reason codes and statements" into a single unified list of denial reasons.

12. What does Medicare say about its goal of "lowering the improper payment rate"?

The following is an edited version of CMS strategy for the past, present, and future in Section 1.3.2, Improper Payment Prevention Goals in the Medicare Program Integrity Manual: Chapter 1, "Medicare Improper Payments: Measuring, Correcting, and Preventing Overpayments and ~~Underpayments"~~ (I crossed out "Underpayments" because, believe me, Medicare is **not** looking for underpayments).

> CMS strives in every case to pay the right amount to a legitimate provider, for **covered, correctly coded** and **correctly billed** services. To achieve the goal of lowering the error rate, CMS follows three parallel strategies: CMS strategy for the **past**, CMS strategy for the **present**, and CMS strategy for the **future.** (Emphasis added.)

13. What does "CMS strives in every case to pay the right amount to a legitimate provider, for covered, correctly coded and correctly billed services" mean?

This statement means Medicare will deny payment if it finds the smallest billing error, even when it is obvious the service was medically reasonable and necessary. This is why the complex review performed by the RACs is the most successful tool in taking back payments from providers.

As an example, if the DME RAC finds a diabetic therapeutic shoe service was successful in healing a limb-threatening/life-threatening diabetic ulcer but only four of five reporting documents are correctly completed and submitted when payment is reviewed—payment for that service is considered "improper" and repayment is demanded.

14. What is the "CMS strategy for the past"?

CMS corrects past improper payments through post-payment claim review by the RACs.

15. What are the different types of claim reviews used by the RACs?

The RACs use both simple and complex claim reviews.

16. What kind of simple claim review is used by the RACs?

The RACs use **proprietary software** to data mine the claims that have been paid by the MACs.

17. Do a lot of RAC-discovered improper payments come through data mining?

No. Data mining reveals the smaller percentage of RAC-discovered improper payments.

18. How do the RACs perform complex claim review?

When a suspected problem arises through **data mining** or other sources, the RACs send requests to the providers for copies of the medical records relied upon for billing. The doctors and nurses who work for the RACs review those medical records and decide whether the claim was correctly paid.

19. What percentage of RAC-discovered improper payments come through complex review?

Complex medical review reveals **over** 80% of RAC-discovered improper payments.

20. Are the RACs allowed to blanket-review any service they want to?

No. The RACs are **not** allowed to blanket-review a specific service unless CMS has reviewed the problem and given the RACs permission to include that service on the **RAC website list of "issues"** (e.g., diabetic therapeutic shoe services are listed as an "issue" on the DME RAC websites).

21. Are all the medical review contractors paid in the same manner?

No. Unlike all the other medical review contractors who are paid on a contract plus costs basis, **the RACs are paid on a contingency fee basis.** As expected, the RACs rake back far more money from the providers as "improper payments" than all the other Medicare medical review contractors combined.

22. What is the "CMS strategy for the present"?

CMS prevents current improper payments through the evaluation of program "vulnerabilities" by the **MACs** and by the **SMRC** (supplemental medical review contractor) and by taking the necessary action to prevent the identified vulnerabilities in the future.

23. What is the "CMS strategy for the future"?

CMS prevents future improper payments by measuring recent improper payments. "The **CERT** (comprehensive error rate testing) contractor program pinpoints the causes of improper payments and calculates the actual service specific, provider type specific, and contractor-specific error rates."

THE MACS

24. What is a MAC?

A MAC (Medicare Administrative Contractor) is a for-profit corporation that contracts with CMS to perform the Medicare fee-for-service (FFS) claims administrative services.

25. How many different types of MACs are there?

There are three separate types of MACs:

A/B MACs: Part A/Part B MACs
DMEPOS MACs: Durable Medical Equipment, Prosthetics, Orthotics, and Supply MACs
HH+H MACs: Home Health & Hospice MACs

26. Who are the MACs?

For a complete list of all the MACs and their jurisdictions, see https://www.cms.gov/Medicare/Medicare-Contracting/Medicare-Administrative-Contractors/Who-are-the-MACs.html#MapsandLists. Each MAC has a geographic area of jurisdiction that usually includes several states.

27. What "administrative" services are performed by the MACs?

- The MACs process (pay or deny all submitted) claims.
- The MACs, on their own, investigate suspected overpayments.
- The MACs demand repayment of overpayments that are revealed by their own investigations.
- The MACs demand repayment of overpayments upon request by the RACs, the CERT, and the SMRC.

The MACs use a graduated menu of enforcement weapons, including the following:

- Provider education/feedback
- Prepayment review of claims
- Post-payment review of claims—with or without extrapolation

- Suspension of provider privileges
- Referral to the UPIC for investigation of fraud

28. What does "the MACs process (pay or deny all submitted) claims" mean?

The MACs decide whether to pay or deny each claim submitted by the providers within a MAC's jurisdiction. The MACs process more than one billion claims a year.

29. How do the MACs initially process claims?

I know you are not reading this book to find out how the MACs perform the initial, non-complex (simple) review of your claims. But for anyone who wants that information, I have moved the questions and answers regarding the initial review of claims to the very end of this chapter.

30. What does the statement "the MACs, on their own, investigate suspected overpayments" mean?

If a suspected overpayment is identified by a MAC through its own claim data analysis, or through other sources (e.g., complaints by a patient or by an employee of the provider), the MAC will perform a complex medical review.

31. What is "complex medical review" of a claim?

In a complex review, the provider's medical records supporting payment of the claim are requested from the provider and are reviewed by a "person" at the MAC. If the MAC needs additional documentation, it will send the provider an **ADR (additional documentation request)** letter.

32. Can you ignore an ADR letter?

No. You must respond to an ADR within 45 days.

33. What happens if you ignore an ADR request?

If you don't submit the requested documentation, or the MAC thinks the documentation is insufficient, the MAC will deny the claim.

In addition, ignoring an ADR request is like waving a red flag at a bull. You are letting the MAC know they should also be looking at you for other billing problems.

34. What does "the MACs demand repayment of overpayments revealed by their own investigations" mean?

When a MAC concludes there has been an overpayment based on its own complex review, the MAC sends the provider a demand for repayment of overpayment.

35. What does "the MACs demand repayment of overpayments upon request by the RACs, the CERT, and the SMRC" mean?

The RACs, the CERT, and the SMRC are constantly hunting for overpayments. When they find an overpayment, they tell the MAC to send a demand for repayment of overpayment to the provider.

36. Do the MACs, the RACs, the CERT, and the SMRC all find the same numbers of overpayments?

No. The RACs are the top predators of complex medical review. You could say the RACs find at least 90% of all overpayments, the MACs find at least 5%, and the CERT and the SMRC find the rest.

37. Are demands for repayment of overpayment ever sent to a provider by a RAC, the CERT, or the SMRC?

No. All demands for repayment of overpayment come from a provider's MAC.

38. How should a provider view the MACs' "enforcement weapons"?

Provider education/feedback is the most benign of the enforcement weapons. Here, a provider is repeatedly doing something wrong and the MAC thinks the provider is doing it out of ignorance. The MAC tells the provider what the provider is doing wrong and then checks later submitted claims to make sure the provider has corrected the billing error.

Prepayment and post-payment review of claims are linked together. The MAC, with or without input from the RAC, the CERT, or the SMRC, thinks you know—or should know—you are billing for something you shouldn't.

Based on a post-payment review of several to many claims, the MAC may ask the provider to repay the overpayments related to just the reviewed claims or may apply its findings to the entire universe of identical claims submitted to Medicare between specific starting and ending dates. When the findings are applied to the universe of identical claims in a practice or business, this is called "extrapolation."

As you can easily imagine—or as you already know—when a billing code is eliminated, or when the complexity of a procedure code or an E&M code is reduced, that "edit" may be applied to hundreds of similar claims by extrapolation. That can result in a big loss of money.

And based on the post-payment review, the MAC may require the provider to submit future claims regarding the problem service for *prepayment review.*

Suspension of privileges is a big step up in the severity of the penalty. But when a provider's billing offenses are glaring enough, and/or when a provider continues to offend despite previous post-payment/prepayment reviews, a MAC can suspend the provider's Medicare privileges. However, as bad as suspension is, this is still a *civil* and not a *criminal* remedy.

Referral to the UPIC occurs when a MAC suspects *criminal fraud.*

39. Can a provider appeal the use of all these enforcement weapons?

Yes. But with the possible exception of provider education/feedback situations, all of the other responses from the MAC require representation by a health care attorney. And if you hear from the UPIC, you are going to want a criminal defense attorney on board as well.

THE RACs (RECOVERY AUDITORS)

40. What do the RACs do?

The RACs do post-payment reviews of the claims paid by the MACs, looking for errors.

41. How many A/B RACs are there?

There are four A/B RACs, and each RAC has been assigned one-quarter of the country.

42. Does each A/B RAC have its own website?

Yes. Each A/B RAC has its own website.

43. How many DMEPOS (durable medical equipment, prosthetics, orthotics, and supplies) RACs are there?

There is one DMEPOS RAC.

44. What happens when a RAC identifies an improper payment?

After a RAC identifies an improper payment, the RAC notifies the provider of the alleged overpayment.

45. What happens when a provider doesn't pay upon notice from the RAC of an overpayment?

If the provider doesn't pay upon receipt of the notice from the RAC, the RAC notifies the MAC. The MAC then sends the provider a demand for repayment of the "overpayment."

46. Are overpayments always collected by the MACs?

Yes. Whether it is the MAC, the RAC, the UPIC, the CERT, or the SMRC that finds the overpayment, it is always the MAC that is responsible for the collection of the overpayment.

47. What does the RAC do when an automated (proprietary software) or semiautomated review reveals an overpayment?

For automated and semiautomated reviews, the RAC sends an informational letter to the provider along with a "request" for repayment.

48. What are RAC automated reviews based on?

Automated reviews are based on claims data analysis only. The RAC sends a letter to the provider that says: "There was an overpayment. This is how much you owe. Please pay it now." With automated reviews, the RAC is certain the overpayment claim is correct. So, with automated reviews, the RAC does not give the provider an opportunity to tell the RAC why the RAC is wrong.

49. What is the difference between a RAC automated review and a RAC semiautomated review?

Semiautomated reviews are based on claims data analysis but the RAC is not certain there has been an overpayment. So, the RAC gives the provider a chance to respond with documentation that will support payment.

50. What is a RAC required to do when an overpayment is discovered as a result of a complex review?

When a RAC discovers an overpayment as a result of a complex review, the RAC is required to send the provider a review results letter with detailed reasons for the improper payment determination.

51. What are complex reviews based on?

Complex reviews are based on a review of the supporting medical records. The reviewer must be a qualified health care coder or clinician based on the type of review. Yup. Billing clerks and LVNs are doing your complex RAC reviews.

52. Who has to approve the RACs' widespread review of a topic?

All new review topics for potential audits (e.g., overpayments for diabetic therapeutic shoes) must be approved by CMS before the RACs can begin widespread review. And "widespread review" means as soon as the DME RAC sees you have billed for a listed issue on the DME RAC website, like diabetic therapeutic shoe services, the DME RAC can send you a request for the medical records supporting that service.

53. What are the topics approved for widespread review by the RACs called?

The approved topics for widespread RAC review are called "**issues**" and all approved RAC "issues" are **listed on all of the RAC websites.**

I don't really have to tell you the RACs want to focus on the problems ("issues") that are the easiest to identify, the most cost-effective to pursue, and that will pay them the most money on a percentage basis, do I?

54. What percentage of appealed RAC "overpayments" are successfully overturned?

About 35% of appealed RAC "overpayments" are successfully overturned.

55. What medical review methods are used by the RACs?

Simple RAC reviews are done by data mining MAC claims with proprietary software. Each RAC develops its own software and uses it to search for overpayments on claims paid by the MACs.

Complex RAC reviews are done by sending an ADR (additional documentation request) for medical records and then reviewing the medical records to see if all the documentation requirements are met for payment.

56. Again, how are the RACs paid?

The RACs are paid on a **contingency** fee basis. What could possibly go wrong?

57. What percentage of your payments do the RACs get to keep?

The A/B RACs get to keep **9.0% to 12.5%** of everything they get back from the providers.

The DME RACs get to keep **14.0% to 17.5%** of everything they get back from the providers.

58. How are the RAC contingency fees determined and what happens to the contingency fee if the "improper payment" is overturned on appeal?

The RACs negotiate their contingency fees with CMS at the time of the contract award.

The RAC must return the contingency fee if an improper payment determination is overturned at any level of appeal.

59. How can you find the Medicare Statement of Work for the RACs?

The statement of work for the four fee-for-service A/B RACs may be found at https://www.cms.gov/Research-Statistics-Data-and-Systems/Monitoring-Programs/Medicare-FFS-Compliance-Programs/Recovery-Audit-Program/Downloads/New_RAC-SOW-Regions-1-4-clean.pdf.

A copy of the statement of work for the one DMEPOS RAC may be found at http://appealacademy.com/wp-content/uploads/2013/04/DME-HHH-Recovery-Auditor-Scope-Of-Work-2013.pdf.

THE UPICS

See Medicare Special Edition Article (SE 1204).

60. What does UPIC stand for?

UPIC stands for "Uniform Program Integrity Contractor."

61. What do the UPIC contractors do?

UPIC contractors are responsible for investigating both Medicare and Medicaid fraud.

62. What actions can the UPICs take?

The UPICs can:

- Request medical records and documentation.
- Conduct interviews.
- Conduct onsite visits.
- Identify the need for prepayment review of a provider's claims.
- Identify the need for prepayment denial of a provider's claims.
- Refer criminal fraud cases to law enforcement.

63. What happens when a UPIC suspects fraud?

The UPICs must refer all cases to the OIG first. If the OIG/OI (Office of Inspector General/Office of Investigations) declines a case that the UPIC believes has merit, the UPIC can refer the case to other law enforcement agencies, such as the FBI. See Chapter 4 of the Medicare Program Integrity Manual, Section 4.18.1.5.

64. Does the UPIC take any direct action against the providers?

No. The UPICs only investigate for fraud.

If the UPIC thinks there is evidence of fraud, the case is referred to the OIG/OI.

If the UPIC thinks the provider just made a billing mistake, the case is referred to the MAC with a request to issue a demand for a repayment of overpayment.

65. Do the UPICs investigate possible fraud in all the Medicare programs?

Yes. The UPICs look at Part A, B, C (Medicare Advantage), and D claims.

THE CERT CONTRACTORS

66. What does CERT stand for?

CERT stands for "comprehensive error rate testing."

67. Which Medicare publications should you read regarding the CERT?

CERT Assignment of Error Categories January 2016
Introduction to Comprehensive Error Rate Testing (CERT) Program
Improper Medicare Fee-For-Service Payments Report—November 2009

68. What is the primary responsibility of the CERT contractors?

The CERT contractors' primary responsibility is to determine a single, national error rate for all Medicare claims.

69. What is the CERT contractors' secondary responsibility?

The CERT contractors' secondary responsibility is to send a request to the provider's MAC to demand a repayment of overpayment when the reviewed medical records do not support the service/supply that was billed and paid. This is a minor responsibility because the CERT contractors are only looking at 50,000 out of more than one billion claims processed by Medicare each year.

70. How many CERT contractors are there?

There are three CERT contractors:

CERT documentation contractor (CERT-DC)
CERT review contractor (CERT-RC)
CERT statistical contractor (CERT-SC)

71. For Medicare appeals, does it matter what each CERT contractor does?

No, it does not matter. So, instead of drilling down on the mechanics of the three CERT contractors' interactions, we will simply refer to all three CERT contractors as "the CERT."

72. How does the CERT determine the national Medicare payment error rate?

Every year the CERT designs its study for the next year and the design includes the following:

1. The CERT will look at approximately 50,000 claims, including both paid and denied claims (as a statistically valid sample of processed FFS claims).
2. The CERT determines which billing codes should be included in the next CERT study.
3. The billing codes (services) that were considered problematic during the previous year are given special attention (e.g., the DME services listed as issues on the DME RAC website).
4. The CERT determines how many claims containing each targeted billing code should be included in the study.
5. The CERT determines how many of these claims should come from each MAC.
6. The CERT then **randomly selects** a predetermined number of these claim types each month from each MAC.
7. Again, although the individual codes to be studied are carefully chosen, the CERT **randomly** selects the actual claims containing those codes.
8. Once a claim has been selected, the CERT requests the medical records from the provider that support payment of that claim.
9. The CERT performs a complex medical review on the records received from each provider and determines whether the claim was properly or improperly paid or denied.
10. For all 50,000 claims, the CERT divides the claims that should **not** be paid into five categories:
    a. The claims that should not be paid because **no documentation was received** from the provider
    b. The claims that should not be paid because the **submitted documentation is inadequate** to support payment
    c. The claims that should not be paid because the **services were not medically necessary** based on Medicare coverage and payment policies
    d. The claims that should not be paid because of **incorrect coding**
    e. The claims that should not be paid because of some **other error** (e.g., duplicate payment, uncovered service, or unallowable service)
11. The CERT applies (extrapolates) its findings to the entire universe of Medicare claims billed during the previous year and comes up with a **national error rate** for all submitted claims.

73. Which Medicare review contractors (MACs, RACs, CERT, UPICs, SMRC) perform random audits?

The CERT review contractor is the **only** Medicare auditor that performs **random** audits. All the other auditors perform targeted or focused audits where suspected or actual problem services, codes, and providers are identified before the audits take place.

74. How does Medicare use the results of the CERT study?

CMS uses the CERT program to identify areas that may be susceptible to improper payment in the FFS program. Then, CMS uses this information to direct future work by the RACs and the MACs.

For example, CMS tells the RACs which type of service claims are more likely to have errors that will lead to the assumption of "improper payment," that will lead to a demand for repayment of overpayment, and that will lead to new "issues" being posted on the RAC websites.

And CMS tells the MACs which services require more billing-restrictive language in the applicable LCD.

75. Do the CERT contractors ever refer a provider for a fraud investigation?

No. As stated in the "Improper Medicare FFS Payments Report November 2009" publication: "Since the CERT program uses random samples to select claims, reviewers are often unable to see provider billing patterns that indicate potential fraud when making payment determinations. The CERT program **does not**, and **cannot**, label a claim fraudulent."

76. How were the CERT review standards changed in 2009?

In 2009, the CERT program was instructed to abandon the "totality of the circumstances" test when reviewing claims and was instead to adopt a "more stringent review" (inflexible checklist) test when reviewing claims for "improper" payments.

You can confirm all of this by searching "Improper Medicare FFS Payments Report November 2009" and then reading page 9 under the heading: "Impact of the More Stringent Review Criteria."

77. Before 2009, under the "totality of the circumstances" test, how did the CERT review medical records?

Under the "totality of the circumstances" test, all available evidence (e.g., other progress notes, test results, billing history) was taken into account by the reviewer to determine whether a claim should have been paid.

78. As of 2009, under the "more stringent review" (inflexible checklist) test, how is the CERT reviewing medical records?

Under the more stringent review test:

1. **The CERT strictly enforces all Medicare rules regarding signature requirements.** For example, if the referring doctor did not sign the progress note or the request for the MRI, and there is no later "attestation statement" from the referring doctor regarding the missing signature, if the referring doctor's signature on the progress note or the request for the MRI is illegible and

there is no "signature log" to establish signature identity, or if the doctor who reads the MRI cannot prove all of the Medicare guidelines regarding electronic signatures were met—payment for the MRI is considered an improper payment.

2. **The CERT strictly enforces all documentation requirements in Medicare regulations, statutes, and policies, including LCD policies.** For example, if payment for diabetic shoes requires completion of five separate documents and only four documents are completed, payment for the diabetic shoes is "improper."
3. **The CERT strictly relies on the medical record documentation from the ordering provider.** The CERT "more stringent review" (inflexible checklist) test removes the history of the claim as a valid source for review information and ignores the medical record documentation from the supplier.

   For example, all the information required to validate payment for an MRI must come from the referring physician. The referring physician's progress note must contain all the clinical information required to order the MRI. The signature on the referring physician's progress note must be present and must be legible or, if present and illegible, must be accompanied by a copy of the referring physician's "signature log" in order to establish the referring physician's signature identity.

THE SMRC

79. What does the SMRC (supplemental medical review contractor) do?

The SMRC does whatever complex medical review CMS wants the SMRC to do. At the request of CMS, the SMRC, StrategicHealth, performs nationwide, complex medical review regarding a service, a type of provider group, or a geographic area. It is the ability of the SMRC to investigate a perceived, specific problem and to quickly drill down on that problem nationwide that gives the SMRC its particular value to CMS in the battle against "improper payments."

See the StrategicHealth website at http://www.strategichs.com/. The website includes a statement that StrategicHealth will **not** reimburse any provider for the cost of copying and sending documents—regardless of the volume of documents—when the provider receives an ADR (additional documentation request) for an SMRC complex review.

In my opinion, every provider should number and fax all documents requested by StrategicHealth—but not necessarily in correct numerical order.

Also see "CMS.gov Supplemental Medical Review Contractor."

The SMRC does nationwide medical reviews, not just medical reviews limited to a specific jurisdiction, such as that performed by the MACs and the RACs. The StrategicHealth website states:

> The SMRC, as a representative of CMS, has a fiduciary responsibility to notify CMS of the outcome of the reviews for assigned projects. At the conclusion of post-payment review, providers and suppliers are provided a Final Review Results Letter from the SMRC. The results letter will stipulate if any overpayment(s) were identified. In addition, your claims may be subject to extrapolation in keeping with the Centers for Medicare and Medicaid Services (CMS) Internet-Only Manual (IOM), Publication (Pub.) 100-08, Chapter 8, Section 8.4.1.4 – Determining When Statistical Sampling May Be Used. The Final Review Results Letter is not a demand letter for overpayment recovery.

Under the direction of CMS, the SMRC provides all identified overpayments to the MAC that is responsible to send the demand letter and recoup the overpayment.

HERE IS HOW MACS PERFORM THE INITIAL, NON-COMPLEX (SIMPLE) REVIEW OF YOUR CLAIMS:

80. When a claim is submitted, how does a MAC decide whether to pay or deny the claim?

In the simplest scenario, the MAC uses a non-complex review to check for claim errors. If there are no errors, the MAC pays the claim. If an error is present, the MAC denies payment.

81. What is a non-complex medical review?

Non-complex (simple) review is review of a claim by computer software only.

82. What non-complex review programs are used by the MACs to process claims?

First, the MACs use Medicare's common working file (**CWF**) software to detect clerical entry errors on submitted claims. See Chapter 27 of the Medicare Claims Processing Manual at https://www.cms.gov/Regulations-and-Guidance/Guidance/Manuals/Downloads/clm104c27.pdf.

The CWF software determines the beneficiary's eligibility and entitlement status and prevents duplicate payments.

83. In addition to the CWF software, what other non-complex (automated) software is used by the MACs to determine whether a claim should be paid?

In addition to the CWF software, the MACs use the National Correct Coding Initiative (NCCI) prepayment claim review programs.

84. What do the NCCI programs include?

The **NCCI** programs include the Correct Coding Initiative (**CCI**) program, the Mutually Unlikely Edits (**MUE**) program, and the **add-on code** program.

85. What is the CCI program?

The CCI prepayment claim review program is a combination of the **PTP** (procedure to procedure) software program and the **MUE** software program.

CCI was developed by CMS to reduce incorrect payments in Medicare Part B claims.

86. What does the PTP software do?

As stated in the CMS publication "How to Use the Medicare National Correct Coding Initiative Tools," the CCI Column 1/Column 2 tables are comprised of **PTP code pairs**.

> If a provider submits two codes of an edit pair for payment for the same beneficiary on the same date of service, the Column 1 code is eligible for payment and the Column 2 code is denied. However, if both codes are clinically appropriate, and an appropriate NCCI-associated modifier is used, the codes in both columns are eligible for payment. Supporting documentation for the use of the modifier must be in the beneficiary's medical record.

87. What does the MUE software do?

The MUE prepayment claim review program uses automated, prepayment edits. An MUE is the maximum number of units of service that a provider would report for a single beneficiary on a single date of service. As an example, a surgeon could not bill a second appendectomy procedure code for the same patient on the same date. The MUE program has now been merged into the CCI program.

88. What does the add-on CPT code prepayment claim review software do?

An add-on code is a CPT code that is only payable when billed with its linked primary CPT code. Medicare Change Request 7501 states: "An add-on code is a HCPCS/CPT code that describes a service that is always performed in conjunction with another primary service. An add-on code is eligible for payment only if it is reported with an appropriate primary procedure performed by the same practitioner. An add-on code is never eligible for payment if it is the only procedure reported by a practitioner."

An example of an add-on code and the primary code it must be billed with would be 26861 and 26860:

> The primary CPT code 26860 is defined as: Arthrodesis, interphalangeal joint (of a finger), with or without internal fixation.
>
> The add-on CPT code +26861 is defined as: each additional interphalangeal joint (of other fingers), with or without internal fixation.

Because it is an add-on code, +26861 is never payable if billed alone. It must always be billed with 26860.

23

Evaluation & Management (E&M) Codes

23a

E&M Code Requirements

OUTLINE

1. What do the 2020 CMS proposed changes to the E&M documentation rules for office/outpatient visits (99201 through 99215) tell us?
2. Is the rest of this chapter based on the proposed changes to the CMS rules?
3. Do your records have to be perfect in order to win an ALJ decision regarding an E&M code?
4. Most of you buy the new CPT Manual every year, but what do you do with it?
5. What will reading the E&M guidelines once a year do for you?
6. How many E&M codes do you use?
7. What about billing the E&M codes of highest complexity for every patient visit?
8. What bad habit do many providers who usually bill the E&M codes of highest complexity have in common?
9. What happens when the ALJ realizes you are cutting and pasting your original H&P into your follow-up progress notes?
10. What effect does cutting and pasting large parts of the original H&P into follow-up notes have on patient care?
11. What if a provider wants to include previous comprehensive history and/or examination findings in a future progress note?
12. What will these words do when you are in front of the ALJ?

13. Why will the ALJ not be offended by the incorporation of findings from a previous history and examination?
14. If an established patient returns with a complex problem and you want to update the "comprehensive history," how can you make yourself audit-proof?
15. Now let's start at the beginning of the patient encounter. Why can't you just walk into a treatment room, take care of the patient, and figure out the E&M billing code later?
16. What is the first thing you must decide when you walk into a treatment room?
17. Why do you have to immediately decide on the complexity of the patient's problem?
18. Isn't this the polar opposite of your training?
19. Once you decide on the complexity of the patient's problem, what does that tell you about the history and the physical examination?
20. What happens to the level of complexity when there are multiple problems and/or a lot of data to review?
21. What happens to the level of complexity in relation to the risk of complications and/or morbidity or mortality?
22. What are the expert physicians on the CPT panels trying to tell you?
23. Are the expert physicians on the CPT panels telling you to up-code?
24. What is the bottom-line message from the expert physicians on the CPT panels?
25. Without looking, can you name the four levels of history described in the CPT Manual?
26. Can you define the four levels of history and examination described in the CPT Manual?
27. What happens when you are in front of the ALJ and you don't know the difference between the four levels of history and examination described in the CPT Manual?
28. If you know the four levels of history and examination, but you don't decide on the appropriate E&M code until the patients are gone, what happens?
29. Does Medicare have "good cops" and "bad cops"?
30. Who are the "bad cops"?
31. Who are the "good cops"?
32. What does Appendix C in the CPT Manual contain?
33. Do the experts who write and edit the CPT Manual use a logical approach in assigning increasingly more complex E&M codes to patient problems?
34. Can we select a single area of clinical interest to illustrate how the complexity of an E&M encounter changes with the clinical facts?
35. Can we use a single clinical problem encountered by the foot and ankle surgeons as our model and then march that problem through all levels of E&M complexity?
36. How should you view and analyze the Appendix C clinical examples for your specialty?
37. Why should the 99201 and 99202 E&M codes never be used for new Medicare patients?
38. Why do all new Medicare patients require at least a detailed history?
39. Returning to our 65-year-old model patient with an infected ingrown toenail, what are the CPT Appendix C foot/ankle examples for a 99203 new patient visit?
40. Can we move the Appendix C, 99203 clinical examples into a Medicare setting?
41. What do these two 99203, Appendix C, foot/ankle clinical examples have in common?
42. How could we make our model patient analogous to these 99203 clinical examples?
43. What are the CPT Appendix C, foot/ankle clinical examples for 99204?

44. How can we move these 99204 clinical examples into a Medicare setting and how should we be thinking about our modified examples?
45. What do these 99204, Appendix C clinical examples have in common?
46. How could we make our model patient analogous to the 99204 clinical examples?
47. What are the differences between the 99203 and 99204 clinical examples?
48. What are the CPT Appendix C, foot/ankle clinical examples for 99205?
49. What do the 99205, Appendix C, clinical examples have in common?
50. How could we make our model patient analogous to the first 99205 clinical example?
51. How could we make our model patient analogous to the second 99205 clinical example?
52. Should you spend time distinguishing the complexity of the E&M codes?
53. Why should the 99211 and the 99212 codes never be used for Medicare patients?
54. What is the Appendix C, foot/ankle clinical example for a 99213 patient visit?
55. How can we characterize the clinical features of the 99213 foot/ankle clinical example?
56. How could we make our model patient analogous to the 99213 clinical example?
57. What is the CPT Appendix C, foot/ankle clinical example for 99214?
58. Can we characterize the clinical features of the 99214 example?
59. How could we make our model patient analogous to the 99214 clinical example?
60. What is the CPT Appendix C, foot/ankle clinical example for 99215?
61. Can we characterize the clinical features of the 99215 example?
62. How could we make our model patient analogous to the 99215 clinical example?
63. Is it okay to decide on the appropriate E&M code when you are dictating the progress note?
64. Why fight your way out of the "I don't have the required E&M code information" billing hole in front of a judge?
65. What happens when you don't get the information during the patient encounter and you are selecting the E&M code later while you are dictating?
66. Until you decide on the correct E&M code, and complete the history and examination requirements for that code, forget about making conversation with the patient.
67. When is it okay to bill for a procedure code and an E&M code on the same day?
68. Should you incorporate the E&M code requirements in your progress notes?
69. How do you take the guesswork out of the E&M code selection process?
70. When you argue for payment of an E&M code, what does the judge want to know?
71. Do the clinical examples in Appendix C just apply to the listed specialty/specialties?
72. What will you do with the Appendix C clinical example during the appeal?
73. Do Appendix C clinical examples cut both ways?
74. In addition to proving that the E&M code was appropriate, what else will you have to prove?
75. Again, where do you find technical requirements for the history, examination, and medical decision-making required for each E&M code?
76. Does Medicare and all the other insurance companies base compensation for E&M services on the content of your progress notes?
77. If you did it but you didn't write it, did it happen?
78. If you did it and you wrote it but your note is illegible, did it happen?
79. If you did it, if you wrote it, if your note is legible—but you didn't sign the note—did it happen?
80. Why should you be thankful for the authors of the CPT Manual?

1. What do the 2020 CMS proposed changes to the E&M documentation rules for office/outpatient visits (99201 through 99215) tell us?

Unlike the current documentation requirements under the 1995 or the 1997 E&M guidelines, the new rules de-emphasize the bulleted history and physical examination requirements and, instead, emphasize medical decision-making as the basis for determining the appropriate level of E&M visit. While these changes are not without controversy, the underlying theme is: It is the level of complexity of the patient's problem(s) that should determine the correct E&M code. That theme is expressed over and over in this chapter.

2. Is the rest of this chapter based on the proposed changes to the CMS rules?

No. This chapter is based on the rules currently in place regarding the E&M codes.

3. Do your records have to be perfect in order to win an ALJ decision regarding an E&M code?

No. But in order for the judge to rule in your favor, the progress note for the date of service at issue must include a description of the patient's problem (the patient's complaint/the reason you are seeing the patient), your findings by history, your examination findings, your conclusions, your treatment, if any, on that day, and your plans for future care.

In other words, your progress note must tell the complete story to the judge. If your progress note is only a partial story, you are far less likely to win the ALJ decision.

4. Most of you buy the new CPT Manual every year, but what do you do with it?

Every yearly edition of the CPT Manual begins with "Evaluation and Management (E/M) Services Guidelines," and every year when you get your new copy of the CPT Manual, you should read that section as though your financial life depends on it—because it does.

5. What will reading the E&M guidelines once a year do for you?

Reading these guidelines takes all the mystery out of the E&M codes. Yet a huge percentage of providers have never read the E&M guidelines at the beginning of the CPT Manual.

If you are in this "huge percentage," stop reading this book right now and get your CPT Manual out. Read the seven or eight E&M guideline pages without marking them. Then, make a copy of the seven or eight pages and read them again very slowly and very carefully, using a yellow highlighter for the parts that apply to your E&M billing problems. Finally, reduce the E&M rules to a bullet list for each of the E&M codes you most often use. Keep the bullet list in front of you as you dictate your progress notes until you have this down pat.

6. How many E&M codes do you use?

Most providers use less than a dozen E&M codes for more than 95% of their patient encounters. How difficult would it be to master the E&M requirements for the six to ten codes you use all the time?

Look in the mirror. Many of you reading this section have the same sheepish look on your face. You are not alone, but you must fix this "relationship" problem you have with your billing—and you are the only one who can fix it.

7. What about billing the E&M codes of highest complexity for every patient visit?

You cannot bill the E&M codes of highest complexity for every patient visit. It just doesn't work. The RAC companies, who see self-targeted providers/suppliers everywhere, are looking for you as you read this. And those Harvard/Stanford MBAs who work for the RACs will find you.

8. What bad habit do many providers who usually bill the E&M codes of highest complexity have in common?

I have been shocked to see how often providers in all specialties are willing to cut and paste whole sections of the initial history and physical examination note into their follow-up progress notes. The RACs have no difficulty spotting this and the ALJs have no difficulty spotting it either.

9. What happens when the ALJ realizes you are cutting and pasting your original H&P into your follow-up progress notes?

You will lose that ALJ appeal, you will lose your credibility with that ALJ for future appeals, and you will be the subject of conversation as the ALJs eat lunch together.

10. What effect does cutting and pasting large parts of the original H&P into follow-up notes have on patient care?

At the very least, a progress note should include what's wrong with the patient, how the patient is responding to treatment, what was done on the date of the progress note, and what the plan is for future care. As an attorney, I know the clients who paste large parts of the original H&P into subsequent progress notes rarely include this basic information in adequate detail in their follow-up progress notes. As a health care provider, I know leaving out this basic information can lead to bad consequences.

Do not cut and paste!

11. What if a provider wants to include previous comprehensive history and/or examination findings into a future progress note?

Here are some magic words you can use:

> *The findings from the comprehensive history and comprehensive examination performed on [date of the previous comprehensive history and examination] are incorporated by reference into this progress note. The following additional findings from today's encounter should be read as modifications of the findings on [date of the comprehensive history and examination].*

12. What will these words do when you are in front of the ALJ?

Because you were smart, you submitted a copy of the previous comprehensive history and examination note, along with the progress note for the date of service at issue, when you submitted your documents to the QIC for the reconsideration appeal. As a result, the ALJ will have both notes in front of her as you are presenting your case. And the ALJ will **not** be offended by your "incorporation" of previous findings into the progress note for the date of service at issue.

13. Why will the ALJ not be offended by the incorporation of findings from a previous history and examination?

Attorneys refer to previous documents and incorporate them "by reference" all the time. There is no problem in doing that. The problem arises when a provider decides to "cut and paste" and only changes an occasional word here and there in order to pass a two- or three-page progress note off as completely original on the date of the service at issue.

14. If an established patient returns with a complex problem and you want to update the "comprehensive history," how can you make yourself audit-proof?

Give the patient another copy of your "new patient questionnaire" and have the patient fill it out. Even if you just sign and date that completed questionnaire and scan it into the patient's medical record, that will be enough to satisfy the "comprehensive history" portion of the 99215 code.

15. Now let's start at the beginning of the patient encounter. Why can't you just walk into a treatment room, take care of the patient, and figure out the E&M billing code later?

This is billing suicide by ignorance. The billing rules must drive what you do in the treatment room rather than allowing what you do in the treatment room to drive your billing.

16. What is the first thing you must decide when you walk into a treatment room?

You must immediately decide on the complexity of the patient's problem.

17. Why do you have to immediately decide on the complexity of the patient's problem?

The complexity of the patient's problem determines how extensive the history will be and how extensive the examination will be.

18. Isn't this the polar opposite of your training?

Yes. But you are no longer in training. And with 99% accuracy, you know within 60 seconds of walking into a room whether you are looking at a patient with a simple problem or a complex problem.

19. Once you decide on the complexity of the patient's problem, what does that tell you about the history and the physical examination?

Once you understand the complexity of the patient's problem, a light should come on in your head that tells you what information you need for the history **on that day**, and how complex the examination must be **on that day**, in order to bill the correct E&M code for the appropriate E&M service you should be providing **on that day**.

20. What happens to the level of complexity when there are multiple problems and/or a lot of data to review?

You already know you can increase the complexity of decision-making by one or even two levels if the patient has a laundry list of separate problems and/or you have a huge amount of data to review.

21. What happens to the level of complexity in relation to the risk of complications and/or morbidity or mortality?

You also know it is the "risk of complications and/or morbidity or mortality" that almost always determines the complexity of decision-making.

22. What are the expert physicians on the CPT panels trying to tell you?

The expert physicians on the CPT panels are **screaming** at you: Use the seriousness of the patient's problem to determine what kind of history and what kind of examination are required for the patient sitting in front of you!

23. Are the expert physicians on the CPT panels telling you to up-code?

Absolutely not. The expert physicians on the CPT panels want you to practice best quality medicine, and when a patient's problem requires a 99205 H&P or a 99215 H&P, the expert physicians on the CPT panels want you to perform a comprehensive history and a comprehensive examination.

The same expert physicians would strongly oppose a decision to perform and bill for a comprehensive history and a comprehensive examination when the patient has a 99203- or a 99213-complexity problem.

24. What is the bottom-line message from the expert physicians on the CPT panels?

You must tailor the history and the physical examination to the complexity of the patient's problem.

25. Without looking, can you name the four levels of history described in the CPT Manual?

The four levels of history described in the CPT Manual are the **problem-focused** history, the **expanded problem-focused** history, the **detailed** history, and the **comprehensive** history.

26. Can you define the four levels of history and examination described in the CPT Manual?

If the answer is no, you need to read the seven or eight pages in the CPT Manual on E&M guidelines once a week until you have this down.

27. What happens when you are in front of the ALJ and don't know the difference between the four levels of history and examination described in the CPT Manual?

Medicare will argue that the contents of your progress note did not justify the level of complexity code you billed. You will be arguing that the seriousness of the patient's problem justified the E&M code even if some of the history and physical examination information is absent.

28. If you know the four levels of history and examination, but you don't decide on the appropriate E&M code until the patients are gone, what happens?

You won't have the H&P information you need for the code you want to bill.

29. Does Medicare have "good cops" and "bad cops"?

Yes. Medicare does have "good cops" and "bad cops."

30. Who are the "bad cops"?

The "bad cops" are the attorneys, coders, and full-time insurance physicians who sit around thinking how they can make the billing rules more restrictive and how they can make appeals less successful.

31. Who are the "good cops"?

The "good cops" are the doctors who sit on the American Medical Association (AMA) panels of experts that review the CPT billing codes. Every specialty in medicine is represented and each representative is a recognized expert in her specialty.

These panels of expert doctors want the providers to practice best-quality medicine. As a result, their E&M clinical examples in Appendix C of the CPT Manual graphically describe the complexity of the patient's problem for each specialty, for each E&M code.

32. What does Appendix C in the CPT Manual contain?

The AMA's committee of expert doctors who write and edit the CPT Manual know the E&M codes are not black and white. As a result, these experts have included "Appendix C—Clinical Examples" for the use of the E&M code across a wide range of specialties.

33. Do the experts who write and edit the CPT Manual use a logical approach in assigning increasingly more complex E&M codes to patient problems?

I think the answer is yes.

34. Can we select a single area of clinical interest to illustrate how the complexity of an E&M encounter changes with the clinical facts?

Yes, and I have selected foot and ankle surgery as our area of focus.

35. Can we use a single clinical problem encountered by the foot and ankle surgeons as our model and then march that problem through all levels of E&M complexity?

Yes, and we will use the example of a 65-year-old patient with an infected ingrown toenail as our model patient in order to illustrate how the complexity of an E&M encounter changes with changing clinical facts.

In addition, we will make the foot and ankle clinical examples in Appendix C analogous to our model patient at each E&M level of complexity.

36. How should you view and analyze the Appendix C clinical examples for your specialty?

Make a table. In one column, list all the E&M codes that apply to your practice in order of increasing complexity. Write the Appendix C examples for your area of practice under each code in that column. In the other column, write the E&M characteristics that apply to each code as we have for the foot and ankle surgery examples in this chapter. This exercise will enable you to understand the logic used by the CPT panel of experts in differentiating one level of complexity code from the next level for your area of practice.

37. Why should the 99201 and 99202 E&M codes never be used for new Medicare patients?

Medicare patients come with too much medical history to qualify for the two lowest level E&M new patient codes. Even if the presenting problem seems very innocent, all new Medicare patients require at least a detailed history.

38. Why do all new Medicare patients require at least a detailed history?

A "problem-focused" or an "expanded problem-focused" history will not effectively reveal the shopping list of medical problems that accrue in the lives of all Medicare-aged patients. And that shopping list of problems may bear directly on the patient's current problem.

39. Returning to our 65-year-old model patient with an infected ingrown toenail, what are the CPT Appendix C foot/ankle examples for a 99203 new patient visit?

The two foot/ankle examples read as follows:

> Initial office visit for a 45-year-old hypertensive female with a two-month history of plantar heel pain.
>
> Initial office visit for a 12-year-old male athlete with retrocalcaneal pain and swelling with no prior treatment.

40. Can we move the Appendix C, 99203 clinical examples into a Medicare setting?

Let's make the first patient a 65-year-old hypertensive female with a two-month history of plantar heel pain. Even though systemic hypertension has nothing to do with plantar heel pain, we can draw a reasonable inference from this clinical example. The CPT committee of experts has given us an example of a patient with a localized foot problem and a systemic condition that is not related to the foot problem—but that you should know about—based on a 99203 "detailed history." A new Medicare patient with a localized foot/ankle complaint requires at least a 99203 detailed history and detailed examination.

Let's make the second patient a 72-year-old male athlete with retrocalcaneal pain and swelling, with no prior treatment. For a 12-year-old male athlete, you would be thinking about Sever's disease (inflammation of the calcaneal growth plate due to pull of the Achilles tendon at its insertion site on the back of the heel bone). For our 72-year-old male athlete, that growth plate has been closed for more than five decades. Instead of Sever's disease, you would be thinking about an insertional Achilles tendonitis with or without a (fractured) enthesophyte, and/or partial Achilles tendon tear. In any event, the CPT committee of experts has given us an example of a patient with a subjective complaint of localized pain with activity and an objective finding of clinically obvious swelling at the site of pain. This patient will require at least a 99203 detailed history and detailed examination, and may require more depending on what is revealed in the patient's history and examination.

41. What do these two 99203, Appendix C, foot/ankle clinical examples have in common?

In both 99203 examples, Appendix C describes a *new* patient with a foot/ankle problem not related to or caused by a systemic disease. And in both examples, there is no threat of loss of limb or loss of life.

42. How could we make our model patient analogous to these 99203 clinical examples?

The 65-year-old patient would present with an infected ingrown toenail but without any comorbidities.

43. What are the CPT Appendix C, foot/ankle clinical examples for 99204?

The two foot/ankle examples read as follows:

> Initial office visit for a 42-year-old female with Charcot-Marie-Tooth disease, pes cavus, and worsening painful hammer toes.
>
> Initial office visit for a 55-year-old male with progressive rheumatoid arthritis and deformity of the ankle secondary to previous injury.

44. How can we move these 99204 clinical examples into a Medicare setting and how should we be thinking about our modified examples?

Let's make the first patient a 65-year-old female with Charcot-Marie-Tooth disease, pes cavus, and worsening painful hammer toes. These facts describe a patient with an inherited neurological disorder (Charcot-Marie-Tooth disease) along with a combination of mechanical foot problems that are related to that neurological disorder (pes cavus and worsening, painful hammer toes).

Let's make the second patient a 65-year-old male with progressive rheumatoid arthritis and a deformity of the ankle secondary to previous injury. Under these facts, the second clinical example describes a patient with a systemic disease (progressive rheumatoid arthritis) and a deformity of the ankle secondary to previous injury, with the injury impliedly made worse by the systemic disease.

45. What do these 99204, Appendix C clinical examples have in common?

In both 99204 examples, the patient has a systemic disease along with foot/ankle symptoms that are impliedly made worse by their systemic disease. But there is no threat of loss of limb or loss of life.

46. How could we make our model patient analogous to the 99204 clinical examples?

Our 65-year-old diabetic patient, with or without diabetic neuropathy, has moderate arterial disease in addition to the infected ingrown toenail. But our 99204 patient would be afebrile and would have no evidence of an ascending cellulitis.

47. What are the differences between the 99203 and 99204 clinical examples?

Both 99204 clinical examples have a systemic disease that directly affects the diagnosis and/or treatment of the patient's foot/ankle problem. By contrast, the 99203 clinical examples do not have a systemic disease that directly affects the foot/ankle problem.

48. What are the CPT Appendix C, foot/ankle clinical examples for 99205?

The two examples read as follows:

> Initial office visit for a 75-year-old febrile female with an infected posterior heel ulceration penetrating to bone with comorbidities of diabetes and peripheral vascular disease.
>
> Initial office visit for a 36-year-old hypertensive laborer with inability to bear weight due to multiple metatarsal fractures and forefoot compartment syndrome stemming from a crush injury suffered two days prior.

49. What do the 99205, Appendix C, clinical examples have in common?

In the first 99205 example, the patient has a foot/ankle problem that is related to or caused by a systemic disease, and there is a threat of loss of limb and possible loss of life without prompt intervention.

In the second 99205 example, a crush injury makes systemic hypertension worse so the patient may require (emergency) antihypertensive treatment. On this basis, the patient has a foot/ankle problem related to their systemic hypertension. In addition, there is a threat of loss of limb if a fasciotomy is not timely performed.

50. How could we make our model patient analogous to the first 99205 clinical example?

Our example would be a 65-year-old diabetic patient with or without neuropathy but with significant arterial disease who presents with an infected ingrown toenail and has an ascending cellulitis.

51. How could we make our model patient analogous to the second 99205 clinical example?

Our example could be a 65-year-old diabetic patient whose diabetes is out of control and who presents with an infected ingrown toenail and ascending cellulitis.

52. Should you spend time distinguishing the complexity of the E&M codes?

If you can reduce the progression of the E&M codes you actually use every day to a story that you can easily remember and that makes complete sense to you, you will be able to walk into a treatment room and immediately decide which version of "the story" applies to the patient in front of you. Once you know which version of your story applies, you will automatically pick the correct level of complexity history and physical examination for that patient on that day.

53. Why should the 99211 and the 99212 codes never be used for Medicare patients?

The 99211 code doesn't require even the presence of a "physician or other qualified healthcare professional." And the 99212 code only requires the briefest description of the complaint and an examination limited to the area of complaint. Medicare patients come with too much history and too many possibilities of significant findings on examination to limit the history and examination to either of these codes.

54. What is the Appendix C, foot/ankle clinical example for a 99213 patient visit?

The "Appendix C—Clinical Examples" section of the CPT Manual gives the following foot/ankle example for a 99213 problem:

> Office visit for a 68-year-old female established patient with unilateral painful bunion.

55. How can we characterize the clinical features of the 99213 foot/ankle clinical example?

Based on the Appendix C example, the 99213 patient has an extremity problem without any comorbidities.

56. How could we make our model patient analogous to the 99213 clinical example?

As with the 99203-model patient above, our 65-year-old patient would present with an infected ingrown toenail but without any comorbidities.

57. What is the CPT Appendix C, foot/ankle clinical example for 99214?

The Appendix C section gives the following foot/ankle example for a **99214** problem:

> Office visit for an established diabetic patient with peripheral vascular disease with a new non-infected deep planter ulceration.

58. Can we characterize the clinical features of the 99214 example?

Like the 99204 examples, the 99214 patient has a systemic disease (i.e., peripheral vascular disease), along with foot/ankle symptoms that are impliedly made worse by the systemic disease. But there is no immediate threat of loss of limb or loss of life.

59. How could we make our model patient analogous to the 99214 clinical example?

We will use the same example we gave for 99204. Our 65-year-old diabetic patient may or may not have diabetic neuropathy but would have moderate arterial disease, as the patient presents with an infected ingrown toenail. Significantly, this 99214 patient would be afebrile and would have no evidence of an ascending cellulitis.

60. What is the CPT Appendix C, foot/ankle clinical example for 99215?

The Appendix C section gives the following example for a **99215** problem:

> Office visit for an established diabetic patient with a cellulitic deep plantar abscess and history of previous forefoot amputation on the contralateral side.

61. Can we characterize the clinical features of the 99215 example?

Like the first 99205 example above, the patient has a foot/ankle problem that is related to or caused by a systemic disease, and there is a threat of loss of limb and possible loss of life without prompt intervention.

62. How could we make our model patient analogous to the 99215 clinical example?

Our example could be a 65-year-old diabetic patient with or without neuropathy but with significant arterial disease who presents with an infected ingrown toenail and with an ascending cellulitis.

63. Is it okay to decide on the appropriate E&M code when you are dictating the progress note?

No! Pay attention: **You must make the decision as to the level of complexity E&M code you are going to bill when you walk into the treatment/exam room.** Otherwise, at best, you will pick the appropriate level of complexity E&M code after the patient has left your office, but you won't have the appropriate level of complexity history and examination details that will support payment of the E&M code at issue.

If you are picking out E&M codes after the patients leave your office, you will be telling the judge that the complexity of the problem determined the correct E&M code, even if you didn't have all the required E&M code information. Sometimes the argument will work but many times it won't.

64. Why fight your way out of the "I don't have the required E&M code information" billing hole in front of a judge?

And if you are in front of an ALJ for a repayment of overpayment case or for an audit, and you are trying to justify the absence of required information for many, many E&M codes, how do you think that's going to go?

65. What happens when you don't get the information during the patient encounter and you are selecting the E&M code later while you are dictating?

You will, most frequently, either "down-code" when you select the E&M code or, if you performed an in-office procedure for the patient's problem, you may not bill an E&M code at all.

Change your habits. You are not practicing best-quality medicine and you are killing yourself financially.

66. Until you decide on the correct E&M code, and complete the history and examination requirements for that code, forget about making conversation with the patient.

For many of you, this will be very hard. But you must do this. The patient is not there to socialize with you, and you will not be paid for the E&M service you are providing unless you complete the history and examination requirements for the appropriate E&M code.

Stated differently, the patient wants you to provide first-class care and you want to get paid.

67. When is it okay to bill for a procedure code and an E&M code on the same day?

You already know you can bill for an E&M code and a procedure code if it is a "new patient" encounter.

I hope you also know you are **always** allowed to bill for an E&M code and a procedure code if the E&M code is for a **different problem** than the problem associated with the procedure code.

You may not know that you can bill for an E&M code along with a procedure code if the E&M required for the patient's problem requires **more** than the E&M included in the procedure code.

68. Should you incorporate the E&M code requirements in your progress notes?

The physicians and nonphysician practitioners who bill appropriately and make the most money always incorporate the E&M code requirements as they dictate their notes. In addition, they understand how to select the highest justifiable E&M code based on the complexity of the patient's problem(s).

69. How do you take the guesswork out of the E&M code selection process?

The only way you can take the guesswork out of the E&M code selection process is to know the rules. Otherwise, you will guess wrong a lot of the time and that means you will be selecting codes of higher complexity than can be justified or you are selecting codes of lower complexity than should be billed. Think about it. You are making yourself a target for RAC audits regarding the higher complexity codes that should not be paid, and you are cheating yourself out of payment for the higher complexity codes you are not billing.

70. When you argue for payment of an E&M code, what does the judge want to know?

If you were the ALJ, what would you want to know right off the bat? You would want to know whether the seriousness of the patient's problem justified the level of complexity of the E&M code billed. By the way, you have the perfect chance to frame this argument in your letter brief.

71. Do the clinical examples in Appendix C just apply to the listed specialty/specialties?

No. At the end of each clinical example in Appendix C of the CPT Manual, the medical or surgical specialty for that clinical example is cited in parentheses as the specialty most likely to be asked to take care of that patient. However, many of the patients in the clinical examples could be seen by specialties other than those cited. Therefore, you must read through the examples rather than just looking at the indicated specialties. This will improve your chances of finding a clinical example analogous to the patient associated with your denied claim.

72. What will you do with the Appendix C clinical example during the appeal?

You will make the CPT Manual clinical example analogous to your patient. This will enable you to convince the ALJ **emotionally** that the denied E&M code was appropriate based on the complexity of the patient's problem. Then, the ALJ will be willing to listen to your argument that you met all the technical requirements for the history, the examination, and the medical decision-making required for that denied code. Here is the basic rule for the selection of appropriate E&M codes: **The seriousness of the patient's problem always drives the selection of the appropriate E&M code.**

73. Do Appendix C clinical examples cut both ways?

Yes. Let's be clear about this. Let's assume a 65-five-year-old Medicare beneficiary is seen by the chairperson of the department of medicine at the Mayo Clinic for a complaint of an isolated wart on one foot. And let's assume Dr. Mayo performs the most beautifully detailed history and physical examination in the history of medicine only to find out that the patient is otherwise completely healthy. Despite the Nobel Prize–like, ten-page, single-spaced H&P report, that patient is not going to qualify for more than a 99203 initial office visit E&M code. Why? The presenting problem simply does not support any higher complexity code.

74. In addition to proving that the E&M code was appropriate, what else will you have to prove?

After you convince the ALJ that the denied E&M code was the appropriate code based on the seriousness of the patient's problem, you will then have to prove you met all the technical requirements for the history and the examination or that the missing information was not relevant.

75. Again, where do you find technical requirements for the history, examination, and medical decision-making required for each E&M code?

The "Evaluation and Management (E/M) Services Guidelines" at the beginning of the CPT Manual is the primary source for this information. For those of you who have older copies of the CPT Manual, you know (or should know) that these E&M Guidelines are republished every year. How many of you have taken the time to read through these guidelines? Based on my experience representing physicians at ALJ hearings, the answer is not very many.

76. Does Medicare and all the other insurance companies base compensation for E&M services on the content of your progress notes?

Yes. And if your notes do not support the level of complexity of the E&M code billed based on the severity of the patient's problem and if your notes do not support the level of complexity of the E&M code billed based on the content of the recorded history, examination, and/or medical decision-making, you will not win payment when the code is denied and you protest the denied payment.

77. If you did it but you didn't write it, did it happen?

Here is another painful Medicare appeals lesson many of you have learned: If you didn't write it, *it didn't happen.*

78. If you did it and you wrote it but your note is illegible, did it happen?

If you did it and you wrote it but your note is illegible, *it didn't happen.* Stop guessing at what the E&M codes require and stop handwriting your progress notes. Your income depends on it. And offshore dictation services charge only 6¢ to 9¢ a line, depending on your volume of dictation.

79. If you did it, if you wrote it, if your note is legible—but you didn't sign the note—did it happen?

If you are the target of a CERT audit, the answer is no. Before 2009, the CERT reviewers used a "totality of the circumstances" test to decide whether a claim should be paid or denied. The reviewers would look at the progress notes for other dates, would look at correspondence, would look at orders for tests and at test results to decide whether an unsigned progress note would support payment.

Beginning in 2009, the CERT review standards were changed to an "inflexible checklist" test and the slightest deviation from all the Medicare billing rules that apply to a claim will result in the conclusion that payment of the claim was "improper." You can confirm this by entering "Improper Medicare FFS Payments Report November 2009" into the search bar and then reading page 9 under the heading "Impact of the More Stringent Review Criteria."

80. Why should you be thankful for the authors of the CPT Manual?

The authors of the CPT Manual are telling you exactly what is required for each E&M code, and they are giving you clinical examples that clarify which code to use depending on the patient's problem. Don't fight this. Learn what is required and use it to your advantage.

23b

E&M Code Letter Briefs

OUTLINE

1. When should a provider appeal denied or down-coded E&M claims?
2. Why do the CPT panel doctors want you to bill the highest complexity E&M code appropriate for the patient?
3. Are the doctors on the CPT panel part of the Medicare group denying or down-coding your claims?
4. What will the ALJ need to decide in your favor when you appeal denied or down-coded E&M claims?
5. Is there a general template you can use for denied or down-coded E&M claims?
6. Should you use the CPT Manual language to describe the history, examination, and complexity of medical decision-making for the E&M codes at issue in an appeal?
7. How many pages can you use for the letter portion of the E&M code letter brief, and how many pages can you use for the attachments?
8. What could a sample letter look like?

1. When should a provider appeal denied or down-coded E&M claims?

If a provider is the target of a Medicare **audit**, with a demand for repayment of overpayment based on the extrapolation of a few E&M codes applied to **hundreds of E&M codes** billed within a range of dates, the provider must fight for payment of every denied or down-coded claim. Because just one E&M code in the audit may represent 100 or more E&M codes that are the subject of the audit.

2. Why do the CPT panel doctors want you to bill the highest complexity E&M code appropriate for the patient?

The doctors who sit on the CPT panel and decide the requirements for the E&M codes want you to use the highest complexity E&M code appropriate for the patient you are seeing, based on the complexity of the patient's problem. Why? Because the doctors who sit on the panel want you to practice **best-quality medicine** at each patient encounter.

3. Are the doctors on the CPT panel part of the Medicare group denying or down-coding your claims?

No. The doctors who sit on that CPT panel are **not** part of the Medicare group (doctors, attorneys, and coders) working to keep you from getting paid for the E&M services you provide.

4. What will the ALJ need to decide in your favor when you appeal denied or down-coded E&M claims?

The ALJs will decide in your favor **if** the progress note proves the complexity of the E&M code was appropriate based on the patient's problem, and **if** the progress note contains the information **necessary** (not required information, just necessary information) for the E&M code billed.

5. Is there a general template you can use for denied or down-coded E&M claims?

Yes. Below, you will find a general example of a letter you can use for E&M codes. But first we are going to revisit two points.

6. Should you use the CPT Manual language to describe the history, examination, and complexity of medical decision-making for the E&M codes at issue in an appeal?

Yes. You want to give the ALJ team **the exact wording the ALJ will want to use** when writing the decision in favor of payment. Make it easy for the ALJ!

7. How many pages can you use for the letter portion of the E&M code letter brief, and how many pages can you use for the attachments?

The letter portion of the brief should be no longer than three pages. The attachments, however, can be as many pages as you think necessary.

If the judge wants to know whether an assertion you make in your letter is correct, the attachments to the letter brief will enable her to immediately read the source document your assertion is based on. Even if your attachments to the letter brief add up to 500 pages, that's okay as long as the letter portion of the brief is no longer than three pages.

8. What could a sample letter look like?

After you define the code(s) at issue in the letter portion of the brief, the attachment for each patient whose E&M code is being extrapolated to a large number of identical E&M codes could read as follows.

Dear QIC,

The E&M code at issue for [first name, last name of Medicare patient] is ________.

That code is defined as ________.

The patient is a _______ year-old male/female with [description of problem], who was seen in the office [or other location] on [date of encounter] as a new patient/established patient, complaining of/for follow-up of [complaint or problem being followed up].

The patient's [expanded problem focused/detailed/comprehensive] history, see Attachment #___, revealed the following: ________.

The patient's [expanded problem focused/detailed/comprehensive] examination revealed the following: ________.

Photographs of the patient's [foot/ankle], with the name of the patient, the patient's Medicare number, and the date of the photographs in the background are enclosed in Attachment # ___.

The diagnosis was ________.

The complexity of medical decision making was [of low complexity/of moderate complexity/of high complexity] based on the [limited/multiple/extensive] number of diagnoses or management options; based on the [limited/moderate/extensive] amount and/or complexity of data to be reviewed; and based on the [low/moderate/high] risk of complications and/or morbidity or mortality. See the patient records in Attachment(s) #____, ____, and ____.

Treatment/the treatment plan included ________.

Treatment guidelines for this problem, as published by the [name of specialty or business organization], are enclosed as Attachment #____.

An article from a peer-reviewed journal, with a diagram (or photograph) of a patient with an (almost) identical problem/deformity is enclosed as Attachment #_____. The article supports the treatment/treatment plan provided for [Mr./Ms. first, last].

Additionally, treatment guidelines for this problem are published in the following textbooks: _________, _________, and _________. Those textbook sections are enclosed as Attachments #____–____.

Based on the above, the Medicare contractor [name of contractor] has incorrectly denied/down-coded the originally submitted CPT code [number of E&M code].

24

Procedure Code Requirements

OUTLINE

1. Can a provider use anything other than HCPCS codes when billing Medicare?
2. Do the HCPCS codes require interpretation?
3. Who writes the CPT Manual, how are the CPT codes written, and where do the CPT codes fit in the HCPCS hierarchy?
4. Who writes the HCPCS II Manual, how are the HCPCS II codes written, and where do the HCPCS II codes fit in the HCPCS hierarchy?
5. When is a CPT (HCPCS I) code used and when is an HCPCS II code used?
6. What are the issues in appeals regarding procedure codes?
7. What will Medicare argue when you appeal a denied or down-coded procedure code?
8. When will an ALJ decide in favor of the provider regarding procedure codes?
9. What do the situations favoring payment of a procedure all have in common?
10. Can a provider rely on the descriptions and definitions for the procedure codes in the CPT Manual and the HCPCS II Manual?
11. When a procedure is denied in whole or in part, what could a sample letter to the QIC look like?

1. Can a provider use anything other than HCPCS codes when billing Medicare?

No. HCPCS is the acronym for Healthcare Common Procedure Coding System. The HCPCS codes must be used when billing for all services provided to Medicare beneficiaries.

2. Do the HCPCS codes require interpretation?

No. The HCPCS I (CPT) codes and the HCPCS II codes are not meant to be tricky. The plain and simple meaning of a CPT code or an HCPCS II code is how the code should be applied.

3. Who writes the CPT Manual, how are the CPT codes written, and where do the CPT codes fit in the HCPCS hierarchy?

The CPT Manual is written by the AMA (American Medical Association).

The CPT codes are numeric (e.g., 77373).

The CPT codes are considered HCPCS Level 1 codes.

4. Who writes the HCPCS II Manual, how are the HCPCS II codes written, and where do the HCPCS II codes fit in the HCPCS hierarchy?

The HCPCS II Manual is written by CMS (Centers for Medicare & Medicaid Services).

The HCPCS II codes are alphanumeric (e.g., G0339).

The HCPCS II Manual codes are Level 2 codes.

5. When is a CPT (HCPCS I) code used and when is an HCPCS II code used?

Medicare providers **must** use the CPT (HCPCS I) code unless an HCPCS II code is more specific in its description of the provided service. As an example, the HCPCS II codes G0339 and G0340 more accurately describe the delivery of robotic stereotactic body radiation therapy (R-SBRT) than does the CPT code, 77373, that describes (non-robotic) stereotactic body radiation therapy (SBRT). Therefore, the G0339 and G0340 codes would be used instead of the 77373 code when billing for R-SBRT.

Most commonly, the HCPCS II codes are used to bill for items and procedures that are not mentioned in the CPT Manual.

6. What are the issues in appeals regarding procedure codes?

The procedure code definitions are never at issue. The fight is always over whether the correct procedure code was billed based on the procedure report, whether the procedure code billed is allowed under the CCI edits, whether the LCD indications for the use of the code are met, and whether the documents required for billing the procedure code are in the patient's file.

7. What will Medicare argue when you appeal a denied or down-coded procedure code?

Most commonly, the contractor and the QIC will argue that the billed procedure code must be down-coded based on the progress note, that the billed procedure code is not allowed under CCI edits (e.g., unbundling), that the billed procedure was "not medically reasonable and necessary" based on the LCD indications, or that the required documents requested by Medicare were not submitted by the provider (e.g., the documents required for billing diabetic therapeutic shoes).

8. When will an ALJ decide in favor of the provider regarding procedure codes?

The ALJ will most likely decide in your favor in all of the following circumstances: You can prove the down-coding was wrong based on the procedure report meeting the requirements of the billed code, the CCI edit was wrong, the billed procedure was medically reasonable and necessary based on the recognized standard of care, and the LCD indication limitation should not be followed (e.g., when digital images confirm the need for the contested service), and there is no question the service was provided.

9. What do the situations favoring payment of a procedure all have in common?

The above list is not all-inclusive, but all these circumstances have the same thing in common. When medical necessity supports the procedure and there is no question the procedure has been performed as billed, the ALJ is likely to find in favor of the provider—even when a Medicare "billing rule" is not obeyed.

10. Can a provider rely on the descriptions and definitions for the procedure codes in the CPT Manual and the HCPCS II Manual?

No. Do not rely on the definitions in the CPT Manual and the HCPCS II Manual. You must read the contractor's LCD and any related Medicare MLN (Medicare Learning Network) article that addresses the service at issue because the applicable LCD and MLN article may add a host of requirements to the code(s) you are billing for the service at issue.

11. When a procedure is denied in whole or in part, what could a sample letter to the QIC look like?

Dear QIC,

The CPT (or HCPCS) code(s) at issue is/are ________.

This/these code(s) is/are defined as ________.

The patient, a ________-year-old male/female with [description of problem], was first seen on [date of encounter] complaining of [complaint]/for treatment of ________.

The patient's history and examination report, as well as the subsequent progress notes that predate the contested procedure(s) was/were performed may be found in Attachment #____.

Photographs of the patient's problem, with the name of the patient, the patient's Medicare number, and the date of the photographs in the background are enclosed in Attachment # ____.

The diagnosis was ________, ICD 10 code(s) ________.

On [date(s) of treatment], the denied/down-coded procedure was performed. A copy of the procedure report is enclosed in Attachment #____.

The [name of contractor] LCD that applies to the contested service is L ___________. The applicable LCD, L________, states: ________.

The MLN article that applies to the contested service is _____________. This article states: "________."

Treatment guidelines for this problem, as published by [name of specialty or business organization], are enclosed as Attachment #___. These treatment guidelines support the treatment for (first, last).

An article from a peer-reviewed journal, with a diagram (or photograph) of a patient with an (almost) identical problem is enclosed as Attachment #___. The article supports the treatment provided for [Mr./Ms. first, last].

Additionally, treatment guidelines for this problem are published in the following textbooks: _________, _________, and _________. Those textbook sections are enclosed as Attachments #___–___.

OR

The service provided for the patient's problem, evident in the submitted photograph, is not included in the LCD indications/is prohibited in the applicable LCD. However, the service was medically reasonable and necessary for the following reasons: ________.

In addition, the service provided is ***as safe as/safer than*** *the indicated service in the LCD because ________. The safety of the provided service is supported by the documents enclosed as Attachments #___–___.*

The service provided is **as effective as/more effective than** *the indicated service in the LCD and this statement is supported by the documents enclosed as Attachments # ___–___.*

The service provided is **no more expensive than/is less expensive than** *the "indicated" service in the LCD as supported by the document(s) enclosed as Attachment #___.*

Based on the above, payment should be awarded for the denied CPT/HCPCS II code/service provided for [Ms./Mr. first, last].

When using the above examples, always **remember to eliminate the unnecessary words, parentheses, underscores, and sentences.**

25

Progress Notes

OUTLINE

1. For an ALJ, what does a progress note have to say to decide in favor of the provider?
2. When is it okay to handwrite progress notes?
3. What bad things happen when you write your notes by hand?
4. What happens when you go to an ALJ hearing with handwritten progress notes?
5. When is it okay to use commercial, templated progress notes?
6. When is it okay to paste the initial H&P note into all of your progress notes?
7. What is the ALJ thinking when you paste the initial H&P as more than 95% of the progress note?
8. When is it okay to use your initial H&P as "the letter" you send to the referring doctor?
9. When should you convert to dictated progress notes?
10. How much does it cost to have your dictated progress notes transcribed?
11. Where can you find an in-office transcriptionist for $1,400 a month?
12. If suitable for your specialty or business, you should use body diagrams.
13. What will body diagrams do for your medical records?
14. Should you scan the body diagram into the patient's medical record?

1. For an ALJ, what does a progress note have to say to decide in favor of the provider?

At an absolute minimum, the provider's progress note for the date in question would have to be legible and would have to contain a description of the patient's problem and what was done for that problem. Without looking at any other document, the progress note should justify payment for the service that was billed and denied.

2. When is it okay to handwrite progress notes?

Never.

It is okay to handwrite your progress notes only if you are able to travel back in time before the year 2010.

3. What bad things happen when you write your notes by hand?

When you write a progress note by hand, you leave out important information because it is too tedious to write everything, and, anyway, your writing is illegible. As a result, your progress notes will be discarded by almost any ALJ you find yourself in front of.

Subtract the difference in time required to dictate your notes from the time you spend writing them and use that time to see one or two more patients during the same day. Assuming a modest payment of $25 per patient visit, do you really think the expense of dictating all your notes at the rate of 6¢ a line isn't covered by the one or two additional patient visits?

Finally, you can speak many times faster than you can write. As a result, your progress note will far more accurately and expansively reflect what happened during each patient encounter.

4. What happens when you go to an ALJ hearing with handwritten progress notes?

The ALJs reject any document that is not readable. In 2010, the Medicare Learning Network (MLN) published the "Evaluation and Management Services Guide" that relies on the 1995 and the 1997 versions of Medicare's "Documentation Guidelines for Evaluation and Management Services."

All three documents include the following: "The medical record should be **legible**."

But even as you read this, Medicare is tightening the rules. So here is the warning worth repeating. If it **isn't documented**, you didn't do it. If it is documented, but your note is **illegible**, you didn't do it. If it is documented and your note is legible but **you didn't sign** the note, you didn't do it. If you didn't do it, the ALJ is not going to award payment for the billed service.

5. When is it okay to use commercial, templated progress notes?

Although I have successfully represented providers at ALJ hearings where commercially available template notes with diagrams have been used, I am always crossing my fingers hoping the judge will allow me to explain what the template forms say and how they are used.

If you want a good idea of how the ALJs sees your template notes, give the template form you are using to a nonmedical friend and have the friend spend five minutes looking at the form. Then have them explain to you what the form says. That is how much time the ALJ will spend on the form and how little the ALJ will understand about the form.

However, it must also be said that the template forms are an improvement over entirely handwritten notes.

6. When is it okay to paste the initial H&P note into all of your progress notes?

Never! When all or most of the initial H&P note is incorporated into **all** of your subsequent progress notes, several bad things happen:

1. You fail to dictate the quantity and quality of information that flows from the patient encounters and would otherwise meet most progress note requirements.
2. The ALJ who, by definition, is an expert on document review, immediately and correctly concludes you are trying to fool the reader into believing all or most of the information in each progress note was obtained on the date of the note.
3. When the ALJ spots the same typo at the same spot in every progress note, the ALJ stops listening.

7. What is the ALJ thinking when you paste the initial H&P as more than 95% of the progress note?

The ALJ correctly concludes your appeal is a scam and decides against you regardless of the rest of the information you present during the hearing.

8. When is it okay to use your initial H&P as "the letter" you send to the referring doctor?

Always! Why would you want to reinvent the wheel every time you write a letter back to a referring doctor regarding a new patient?

Send a copy of your initial H&P along with a note that says something like:

Dear Dr. ________, Enclosed, please find a copy of my initial patient encounter notes regarding ________. Thank you for the referral and please don't hesitate to call if there are any questions regarding my findings and/or treatment plan.

9. When should you convert to dictated progress notes?

Yesterday. There are providers in your community who already use HIPAA-compliant dictation services in India, Pakistan, and so on. The transcription rates are unspeakably cheap, and the notes come back within 24 hours in Microsoft Word with any questionable words highlighted in bold.

10. How much does it cost to have your dictated progress notes transcribed?

Currently, the transcription rates are between 6¢ and 9¢ a line, depending on the volume of work and your negotiating abilities.

11. Where can you find an in-office transcriptionist for $1,400 a month?

There were three providers in my podiatry practice, and I paid all the overhead expenses, including our transcription service based in Islamabad, Pakistan. All three doctors dictated every progress note and letter, and my monthly bill for transcription never exceeded $1,400, based on a per line rate of $.06. Where are you going to hire an in-office transcriptionist for $1,400/month?

12. If suitable for your specialty or business, you should use body diagrams.

For those of you who practice or work with a specific body area, and many or most of the problems you address can be circled on a diagram of that body area, you need a template diagram that can be incorporated (scanned) into your progress notes.

For example, if you are a foot and ankle surgeon, you need a single page "template" for each patient encounter that has the name of the patient and the date of the encounter at the top of the page and diagrams of dorsal and plantar views of both feet and medial, lateral, anterior, and posterior views of both feet/ankles/lower legs, along with some lines on the page for writing.

Number the areas of complaint, using number 1 for the problem the patient is most concerned about.

13. What will body diagrams do for your medical records?

The purpose of the handwritten single page of diagrams is to provide you with a reminder of all the problems, exam findings, and treatment recommendations using abbreviations or marks indicating specific types of problems. You will refer to these notes when dictating.

14. Should you scan the body diagram into the patient's medical record?

Yes. The diagram template with handwritten notes for each encounter should be scanned into the patient's electronic file. This is your best defense against inaccurate dictation at the end of the day and is a defense that rings true in front of an ALJ.

26

How to Win Medicare Appeals

OUTLINE

1. Know the E&M codes you use every day.
2. Read the CPT requirements for those E&M codes.
3. Do not handwrite your progress notes.
4. Do not cut and paste your initial H&P into subsequent progress notes.
5. If appropriate, use photos of the patient's problem for the Medicare appeal.
6. You must authenticate photos of the patient's problem.
7. One person should enter all information on appeals into the office computer.
8. Create and maintain a computer file of authoritative documents supporting the services that have been denied by Medicare.
9. Maintain a continuously running spreadsheet for all Medicare appeals.
10. Review the Medicare Remittance Advice statements every day.
11. Do not make a CCI edit mistake twice.
12. Respond immediately to Medicare demands for documents regarding unpaid claims.
13. Respond immediately to Medicare demands for documents regarding paid claims.
14. When up against an appeal deadline, send the appropriate Medicare form—without anything else—with proof of delivery and by overnight mail.
15. Submit a letter brief when you request the reconsideration appeal.
16. Personally review all the documents before the QIC appeal packet is mailed.
17. Always request a video teleconference ALJ hearing.
18. Do not rely on your attorney to write the letter brief without your help.
19. When the QIC raises new issues, restrict your second letter brief to those issues.
20. You must always be prepared to prove medical necessity.
21. Never argue a Medicare rule is "unfair."
22. Never go to an ALJ hearing thinking you can wing it.
23. When the judge starts talking, you stop talking.
24. Answer the question the judge is asking.

The following statements are based on common sense and are covered elsewhere in the book. But read these three pages. They are the reason you bought the book.

1. Know the E&M codes you use every day.

You do not have to know the requirements for the E&M codes you do not bill. You must know the requirements for the E&M codes you do bill. And most likely, you bill fewer than ten E&M codes 95% of the time.

2. Read the CPT requirements for those E&M codes.

The CPT requirements for the E&M codes are spelled out in detail at the very beginning of the CPT Manual. Read those six or seven pages slowly and carefully once a year when you get your new CPT Manual. Like the CPR course you used to take every couple of years, you will be amazed at how much you have forgotten.

And when you get the new CPT Manual each year, read the Medicare Articles and the LCDs that are published by your contractor regarding all the services you commonly provide.

3. Do not handwrite your progress notes.

Do not handwrite your progress notes. Dictate your notes and have them transcribed. It's cheap, it's effective, and it's efficient. Offshore transcription costs as little as 6¢ a line. You can dictate five times as much information about a patient visit in the time it takes to handwrite an unreadable and incomplete progress note.

4. Do not cut and paste your initial H&P into subsequent progress notes.

Never use the initial H&P note over and over again as a "new" progress note. At the very least, your dictated progress note should include a description of the patient's problem, what you did, why you did it, and what your plans are for future care.

5. If appropriate, use photos of the patient's problem for the Medicare appeal.

When you provide care for problems that can be visualized in a photograph, and photographs of the patient's problems can appropriately be shown at an ALJ hearing, take digital images of the patient's problem(s).

6. You must authenticate photos of the patient's problem.

If you take photographs of a patient's problem, authenticate the images by using a letter-sized piece of computer paper as a background with the patient's initials, Medicare number, and the date of the photograph printed on the sheet of computer paper in a large enough font size to read easily.

7. One person should enter all information on patient appeals into the office computer.

Put an office system in place to appeal denied claims and put one person in charge of maintaining the computer entries and the appeals for all denied claims.

8. Create and maintain a computer file of authoritative documents supporting the services that have been denied by Medicare.

Create a computer file for each of the commonly denied procedure codes you bill. Place copies of the articles and textbook sections you will use to fight payment denials in each procedure code computer file.

9. Maintain a continuously running spreadsheet for all Medicare appeals.

Use a continuously running spreadsheet for all Medicare appeals and review the spreadsheet once a week—for five minutes—with the person who maintains the spreadsheet.

10. Review the Medicare Remittance Advice statements every day.

Review the Medicare Remittance Advice statements every day. Highlight any denials or down-codes. Have the highlighted RAs scanned into your office computer in a separate Medicare file.

11. Do not make a CCI edit mistake twice.

Read the CCI edits for any procedure code where payment is denied based on a CCI edit. Don't make the same mistake twice.

12. Respond immediately to Medicare demands for documents regarding unpaid claims.

You won't get paid until Medicare receives the requested documents and determines payment should be made for the service in question.

13. Respond immediately to Medicare demands for documents regarding paid claims.

Assume one of the Medicare contractors (MAC, RAC, CERT, SMRC, UPIC) is opening up an audit.

14. When up against an appeal deadline, send the appropriate Medicare form—without anything else—with proof of delivery and by overnight mail.

If you are up against a timeline for an appeal, send the appropriate Medicare form for that appeal with proof of delivery by overnight mail.

Appeal all initial claim denials within one week of receiving the initial claim denial.

Appeal all redetermination denials within one week of receiving the redetermination denials.

15. Submit a letter brief when you request the reconsideration appeal.

In a letter less than three pages, explain what you did and why you did it, how you know it was the correct thing to do, and why the contractor's denial reasons are wrong, and staple it to copies of the patient's medical records. When you request the QIC appeal, submit all of your evidence supporting payment: a copy of **all related patient records** (hard copies of digital [e.g., iPad or smartphone] images that show the patient's deformities/problems); the progress note, procedure report, imaging report, and/or lab findings for the service date at issue; other progress notes (e.g., initial H&P and/or letters from referring or co-treating doctors); published statements by specialty organizations supporting the service you provided; peer-reviewed journal articles supporting the service you provided; and textbook section(s) supporting the service you provided.

Your best arguments should always come first in the letter!

16. Personally review all the documents before the QIC appeal packet is mailed.

Make sure all necessary documents are signed and included in the reconsideration appeal packet sent to the QIC. Do not allow a QIC evidence package to go out the door until you have personally reviewed the contents.

17. Always request a video teleconference ALJ hearing.

Always request a video teleconference ALJ hearing. You want to make sure you and the judge are on the same page at the same time during the hearing. And you want to make sure the judge is not distracted by something happening out of view of the camera as you are arguing and/or while your witness or patient is testifying.

18. Do not rely on your attorney to write the letter brief without your help.

Even if you are represented by an attorney, do not rely on the attorney to write the prehearing letter brief without your assistance. The attorney knows as much about your specialty or your business as you know about law, which is to say, nothing. Write the medical portion of the three-page prehearing brief using the same language you would use to explain the patient's problem to the patient. Trade the prehearing brief back and forth with your attorney until you are both satisfied the brief accurately and concisely explains the patient's problem and your treatment of that problem in easy-to-understand language.

19. When the QIC raises new issues, restrict your second letter brief to those issues.

When the QIC raises **no new issues** in the reconsideration denial letter, do not bring up and do not write about any issues other than those listed in the redetermination denial letter.

When the QIC raises **new issues** in the reconsideration denial letter, submit a second letter brief to the ALJ but do not bring up and do not write about any issues other than the new issues raised by the QIC.

20. You must always be prepared to prove medical necessity.

You must always be prepared to explain to the judge why your denied treatment was "medically reasonable and necessary."

21. Never argue a Medicare rule is "unfair."

Arguing a Medicare rule applied to your claim is "unfair" is a sure loser. The judge has to follow the Medicare rules. Instead, tell the judge why the Medicare rule cited by the contractor and/or QIC as the reason for denial should not be applied to the claim at issue.

22. Never go to an ALJ hearing thinking you can wing it.

Never go to an ALJ hearing without preparing your presentation. As soon as you begin to ramble, the judge begins to think about lunch.

23. When the judge starts talking, you stop talking.

During the ALJ hearing, do not interrupt the judge and do not talk over her. You will **always** stop speaking as soon as the judge starts speaking.

24. Answer the question the judge is asking.

When the ALJ asks you a question, answer the question asked by the judge. Do not answer the question you think she should be asking. You will get the chance to say what you want to say during the hearing and the judge will understand she is "missing the point" as you present your argument.

27

How to Lose Medicare Appeals

OUTLINE

1. Don't bother reading the CPT requirements for the E&M codes you use. You know what you need to know from residency training.
2. If you want to use the 99205 code for all new patients, that's your business.
3. Don't waste your time reading CCI edits.
4. You're right: The LCDs are also a waste of time.
5. You should cut and paste your initial H&P for future progress notes. It always looks great!
6. Your handwritten notes are perfectly adequate.
7. Just because a service you provide is flagged as an "issue" on the RAC website does not mean you have to take special care when billing for that service.
8. Your time is too valuable to waste on reviewing the Remittance Advice statements from Medicare.
9. Medicare appeals are simple. You don't need a special plan.
10. Even if you don't send the documents your contractor is requesting, the contractor will still pay you for those services.
11. Don't worry about submitting any evidence before you request an ALJ hearing.
12. If the deadline for an appeal is approaching, just ask for an extension.
13. You don't have to send a letter to the QIC explaining your evidence (patient care documents) and why you should be paid.
14. Let your attorney do all the preparation for the hearing. That's what she is paid to do.
15. If you think the judge needs to hear about issues not raised by the QIC, by all means, let her know.
16. If you think a Medicare rule is not fair, tell the judge all about it.
17. Do not bother preparing your presentation for the judge. You will do a better job if you are relaxed.
18. If you have something important to say during the hearing, interrupt the judge and say it.
19. If you need to reframe the judge's question in order to keep the hearing on track, reframe the question and then answer it.

1. Don't bother reading the CPT requirements for the E&M codes you use. You know what you need to know from residency training.

Don't bother reading the CPT requirements for each of the E&M codes you use. The definition of each code tells you everything you need to know.

2. If you want to use the 99205 code for all new patients, that's your business.

If you want to use the 99205 code for all new patients, and if you want to use the 99215 code for all established patients, it should be your privilege to do so. Remember, you are board certified.

3. Don't waste your time reading CCI edits.

Don't bother reading the CCI edits for the procedure codes you commonly bill. Bill whatever you think is fair.

4. You're right: The LCDs are also a waste of time.

Don't bother reading the LCDs published by your contractor regarding the services you provide. You're a specialist and you know what your patients need.

5. You should cut and paste your initial H&P for future progress notes. It always looks great!

Use the initial H&P note over and over again as "new" progress notes for the same patient, changing only a word here and there. It will save time and looks impressive.

6. Your handwritten notes are perfectly adequate.

Handwrite your progress notes. It's okay.

7. Just because a service you provide is flagged as an "issue" on the RAC website does not mean you have to take special care when billing for that service.

When you provide services that are flagged as "issues" on the RAC websites, such as diabetic therapeutic shoe services, don't bother filling out the reporting forms required in the LCD and don't waste time taking digital images of the patients' ulcers, hemorrhagic keratomas, hammertoes, and so on. The ALJ will take your word that the patient needed the service.

8. Your time is too valuable to waste on reviewing the Remittance Advice statements from Medicare.

Don't bother reviewing the Medicare Remittance Advice (EOMB) statements every day. Let your front office staff do it. After all, that's what they are paid to do.

9. Medicare appeals are simple. You don't need a special plan.

Don't bother putting a system in place to appeal denied claims. Just appeal when it occurs to you.

10. Even if you don't send the documents your contractor is requesting, the contractor will still pay you for those services.

Don't respond to demands for documents that you receive from your Medicare contractor regarding unpaid claims. The contractor will pay you without those documents.

11. Don't worry about submitting any evidence before you request an ALJ hearing.

Don't bother submitting all of your evidence supporting payment when you request the QIC appeal. If the QIC denies payment, you can always submit your additional evidence later to the ALJ.

12. If the deadline for an appeal is approaching, just ask for an extension.

If you are up against a timeline for an appeal, just ask for an extension to get the appeal documents submitted.

13. You don't have to send a letter to the QIC explaining your evidence (patient care documents) and why you should be paid.

Don't bother submitting a prehearing brief to the QIC. You can "wing it" and still win.

14. Let your attorney do all the preparation for the hearing. That's what she is paid to do.

Once you have an attorney, relax. The attorney is expected to do all the work in preparation for the ALJ hearing.

15. If you think the judge needs to hear about issues not raised by the QIC, by all means, let her know.

If you think there are issues that were not raised by the QIC in the reconsideration denial letter, and those issues should be fully addressed, by all means, bring those issues up at the ALJ hearing.

16. If you think a Medicare rule is not fair, tell the judge all about it.

If you think a rule that Medicare applied to your denied claim wasn't fair, argue why the rule is unfair and whine that the judge should award payment based on the "unfairness" of the rule.

17. Do not bother preparing your presentation for the judge. You will do a better job if you are relaxed.

You can go to an ALJ hearing without preparing a presentation. After all, you know what happened with the patient and can explain it to the judge.

18. If you have something important to say during the hearing, interrupt the judge and say it.

During the ALJ hearing, if you think you have something important to say and you want to say it before you forget it, go ahead and interrupt the ALJ. Judges like that.

19. If you need to reframe the judge's question in order to keep the hearing on track, reframe the question and then answer it.

When the ALJ asks you a question and you think the judge is missing the point, don't answer the question. Instead, tell the judge the question she should be asking based on the point you want to make. The judge will appreciate your help.

28

Medicare Forms You Should Be Using

LIST OF MEDICARE FORMS NEEDED FOR APPEALS

Form CMS-1696: Appointment of Representative
Form CMS-R-131: Advance Beneficiary Notice
Form CMS-20027: Medicare Redetermination Request Form
Form CMS-20033: Medicare Reconsideration Request Form
OMHA-100: Request for ALJ Hearing or Review of Dismissal (by the QIC)
OMHA-100A: Request for ALJ Hearing or Review of Dismissal—Multiple Claim Attachment
HHS-719: Request for Copy of Records in the (ALJ) Case File
HHS-724: Request to Correct, Amend, or Delete a Record
HHS-727: Extension Request to File a Request for an ALJ Hearing
HHS-728: Filing of New Evidence (after the QIC has issued the reconsideration decision)
HHS-729: Response to Notice of Hearing
HHS-730: Withdrawal of Request for an ALJ Hearing
Form DAB-101: Request for Review of ALJ Medicare Decision/Dismissal (sent to the HHS Departmental Appeals Board, Medicare Appeals Council)

HOW TO FIND THESE MEDICARE FORMS ON THE COMPUTER

In the Internet search bar, put the word "Medicare" in front of the form you are looking for and click. For example, if you want the form to request a redetermination appeal, put "Medicare Form CMS-20027" into the search bar and click.

Yes, I know the younger readers are laughing as they read this.

Glossary

A/B MACs Part A/Part B Medicare Administrative Contractors.
ACT "The Act" in this book refers to the Social Security Act.
Add-on code software An add-on code is a CPT code that is only payable when billed with its linked, primary CPT code. Add-on code software makes sure the linked primary CPT code has been billed before payment is allowed for the add-on code. See Chapter 22, "Medicare Audits."
ADR Additional Documentation Request.
AIC Amount in controversy. The AIC is the amount of money that must be at issue to qualify for an ALJ hearing. The 2020 AIC is $170. The AIC is the amount Medicare will actually pay you if you win the ALJ decision. See Chapter 20a, "Submitting the Request for an ALJ Appeal."
ALJ Administrative Law Judge.
ALJ appeal An ALJ appeal is the third level of appeal and is the next step in the appeals process after the reconsideration appeal. The ALJ appeal is the only point in the appeals process where the denied payment is reviewed by a neutral third party.
ALJ hearing An ALJ hearing for underpayments or overpayments occurs before an ALJ, usually by phone, sometimes by video teleconference and, rarely, in person.
ALJ team Each ALJ has a team that usually consists of the ALJ, two attorney advisors, and two legal assistants.
APA Administrative Procedures Act. This is a federal law that controls how the rules for Medicare appeals are written and enforced. The exhaustion of remedies doctrine is part of the APA.
Appeal A provider (provider/supplier) has the right to appeal underpayments and overpayments.
Articles The Medicare Learning Network articles (MLN Matters) explain national Medicare policy in an easy-to-understand format. However, Medicare has not provided an easy-to-use list of topics that would help a provider find the MLN article on the topic being searched. MLN articles focus on coverage, billing, and payment rules for specific provider types.
Beyond a reasonable doubt This is the standard of proof applied in criminal law. For teaching purposes, "beyond a reasonable doubt" means it is 95% more likely one party's evidence should prevail as opposed to 5% that the other party's evidence should prevail. The standard of "beyond a reasonable doubt" is used as hyperbole in this book to emphasize the need for overwhelming proof in some circumstances (e.g., when a provider is appealing an ALJ denial to the Medicare Appeals Council).
Black letter law This refers to the word-for-word statutes, regulations, and policies that apply to payment disputes.
Blanket review (by the RACs) Blanket reviews of specific services (e.g., diabetic therapeutic shoes) are allowed only after the RACs have proved to CMS that billing for the service in question has been "improper" on a widespread basis. CMS must give its approval before a blanket review can be conducted, and the topics approved for blanket reviews are listed as "issues" on the RAC websites.
CAC representative Carrier Advisory Committee representative. Every MAC has CAC representatives for every specialty. Call your state professional organization to find out the names of your CAC reps.
CARC Claims Adjustment Reason Code. A Remittance Advice Remark Code (RARC) is a shorthand reason for denial. A CARC is a longer explanation of a denial along with what you have to do to get paid. Also see the book *Denial Codes Plain English Descriptions* by DecisionHealth.
CBO Congressional Budget Office.
CCI Correct Coding Initiative. The CCI software includes the PTP (procedure-to-procedure) software program and the MUE (mutually unlikely edits) program.

CCS Certified coding specialist.

CERT Comprehensive Error Rate Testing. The CERT audit program is managed by two contractors, the CERT statistical contractor (CERT-SC) and the CERT review contractor (CERT-RC).

Certificate of mailing A certificate of mailing is USPS Form 3817. This proves a document has been sent but does not prove a document has been received by the addressee.

CERT-RC The CERT review contractor requests the medical records from providers; determines whether the records comply with Medicare coverage, coding, and billing rules; and determines whether the claim was correctly paid or if there has been an underpayment or overpayment.

CERT-SC The CERT statistical contractor determines how claims will be sampled and calculates the improper payment rate.

CFR Code of Federal Regulations. The 42 CFR Section 405 contains all the rules regarding Medicare claims and appeals. The daily published Federal Register rules are codified into final rules, and the final rules are published as the Code of Federal Regulations.

Circumstances beyond the provider's control When applied to Medicare appeals, this phrase usually means an act of God, such as a fire, flood, or earthquake.

Clear and convincing (standard of proof) This is the standard of proof applied in civil lawsuits where more than money is at stake. Examples would include a restraining order or the probate of a will. Although the standard of proof in ALJ hearings is supposedly by a "preponderance of the evidence," the standard of "clear and convincing" is used in this book to describe the heightened level of proof needed to convince an ALJ to overturn a claim denial when the applicable LCD policy prohibited the denied service.

Clerical errors A clerical error is a data entry error. In this book, clerical errors most commonly refer to mistakes on the originally submitted claim form. See the Medicare Claims Processing Manual, Chapter 34, Section 10.4—Reopenings Based on Clerical or Minor Errors and Omissions.

CMS Centers for Medicare & Medicaid Services.

CMS-855 form The CMS 855 revalidation form has to be submitted every five years by the A/B providers and has to resubmitted every two years by the DMEPOS providers.

CMS-20027 form The CMS-20027 form is used to request a redetermination, first-level appeal.

CMS-20031 form Transfer of appeal rights form.

CMS-20033 form The CMS-20033 form is used to request a reconsideration, second-level appeal.

CMS regional office When your appeal is incorrectly dismissed and the MAC or the QIC refuses to take a second look, contact your regional CMS office. The regional offices are listed at: https://www.cms.gov/About-CMS/Agency-Information/RegionalOffices/index.html. If the regional office won't help, submit an email complaint to the Medicare fee for service appeals office at: MedicareFFSAppeals@cms.hhs.gov.

Complex claim review Review of medical records by a person (as opposed to simple claim review done by a software program).

Contingency fee The RACs are the only medical review contractors who work on a contingency fee basis. Each RAC negotiates its contingency fee arrangement with CMS when the RAC is hired. When a RAC successfully claws back money from a provider, the RAC gets to keep its contingency fee amount. When a provider successfully appeals an overpayment, the RAC has to return all the recouped payments and interest to the provider.

Contractor When used by itself in the book, the word "contractor" usually refers to the Medicare Administrative Contractor. However, the phrase "Medicare contractors" includes MACs, RACs, CERT, SMRC, and UPICs.

Cost-plus contract With the exception of the RACs who work on a contingency fee basis, the other medical review contractors (MACs, CERT, UPICs, and SMRC) sign cost-plus contracts with CMS and are paid actual expenses plus a predetermined profit.

CPC Certified Professional Coder.

CPT Manual The Common Procedural Terminology Manual, written by the AMA, is also referred to as the HCPCS I Manual. A HCPCS II code is only to be used when the HCPCS II code more accurately describes the provided service.

CR Change Request. This refers to a Medicare policy rule published after an initial rule is published. An example would be Change Request 8501 that lists the issues CMS and the contractor look at in deciding whether to participate in an ALJ hearing:

- The policy implications in the case
- The amount of money at issue
- The source of the denial
- Program integrity matters in the case
- The extent to which the case is about a recurring issue

CV Curriculum Vitae. The résumé of any expert who will testify on your behalf at the ALJ hearing. You must always send your expert's CV to the judge before the hearing.

CWF Common working file. All Medicare contractors must enter their billing and claims data on beneficiaries and providers into the CWF.

Date of a Medicare denial document The date of a Medicare denial document is *not* the typed date on the document. The date of a Medicare denial document is the postmarked date on the envelope containing the document.

Denial Code Dictionary DecisionHealth sells a dictionary of the denial codes written in plain English. The dictionary costs about $140 and is worth it. Otherwise the following link provides a no-cost list of the Remittance Advice remark codes: http://www.wpc-edi.com/reference/codelists/healthcare/remittance-advice-remark-codes/.

De novo hearing ALJ hearings are de novo reviews. This means the ALJ uses the records from the MAC and the QIC, but reviews the evidence and the law (Medicare rules) from the beginning—without regard to the denial decisions of the MAC and the QIC.

Dismissal An appeal can be dismissed by the MAC, by the QIC, or by the ALJ for two reasons: Either the appeal request does not contain all the required information, or the appeal was submitted too late—or both. Unless a dismissal is vacated (reversed), the appeal is over. See Chapter 16, "Dismissals."

DMEPOS Durable medical equipment, prosthetics, orthotics, and supplies. See Chapter 22, "Medicare Audits."

DMEPOS MACs Durable medical equipment, prosthetics, orthotics, and supply Medicare Administrative Contractors. They are called DME MACs for short.

DOJ Department of Justice.

DRG Diagnosis Related Group

E&M Evaluation and Management.

EIN Employer Identification Number. This unique nine-digit number is assigned by the Internal Revenue Service (IRS) to business entities operating in the United States for the purposes of identification.

ERRP Error Rate Reduction Plan. The cornerstone of the MACs' efforts to prevent improper payments is each contractor's ERRP, which includes the following:

1. Targeted provider education to items or services with the highest improper payments.
2. Prepayment and post-payment claim review targeted to those services with the highest improper payments. In addition, in order to encourage providers to submit claims correctly, MACs can perform extrapolation reviews as needed.
3. New or revised LCDs, articles, or coding instructions to assist providers how to correctly submit claims and under what circumstances the services will be considered "reasonable and necessary."

Exhaustion of remedies doctrine This doctrine is contained in the Administrative Procedures Act and requires a provider to complete a redetermination appeal before the provider may proceed to a reconsideration appeal and to complete the reconsideration appeal before the provider may proceed to an ALJ appeal.

Ex parte communication The phrase "ex parte" means "on one side only" and refers to an illegal communication between a party and the ALJ. Once an ALJ hearing is requested, any communication between the provider and the ALJ, or between a Medicare contractor and the ALJ, must be shared with the other party.

Experimental/Investigational Amazingly, Medicare does not define "experimental/investigational." Thankfully, Blue Cross/Blue Shield does and the BCBS definition can be used in Medicare appeals.

Extension When a provider requests an extension, he or she is asking for more time to submit a MAC, QIC, or ALJ appeal than is allowed under the Medicare rules. Usually, extensions are only granted when an act of God (e.g., fire or flood) has prevented the timely submission of the appeal request. See Chapter 15, "Extensions."

Extrapolation This is a statistical sampling of a provider's claims to produce an overpayment estimation.

Findings of fact Findings of fact in the ALJ decision refer to the patient's medical history (medical findings of fact) and the findings related to the denied service or supply.

Framing the argument This refers to telling the story the way you want the ALJ to view the dispute.

Fujitsu ScanSnap This is the desktop scanner I use and recommend. It's fast, reliable, takes up little space, and is moderately priced at about $500.

GAO Government Accountability Office.

Good cause See Chapter 13, "'Good Cause' Does Not Mean What You Think It Means."

"Good cause" for an extension The 405.942 "good cause" requirements for an extension means unavoidable circumstances beyond the physician's control.

"Good cause" for reopening See 405.980, 405.986, and the MCPM, Chapter 34, Section 10.6.2. Good cause for a reopening is defined in 405.986: "There is good cause for reopening when there is evidence that was not considered and that evidence may result in a different conclusion or the evidence that was considered clearly shows on its face that an obvious error was made."

"Good cause" for the submission of new evidence at the time of an ALJ hearing See 405.966 and 405.986. Most of the time, a provider will have great difficulty establishing "good cause" for the late submission of evidence. And every time an ALJ allows late-submitted evidence, that ALJ must explain in her written decision how "good cause" was met.

"Good and sufficient cause" to vacate (reverse) a dismissal Good and sufficient cause to vacate (reverse) a dismissal includes 405.986 "good cause" requirements plus a reason so substantial that it would be unreasonable to deny the request to reverse the dismissal. Also, see 405.952, 405.972, 405.1004, and 405.1052.

HCPCS I Manual Healthcare Common Procedure Coding System Manual. This is the CPT Manual and contains level 1 codes. The CPT codes are numeric.

HCPCS II Manual Healthcare Common Procedure Coding System II Manual. While the CPT Manual is written by the AMA, the HCPCS II Manual is written by CMS. HCPCS level II codes are used to describe and identify health care equipment and supplies that are not identified by the HCPCS level I, CPT codes. The HCPCS II codes are alphanumeric.

HHH Home health and hospice.

HH+H MACs Home Health & Hospice MACs.

HHS-725 form Request for ALJ to review dismissal by the QIC.

HICN Health Insurance Claim Number. This is the patient's Medicare number.

HIPAA Health Insurance Portability and Accountability Act.

H&P History and physical examination.

ICD-10 International Classification of Diseases. The ICD-10 is the tenth revision of the International Statistical Classification of Diseases and Related Health Problems.

Improper payment A Medicare payment that violates any Medicare rule is considered to be an improper payment.

Incorporate by reference "Incorporate by reference" is the act of including the first document within a second document by just mentioning the first document. For example, "The findings in the initial H&P are incorporated by reference in this progress note, with new findings noted as additions or changes to the initial H&P."

Investigational See *Experimental/Investigational* above.

IOM Internet-Only Manuals. The entire Medicare Manual, previously published on paper, is now available online as the IOMs. P40 #2.

IPR Improper payment rate.

IPRS Improper payment reduction strategy. See MPIM Chapter 7.

Krames pamphlets The Krames company publishes pamphlets that explain medical and surgical problems for patients. The pamphlets are well illustrated and are helpful when explaining a patient's problem to an ALJ.

LCD Local Coverage Determinations. These are medical care policies written by the MACs. LCD policies are not binding on an ALJ.

Legal framework The Medicare rules, regulations, and statutes that apply to the service at issue are the legal framework of an ALJ decision.

Letter brief A letter brief is an informal legal brief written to convince the ALJ to order payment of your denied claim.

MAC Medicare Administrative Contractor.

MAC Medicare Appeals Council. The Medicare Appeals Council is part of the HHS Departmental Appeals Board. Because of the confusion with the Medicare Administrative Contractors, the Medicare Appeals Council is now referred to as **"the Council."**

MCPM Medicare Claims Processing Manual (an IOM manual).

Medically reasonable and necessary This term of art comes from Section 1862(a)(1)(A) of the Social Security Act. The elements of the phrase "medically reasonable and necessary" are detailed in Section 13.5.1 of the Medicare Program Integrity Manual: "Contractors shall consider a service to be reasonable and necessary if the service is: safe and effective; not experimental or investigational, and appropriate."

Medical review contractors The businesses contracted with Medicare to review medical claims include A/B MAC, A/B RAC, DME MAC, DME RAC, CERT, UPIC, and SMRC.

Medicare Appeals Council appeal The Medicare Appeals Council is part of the Department of Health and Human Services Departmental Appeals Board. Don't bother appealing an ALJ denial to the Medicare Appeals Council unless the ALJ has made an obvious error based on the applicable rule (e.g., the LCD at the time of the denied service allowed the denied service).

Medicare articles These explain Medicare's medical policies. Like LCDs, Medicare articles are not binding on ALJs. Medicare articles are published on the Medicare Learning Network page of the Medicare website.

Medicare documents For the letter brief submitted to the QIC, a Medicare document is a document written by or relied upon by Medicare (e.g., CPT Manual, IOMs, and LCDs). Also see *Non-Medicare documents* below.

Medicare number The old Medicare number (HICN or Health Insurance Claim Number) was the person's social security number plus a letter. The new Medicare numbers are not related to any other identifier.

Medicare provider For this book, the word "provider" refers to both providers and suppliers. See 400.202.

MLN Medicare Learning Network. The MLN has hundreds of articles that address Medicare issues. These articles "explain national Medicare policy in an easy-to-understand format. They focus on coverage, billing, and payment rules for specific provider types." Search online "Medicare MLN."

More stringent review test This phrase refers to the test used by the CERT after 2009 to determine whether a Medicare payment was correct.

MPIM Medicare Program Integrity Manual. This is an Internet-only manual and is part of the complete Medicare manual.

MR Medical review. See Chapter 22, "Medicare Audits." There are two basic types of MRs: simple medical reviews performed by software programs and complex medical reviews performed by people.

MUE Mutually Unlikely Edits. MUE software prevents payment of more than the maximum number of units of service allowed. As an example, a surgeon could not bill a second appendectomy procedure code for the same patient on the same date. See Chapter 22, "Medicare Audits."

NCDs National coverage determinations. NCDs are medical care policies written by Medicare. NCDs are binding on providers and suppliers, the MACs, the QICs, and the ALJs.

NCCI National Correct Coding Initiative. The NCCI includes the CCI program, the MUE program, and the add-on code program.

Non-Medicare documents For the letter brief submitted to the QIC, non-Medicare documents are documents that were not written by or relied upon by Medicare (e.g., patient care records, articles, textbook sections, and authoritative policy statements).

Notice of Hearing letter See 405.1022. The Notice of Hearing letter is sent to the provider by the ALJ approximately three weeks before the hearing and states the type of hearing, the issues to be decided, and a request for detailed information regarding any witnesses.

NPI National Provider Identifier. This is a unique identification number for covered health care providers.

OIG Office of Inspector General.

OIG/OI Office of Inspector General/Office of Investigations.

OMHA-100 form The OMHA-100 form is used to request the third-level ALJ appeal.

OMHA-100A form The OMHA-100A form is used along with the OMHA-100 form when there are multiple beneficiaries in a single ALJ appeal.

On the record decision An ALJ can make an "on the record" decision, a written decision based on the records—without a hearing—when the decision is completely favorable for the provider. See 405.1000.

Orthotic In this book I have used the word "orthotic" when writing about the custom support used in diabetic therapeutic shoes.

Overpayment An overpayment occurs when a provider (provider/supplier) is paid more for a service than the provider should be paid.

PHI Protected Health Information.

Physician's signature log If you initial your notes, or your signature is illegible, create a signature log that your billing department has available to use whenever Medicare requests authentication of the signature or initials on a patient care document. The signature log will be in table form on your office letterhead. The signature log should include the identifiers for each person in your practice. The table will look as follows:

Name	Credentials	Signature	Initials	Date
David Mullens	DPM	David Mullens	DM	07/16/2019

For more information on signatures, see the CMS IOM, MPIM (Medicare Program Integrity Manual), Chapter 3, Section 3.3.2.4—Signature Requirements.

POE Provider Outreach and Education.

Position paper CMS contractors can submit a "position paper" to the ALJ regarding the service at issue. Although the contractor is required to send you a copy of any position paper submitted to the ALJ (see 405.1012), in my experience, that may not happen. When you submit your request for the ALJ hearing, **ask the ALJ in writing to send you a copy of any position paper submitted by any contractor.** A week before the hearing, call the ALJ's assistant and ask if a position paper has been submitted to the ALJ by any of the Medicare contractors.

Prepayment and post-payment review of claims Claim reviews that are linked together. The MAC, with or without input from the RAC, the CERT, or the SMRC, thinks you know you are billing for something you shouldn't and is (complex) reviewing your claims before payment is made and is (complex) reviewing your claims after payment is made.

Preponderance of the evidence The standard of proof that applies to ALJ hearings is "preponderance of the evidence." This means for a provider to win an ALJ decision, the ALJ must conclude the provider's evidence is at least 51% more likely to be persuasive than the contractor's 49%. (standard of proof) p37 #2.

Principles of law in an ALJ decision For **procedural** denials, the principles of law are usually the 42 CFR sections. For **substantive** denials, the principles of law are usually Medicare policies found in LCDs and in Medicare articles.

Procedural denial Procedural denials are usually claim denials based on entry errors on claim forms or denials based on late submissions.

Progress notes For this book, the phrase "progress notes" refers to all patient care documents authored by the patient's doctors (e.g., the initial H&P and all follow-up visit notes).

Proof of delivery mail Proof of delivery is confirmed by an emailed response letter containing the delivery information, the recipient's name, the tracking number, an image of the recipient's signature, and the printed name and address.

Proof of mailing certificate "Proof of mailing" is not the equivalent of "proof of delivery" mail. When you send copies of appeal requests, letter briefs, and proposed decisions to the Medicare beneficiaries whose claims are at issue, you can send these documents with "proof of mailing" only. When you send any documents to the QIC or ALJ, you should send them by "proof of delivery" mail. Proof of delivery is more expensive than proof of mailing.

Proposed decision A "proposed decision" is written by the provider and is what the provider would like to receive from the ALJ: a favorable decision ordering payment to the provider for a denied service or supply, or a favorable decision that rejects Medicare's demand for repayment of overpayment.

Provider See *Medicare provider* above.

Provider education/feedback The most benign of the MAC enforcement weapons. Here, a provider is repeatedly doing something wrong and the MAC thinks the provider is doing it out of ignorance. The MAC "tutors" the provider and then monitors subsequent claims.

PTAN Provider Transaction Access Number. This is a Medicare-only number issued to providers by MACs upon enrollment to Medicare. A PTAN's use should generally be limited to a provider's communication with their MAC.

PTP software The Correct Coding Initiative (CCI) prepayment claim review program is a combination of the **PTP (procedure to procedure)** software program and the **MUE** (Mutually Unlikely Edits) software program. The CCI Column 1/Column 2 tables are comprised of **PTP code pairs.** If a provider submits two codes of an edit pair for payment for the same beneficiary on the same date of service, the Column 1 code is eligible for payment and the Column 2 code is denied. However, if both codes are clinically appropriate, and an appropriate NCCI-associated modifier is used, the codes in both columns are eligible for payment. Supporting documentation for the use of the modifier must be in the beneficiary's medical record."

QIC Qualified Independent Contractor. The QIC is the contractor responsible for the second-level reconsideration appeal determinations.

RA Remittance Advice. The RA notice is the form you receive from Medicare telling you what was paid and what was denied on the originally submitted claim.

RA Recovery Auditor. This is the new acronym for a Recovery Audit Contractor (RAC).

RAC Recovery Audit Contractor.

RAC issues CMS approved topics for widespread RAC review are called "issues" and all approved RAC "issues" are listed on all of the RAC websites.

RAC reviews

RAC automated reviews. With automated reviews, the RAC is certain the overpayment claim is correct so the RAC does not give the provider an opportunity to tell the RAC why the RAC is wrong.

RAC semiautomated reviews. Semiautomated reviews are based on claims data analysis but the RAC is not certain there has been an overpayment. So, the RAC gives the provider a chance to respond with documentation that will support payment.

RAC complex reviews. Complex reviews are based on a review of the supporting medical records and the reviewer must be a qualified health care coder or clinician based on the type of review.

Random claim review Only the CERT performs random claim review. All other claim review is targeted to a specific geographic area, MAC, service, or group of providers.

RARC Remittance Advice Remark Code.
Reconsideration appeal A second-level appeal performed by a QIC after a redetermination appeal is denied.
Reconsideration Appeal Number The reconsideration appeal decision denial letter will have a number on the first page. You will have to use that number when you submit the ALJ appeal request.
Recoupment When Medicare says an overpayment has occurred and the provider appeals the alleged overpayment, Medicare recoups the overpayment amount plus interest from the provider's future Medicare earnings.
Redetermination appeal A first-level appeal performed by the same Medicare Administrative Contractor that denied the initially submitted claim.
Redetermination Appeal Number The redetermination appeal decision denial letter will have a number on the first page. You will have to use that number when you submit the reconsideration appeal request.
Remark codes These are the codes on a Remittance Advice notice that tells the provider why a claim was denied.
Reopenings See 405.980–405.986. A claim may be reopened by Medicare or at the request of a provider. Medicare reopens paid claims to determine whether the payment was improper. Providers request reopenings of claims thought to be incorrectly denied. See Chapter 17, "Reopenings," and also see the MCPM, Chapter 34, Section 10.6.2.
RRL Review results letter. This is the letter sent by the RAC after a complex claim review. The letter states the review is complete, and there is an overpayment or underpayment finding. The letter gives the provider a detailed rationale to support the finding, the amount of the impending adjustment, and the next steps the provider can anticipate.
SAR Strategy Analysis Report.
Section The word "section," as in CFR section, may be indicated by the symbol §.
Simple claim review Claim review done by a software program (as opposed to complex claim review of medical records by a person).
Smoking gun evidence This phrase describes a piece of evidence so powerful that it is considered conclusive and should determine the outcome of the case.
SMRC Supplemental medical review contractor. The current SMRC is StrategicHealthSolutions, LLC.
SOL Statute of limitations. This is the time limit by which you must get something done, such as submitting an appeal.
SSA The Social Security Act.
SSN Social Security Number.
Standard of Proof The burden of proof required in a particular type of case. In a criminal case, the prosecution has to meet the standard of proof "beyond a reasonable doubt" (95% certainty). In some civil cases (e.g., fraud, wills and inheritances, or withdrawing life support for a relative), the plaintiff has to meet the standard of proof by "clear and convincing evidence" (75% certainty). In most civil cases the plaintiff has to meet the standard of proof (51%) by a "preponderance of the evidence."

Although Medicare supposedly requires the preponderance of the evidence standard when a plaintiff (provider or supplier) appeals an underpayment or a demand for repayment of overpayment, the actual standard of proof will vary with the type of appeal. If the plaintiff can show the wrong LCD requirement was applied, the standard of proof will be "by a preponderance of the evidence." If the plaintiff is trying to convince an ALJ that the actual (correct) LCD requirement should not be applied because the provided treatment was medically reasonable and necessary and was safer and more effective than the LCD indicated treatment, the standard of proof will be at least "by clear and convincing evidence" and may even require "beyond a reasonable doubt" evidence in order to convince the ALJ to order payment.
Substantial deference This refers to the 405.1062 requirement for the ALJ to give "substantial deference" to the nonbinding Medicare rules that were the reason for the claim denial—unless the ALJ concludes the facts in favor of payment outweigh the Medicare rules against payment. The ALJ is required to state in the written decision how substantial deference was paid to the Medicare rules and why the ALJ awarded payment despite the rules. Medicare does not define the phrase "substantial deference."
Substantive denial Claim denials based on a violation of a published Medicare rule or policy.
Suspension of billing privileges When a provider makes an entry error on the CMS855 revalidation form, Medicare may suspend the provider's billing privileges from the date the CMS855 form is due until the date the corrected CMS855 form is received.
Suspension of Medicare privileges When a provider's billing offenses are glaring enough, and/or when a provider continues to offend despite previous post-payment/prepayment reviews, a MAC can suspend the provider's Medicare privileges.
Target audience The target audience of an appeal is always the ALJ.

TIN Federal Tax Identification Number.

Totality of the circumstances test A test used by the CERT before 2009 to determine whether a Medicare payment was correct. The "more stringent review" test has been used by the CERT since 2009 to determine whether a Medicare payment was correct.

Underpayment An underpayment occurs when Medicare pays less for a service than Medicare should pay.

Universe of claims For our purposes, the phrase "universe of claims" applies to Medicare's use of statistical sampling where all of the claims between a definite starting date and end date are subjected to extrapolation. The findings (conclusions) regarding a small random sample of claims from this universe of claims are applied to all of the claims in the universe.

Here are Medicare's rules regarding an overpayment case where a universe of claims are subjected to extrapolation:

1. There must be a minimum of 250 claims in the universe.
2. Up to 10,000 claims can be accommodated in a single universe.
3. All claims must fall into only one of the following categories:
   a. A universe of claim appeals is limited to all prepayment or all overpayment claims, but not a combination of both.
   b. A universe of overpayment claim appeals is limited to all Recovery Audit Contractor (RAC) claims or all non-RAC claims, but not a combination of both.
   c. A universe of RAC claims is limited to claims adjudicated by a single RAC. If the sample is spread among RACs, the benefits of joining the initiative are lost, as the appellant would have to attend multiple hearings.

The provider or supplier has a choice. The provider or supplier can appeal every individual claim in the universe before the ALJ or can appeal the randomly selected claims and then have the ALJ apply her conclusions regarding those randomly selected claims to the universe of claims. The choice will be based on the provider's/supplier's analysis of the small number of claims randomly selected by the RAC.

UPIC Unified Program Integrity Contractor. The UPICs investigate possible fraud for both Medicare and Medicaid.

USPS U.S. Postal Service.

Vacating dismissals See Chapter 16, "Dismissals."

VTC hearing Video teleconference hearing. A provider should always ask for a video teleconference ALJ hearing at an approved video teleconference center as opposed to a telephone hearing.

http://www.medicare.gov/. The website for beneficiaries.

http://www.cms.gov/. The website for providers. Click on the Medicare tab at the top of the page and then scroll down to find the topic you want.

ZPIC Zone Program Integrity Contractor. The ZPIC program (for Medicare only) has been phased out and the UPIC program (for Medicare and Medicaid) has been phased in.

About the Author

David Mullens, B.S., D.P.M., J.D. In 1966, after completing three years at Syracuse University, Dr. Mullens received early admission to the California College of Podiatric Medicine (CCPM) in San Francisco. Dr. Mullens received his B.S. degree in 1967 and received his DPM degree in 1970. He completed his residency at Jewish Memorial Hospital in New York (1970–1971) and at the Podiatry Hospital in San Francisco (1971–1972). He then did a post-doctoral fellowship in dermatology and vascular disease at Stanford University Hospital (1972–1973). Dr. Mullens started the podiatric surgical residency program at the Palo Alto Veterans Administration Hospital in 1975 and established the podiatric surgical service at Stanford University Hospital in 1976. He is a fellow of the American Board of Podiatric Surgery and has authored articles and book chapters on lower extremity problems. He has served as a Clinical Associate Professor at the Stanford University School of Medicine and as a Professor with dual appointments in Basic Science and Podiatric Medicine at the California College of Podiatric Medicine. He was a community surgeon in the Orthopedic Department of Stanford University Hospital from 1976 through 2011. He earned his J.D. at Peninsula University Law School in 1997 and was an associate attorney with Alexander Hawes and Audet in San Jose, CA until 2004. He established his own law practice in Palo Alto in 2004 and represents health care providers regarding payment for services by Medicare and the for-profit insurance companies. To date, Dr. Mullens has successfully prosecuted the collection of several thousand CPT and HCPCS codes previously denied for payment by Medicare and the for-profit insurance companies.

To access downloadable templates for key form letters discussed in this text, please visit http//:ambar.org/htwma-downloads.

Index

Note: *f* indicates figure; *n*, note; and *t*, table

D

E

N

O

P

S

T